The Banana Wars

LESTER D. LANGLEY

The Banana Wars

United States
Intervention in the
Caribbean, 1898-1934

THE UNIVERSITY PRESS OF KENTUCKY

For Charles and Jonathan

The University Press of Kentucky

Scholarly publisher for the Commonwealth,
serving Bellarmine College, Berea College, Centre
College of Kentucky, Eastern Kentucky University,
The Filson Club, Georgetown College, Kentucky
Historical Society, Kentucky State University,
Morehead State University, Murray State University,
Northern Kentucky University, Transylvania University,
University of Kentucky, University of Louisville,
and Western Kentucky University.

Editorial and Sales Offices: Lexington, Kentucky 40506-0024

Library of Congress Cataloging in Publication Data

Langley, Lester D.
    The banana wars.

    Bibliography: p.
    Includes index.
    1. Caribbean Area—Foreign relations—United States.
2. United States—Foreign relations—Caribbean Area.
3. Caribbean Area—Military relations—United States.
4. United States—Military relations—Caribbean Area.
5. Caribbean Area—History. 6. United States—Foreign
relations—20th century I. Title.
F2178.U6L34 1983   972.9′051   85-664
ISBN 0-8131-1548-5

CONTENTS

ILLUSTRATIONS

PHOTOGRAPHS

MAPS

Acknowledgments

My thanks to the University of Georgia History Department for summer research grants that facilitated completion of this study; Paul Nagel, former head of the department, who appreciates the perils of intervention (of the academic rather than the military variety), for innumerable courtesies; Sandy Herbelin, Ann Saye, Kathy Coley, Gloria Davis, Linda Green, Patsy Buffington, Nancy Heaton, and Cathy Cartey, for an efficient job of typing the manuscript; several colleagues—Lee Kennett, William Leary, and Earl Ziemke—who tolerated my often simple questions about military history; Charles Wynes, who read an early draft of the manuscript; and Nash Boney, for endlessly delightful and occasionally profound discussions about the nature of Anglo-Saxon and Hispanic cultures.

The staffs of the Library of Congress Manuscripts Division and the National Archives assisted in my trek through the maze of military records and private papers of soldiers and sailors. Richard Sommers pointed out relevant materials I would otherwise have missed in my visit to the U.S. Army Military History Institute, Carlisle Barracks, Pa. Dean Allard of the Naval Historical Division, Washington Navy Yard, generously shared his knowledge of the "old Navy" and its role in the Caribbean. Across the street at the United States Marine Corps History and Museums Division, Brig. Gen. E.H. Simmons, USMC (ret.), and his colleagues superbly maintain a rich collection of Marine Corps materials in a setting conducive to research and were unfailingly helpful to a civilian obviously fascinated by the exploits of the "banana warriors." A special acknowledgment goes to Benis Frank, keeper of the Oral History Collection; Charles Wood, Personal Papers Division; and especially Jack Shulimson, for always interesting conversation about Marine Corps history. Col. John Greenwood greatly assisted my research by providing a copy of a Marine Corps history of the Haitian intervention, then "in press." Lester D. Stephens, Head, History Department; and Robert Anderson, Vice-President for Research, University of Georgia, facilitated my research in the latter stages of the manuscript.

Lt. Gen. Merwin Silverthorne, USMC (ret.), Gen. Robert E. Hogaboom, USMC (ret.), and Gen. Gerald C. Thomas, USMC (ret.) extended permission to use materials from their oral histories. Harriette Byrd Smith provided the same courtesy for use of the Julian C. Smith Oral History. Capt. Edward L. Beach, USN (ret.), a distinguished author, added to my knowledge of his father, who figured importantly in the Haitian intervention of 1915. Thomas Butler graciously permitted me to look at his father's voluminous correspondence at the elegant family home in Newtown Square, Pa.

My appreciation also goes to the staffs of the Archivo de Relaciones Exteriores, Mexico City; Archivo General de la Nación, Santo Domingo, Dominican Republic; and the Institute de Frères de Instruction Chrétienne, Port-au-Prince, Haiti, which houses a splendid collection of Haitian materials. I regret that despite the efforts of Dane Bowen, Department of State, and the U.S. Interests Section, Havana, I was unable to secure access to the Cuban national archives.

And, finally, a belated acknowledgment to Ray O'Connor, who many years ago tried to impress upon a seemingly unimpressionable graduate student the relationship between force and diplomacy.

Introduction

The day was, he remembered, "a fine clear day, the best sort of Cuban day."

LEONARD WOOD, Diary, May 1902

For sixteen months—ever since December 1899 when President William McKinley had named him military governor—Leonard Wood had exercised supreme power in Cuba. Physically imposing, he looked every inch the stereotypical American soldier of empire engraved in the national consciousness, but his demeanor on this day revealed none of the relentless energy that had characterized his proconsular rule. Now he was about to turn power over to an old man, Tomás Estrada Palma, reverently called Don Tomás by his countrymen. Estrada had been at various times in his long life, a Cuban rebel, a Spanish prisoner, and a schoolmaster. At noon he would become the first president of the hemisphere's first republic in the new century.

Estrada Palma had arrived in the capital only a month before his inauguration, and despite the fact that he was not a member of the rebellion's pantheon of warriors, the Habaneros gave him an enthusiastic welcome. Wood dutifully convened the new Cuban congress to approve the electoral vote for president and vice-president and then undertook to educate his successor in the responsibilities of rule. He found his pupil compatible but somewhat insensitive to Anglo-Saxon political tradition. Wood had earlier decreed that certain officers of the judiciary were protected from executive interference in the exercise of their duties. Estrada wanted to rescind this provision—for what reasons he did not reveal—and Wood dissuaded him only by pointing out that such a regulation had been included in the republic's new constitution.

Havana had been celebrating for a week. Flags were still at half-mast in honor of José Martí (who had been killed in the first weeks of the 1895 rebellion and was already a Cuban martyr) and other slain patriots. But in the evenings crowds thronged the streets, shouting, singing, blowing horns, and popping firecrackers in anticipation of the ceremony when the Cuban banner would fly proudly over the buildings that for almost four centuries had housed the Spanish oppressor.

Wood himself had been honored with a sumptuous banquet at the

Tacón Theater, where 350 admirers had spontaneously jumped to their feet
when the general stood to deliver his speech. For the first time in four years,
wrote an associate, Leonard Wood was speechless. He and Mrs. Wood had
been showered with gifts—even from the Spanish residents who had remained after the humiliation of 1898. An association of Cuban veterans
presented a machete, symbol of the cane worker and Cuban rebel, beauti-
fully engraved with the arms of Cuba and a star of gold.

Such gestures perhaps made the general less unsure about the republic
and its new leader as he stood now before Estrada, the Cuban congress, his
fellow officers, and the papal delegate in the Palacio nacional. When the
clock struck twelve he began reading the document of transfer. There was
no emotion in his voice—he could very well have been reading a sentence
of execution to a condemned man—but he could sense the drama of the
moment by glancing at the eyes of his listeners. Outside, the air reverberated
from the thundering guns of the American warships in the harbor. Wood's
statement and Estrada's brief reply required no more than ten minutes.
When they had finished, a detachment of American soldiers on the roof
began slowly lowering the American flag and hoisting the Cuban colors, to
the salute of the Seventh Cavalry and the Cuban Rural Guard in the Plaza
de Armas below and the warships in the harbor.

Wood had wanted the American officer on the roof to raise the Cuban
flag slowly so as to permit the aging general Máximo Gómez, the Dominican who had commanded a Cuban army, to climb to the roof and give the
final tug on the rope. But when Wood, who was ahead of him, got to the
roof he saw that the Cuban flag was already flying at full staff. He immediately ordered the flag lowered so that Gómez would not be denied. Gómez
soon appeared and with Wood's help hoisted the Cuban banner. As the flag
approached the top the halyards snapped, and it had to be lowered, secured,
and raised again. "This seemed an inauspicious sign," Wood observed later,
"although no one spoke of it at the time though some did later."[1] When
they were finished, the general made his way back downstairs and out of
the palace and proceeded to the dock, where a launch waited to take him
to the *Brooklyn*. On the way the entourage observed a kneeling man—who,
it was learned, had lost three sons in the struggle for independence—
blessing the Americans for allowing him to die in peace. Another "distraught Cuban" embraced a young American naval officer from the *Eagle*,
kissed him on both cheeks, and blurted alternately in English and Spanish,
"I never thought I would live to see this day!"

As the launch plowed through the waters of Havana harbor, Wood
looked back at the Cubans crowding the shoreline, still cheering. Some of
them, the "better class of people," he noted later, watched the Americans
leave with sincere regret.

He was glad his work was done. His labors in Cuba had been monumental, as Secretary of War Elihu Root proudly observed in rendering the official gratitude of the president: "Out of an utterly prostrate colony a free republic was built up, the work being done with such ability, integrity, and success that the new nation started under more favorable conditions than has ever before been the case in any single instance among her fellow Spanish-American republics. The record stands alone in history, and the benefit conferred thereby on the people of Cuba was no greater than the honor conferred on the people of the United States."[2] Leonard Wood never returned to rule Cuba, but when he departed Havana harbor that stunningly beautiful day in May 1902 he believed its American governors would one day return. They would return either as conquerors, as they had arrived in 1898, or, preferably, as benevolent guardians of a people Wood and his generation considered likable, educable, but lacking that indefinable quality of self-sufficiency the Anglo-Saxons believed they had acquired through experience and their distinctive culture.

A special American definition of empire had already been set down to distinguish what the United States was doing in the Caribbean and in Asia from what Europeans had implanted in their empires. Americans of Wood's day resented comparisons of their emerging Caribbean empire with the great imperial ventures of European powers on the African and Asian continents in the late nineteenth century. The United States had only recently liberated Cubans from their Spanish oppressors, Americans boasted, and had no intention of incorporating the island into American domain in the way the British Empire had absorbed Kenya. Puerto Rico had been taken as reparation for the cost of waging war against Spain. The Philippines, the American people were convinced, had been annexed to prepare the Filipinos for democracy's moral and material benefits. And nowhere in the burgeoning American governmental bureaucracy was there anything that rivaled in either scope or purpose the British Colonial Office from which Britain ruled its empire.

Europeans looking at the advance of American interests and influence in the Caribbean ridiculed such arguments, as had old-line antiimperialists who had scoffed at the sanctimony characterizing senatorial annexationist speeches in 1899. The European world of 1900 was made up of dynamic, competing empires—British, French, and German—which had carved out new land and commercial frontiers in Africa and Asia, and European statesmen commonly assumed that their American counterparts, cleverly exploiting anti-Spanish sentiment and disgust over the horrors of the Cuban rebellion (as cynical British imperialists had convinced pious Victorians that it was Britain's duty to uplift the Kenyans), were bent on staking out an American empire in the Western Hemisphere and the western Pacific.

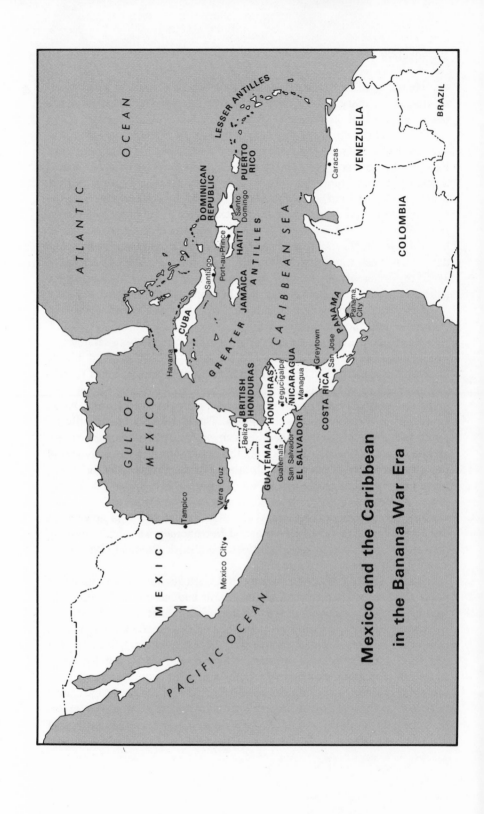

Mexico and the Caribbean
in the Banana War Era

The United States had not been unwillingly thrust into empire, European observers argued, but had consciously chosen that path. Yet the Caribbean empire that emerged after the war with Spain was unlike any of the great European empires of the day. The approach to empire was, to use a snide European phrase, "typically American." Puerto Rico, technically a colony, was virtually ignored (except for a declaration that the Constitution did not follow the flag to the island) until World War I; Cuba, promised its independence, was burdened with American rules governing its domestic and international political behavior and thoroughly penetrated by American capital. But elsewhere the role of capital, which constitutes an important measure of imperial control, was noticeably weaker than American political or military involvement. Not always, to deny a fundamental tenet of John Hobson's classic treatise on imperialism, did the dollar follow the flag. Haiti was as severely ruled as Nicaragua, but American investment played a negligible role in the decision to intervene in Haitian affairs in 1915. Even in Nicaragua, where Wall Street certainly had an important stake, economics played an inferior role to politics in charting the direction of American policy.

If economic motives provided a weak incentive for American empire in the Caribbean, strategic considerations offered a compelling and—considering that this era witnessed the construction of one of America's great engineering achievements, the Panama Canal—justifiable argument for interfering in the internal affairs of disorderly Caribbean societies. Theodore Roosevelt may never have said, "I took the Canal Zone while Congress debated," but the highly publicized boast underscored prewar America's obsession with the canal and the American military's assigned task of protecting it. In the reams of political analysis of Caribbean affairs ground out by diplomats of these years, safeguarding of the "vital waterway" always served as unassailable reason for the sometimes objectionable practice of "gunboat diplomacy" that seemed to characterize American policy. Yet, paradoxically, in only one instance in the military interventions in the Caribbean in this era was protection of the canal—or, more precisely, the canal route—the issue determining American action: in Roosevelt's use of the navy to guarantee the success of the Panamanian revolution by having it "protect the isthmian passageway," a task the navy had been carrying out since the mid-nineteenth century. The factious Haitians or warring Dominicans or bickering Cubans no more threatened the Panama Canal than they menaced the Brooklyn Bridge.

In the Caribbean empire of the age framed by the two Roosevelts, political turbulence in the republics *and* the American military's response to political conditions are closely related, and too little appreciated, elements in explaining the course of American involvement. To be sure, policies, whether military or political (and in this century the two are scarcely distinguishable), were set down in Washington. General goals were articulated and translated into specifics and passed down the line to diplomats in Port-au-Prince or naval officers aboard light cruisers off Santo Domingo. But action was taken without prompt direction from Washington, sometimes because the technical capacity to transmit it swiftly did not exist, and in decisions to intervene in presumably sovereign societies American officers had to plot their moves as the situation called for or as tradition dictated. Theodore Roosevelt sent his secretary of war to Havana in 1906 in a vain effort to resolve the Cuban political crisis, but American officers "using their own judgment," as they had since the beginning of American naval ventures into the Caribbean, were already disembarking troops to quell disorders. Long before Roosevelt declared that the United States would play the role of policeman in the tropics, the navy was policing the tropics. Woodrow Wilson was determined to bring down Victoriano Huerta in Mexico, but an arrogant American naval officer, overreacting to a trivial incident between his own men and some Mexican troops, provided the excuse for action.

"War is the continuation of politics by other means" is dictum appropriate to American prosecution of the "banana wars," as the marines cynically referred to these military interventions in the Caribbean between 1900 and 1934. When in the span of two decades Roosevelt dispatched seven thousand troops to Cuba, Woodrow Wilson, an ardent critic of European imperialism, launched a military invasion of Mexico and Hispaniola, and even Calvin Coolidge, who despite his provincial outlook on Caribbean politics, vaguely understood the implications of sending five thousand marines to chase a Nicaraguan "bandit," the American military intervened with large numbers of troops in four situations and with smaller forces on numerous other occasions, in not one of which—if one excludes the border troubles growing out of the Mexican revolution of 1910–20—was there a direct threat to American security.

Presidents and their secretaries of state, constitutionally responsible for shaping American policy and seeing to it that it was carried out, could try to direct affairs in these political crises; yet in virtually every case of American military involvement in the Caribbean during these years, long-standing military tradition and practice played an equally critical role in determining the course of these interventions. And it was the soldier, not the civilian, who left the most lasting imprint on the occupied. Thus it is largely the military experience of American rule in the Caribbean that reveals the inner history of American empire. Whichever service—Army, Navy, or Marine Corps—the United States employed to exercise its will in America's tropical empire (and on occasion it used all three), the traditions of each service, their sometimes intense rivalries, and the social and political values of the officers and men who carried out American military interventions in the Caribbean noticeably affected the character of American rule.

Naval officers were steeped in the nineteenth-century tradition of their role as diplomats and protectors of the sea lanes. Their predecessors had distinguished names like Porter or Farragut and usually came from proud old families with a strong admiration for the British navy and its role in protecting the empire and chastising those who threatened it. Long before the birth of America's Caribbean empire they had grown accustomed to their reputation as vigilant protectors of American (and, if called upon, European) citizens and their property in the tropics. It was a tradition carried over into the age of battleships and radio communication.

The army lacked the navy's traditions in diplomacy or tropical patrol but compensated with its combat experience in the Spanish-American War and afterward in the grisly pacification of the Filipino rebels and by its selection of energetic, capable, and ambitious men such as Leonard Wood and Frederick Funston to rule occupied Cuba in 1899 and Veracruz in 1914. Though Theodore Roosevelt's choice to direct the Cuban "pacification"— the president consciously avoided calling the dispatch of seven thousand troops to the island in 1906 an "occupation"—was a civilian, army officers such as Robert Bullard and Enoch Crowder served as Cuba's imperial proconsuls.

After the war with Spain the Marine Corps was a small assault force that came under sharp attack from the army and navy but was saved by aggressive politicking on its behalf and by its manifest usefulness in subduing Haiti and the Dominican Republic in 1915 and 1916 and policing Nicaragua in the "last banana war" in the late 1920s and early 1930s. The marines had little of the genteel traditions of the navy or the bureaucratic capabilities of the army. The marines were conscious (and resentful) of their secondary status in America's imperial bureaucracy. The corps not only had no separate department in the executive branch but was tossed back and forth between navy and army command depending on whether its forces were on sea or on land, and none of its commandants in the banana war era rose above the rank of major general. The marines' experience was in taking towns, not running them or negotiating with local bigwigs, but after 1915 the corps became occupier and proconsul of America's Caribbean domain. And the marines rendered a physical imprint to American rule in the Caribbean, as the experience of the most flamboyant banana warriors, Smedley Butler and L. W. T. Waller, Sr., testified.

Despite the antagonisms among the three services, their officers shared several convictions about America's tropical empire. They believed the

8   Introduction

racist canards of their generation that professed the inferiority of Caribbean
peoples, and they acknowledged, though occasionally grudgingly, America's obligation to police what their countrymen called "turbulent little
republics." Their role was to inculcate respect for rule in what they saw as
unruly societies. Such a mission went beyond the grand strategy of safeguarding the Panama Canal or Wall Street's investments. It meant policing
governments that Americans believed incapable of policing themselves or
their people. It meant ultimately the creation of governments in small
countries plagued by discord that could accomplish on the national level
what Americans expected from their local government—an orderly society
populated by the law-abiding. These were the values not of Wall Street but
of Main Street.

   This work surveys American diplomatic and military involvement in
the Caribbean, including the Veracruz intervention in Mexico in 1914,
which constituted an important phase of the banana wars, from 1898, when
an army for empire was created, until 1934, when the last marine occupiers
quietly left Haiti. Four major episodes in America's penetration of the
tropics span these thirty-six years. The first was the Cuban experience, in
which political and military leaders sought to implant in the island what
they but not all Cubans considered as vital political institutions for a successful republican experiment. In the second, American efforts to influence
political events in Central America and Mexico through civilian policies
shaped largely in Washington ultimately became the responsibility of military arbiters. The third major episode in America's imperial experience
came in Hispaniola, where by the time of American entry into World War
I the American military had virtually exclusive control over two disparate
cultures locked on the same island. And, finally, in the late 1920s, as the
booming prosperity of American capitalism collapsed, the country found
itself mired in its last banana war, a savage conflict in Nicaragua that
exhibited strikingly similar parallels to the guerrilla wars of our time.

   The perspective throughout is largely, though not exclusively, the vision of empire—and the revealing prejudices—held by army, navy, and
marine officers who led their commands into alien and often hostile Caribbean societies to quell disorders or "protect American interests" and ruled
as occupiers in these cultures. They fought America's banana wars and
shaped the character of its empire.

PART I

The Cuban Experience

1. Leonard Wood and the White Man's Burden

Almost exactly two months after the declaration of war against Spain in 1898, the United States launched a military invasion of Spanish Cuba. Still flushed with pride over Adm. George Dewey's tremendous victory over the Spanish at Manila Bay on May 1, the American people expectantly awaited an equally glorious triumph in Spain's New World empire. Their perspective of the Cuban rebellion, shaped by exaggerated tales of Spanish wickedness and Cuban resourcefulness, almost unquestioningly followed the accounts of the sometimes rabidly pro-Cuban press and the propaganda dispensed by the Cuban juntas scattered along the east and Gulf coasts. The war on the island, the president had solemnly declared, had by spring 1898 deteriorated into a gruesome spectacle that shook America's moral sensibilities, and it was our humanitarian duty to end it. A conquering army of a republican nation would be dispatched to complete the campaign begun by the Cuban rebels: to destroy the four-hundred-year Spanish empire on the island and, because Congress had declared we were waging a war of liberation and not of conquest, to lay the foundation for a new republic.

The army that landed in eastern Cuba in June 1898 was typically American in its makeup of volunteers and a small cadre of career officers. It had no experience in tropical war. Its officers were either aging veterans from the Indian campaigns or thrill seekers like Theodore Roosevelt. Its leader was a three-hundred-pound, gout-ridden brigadier general, William Rufus Shafter, whom Roosevelt considered "criminally incompetent." The secretary of war, Russell Alger, a well-intentioned but irascible Michigan politician, was incapable of directing the war with the chaotic bureaucracy of the War Department. Alger quarreled so incessantly with the commanding general of the army, Nelson A. Miles, that President McKinley eventually bypassed both and directed the war himself.

The mission of this army was the defeat of Spain and Spanish authority on the island of Cuba, not the expansion of American territorial domain. But it would become in the course of the war an army for empire. Its troops would storm El Caney and San Juan Hill, take Puerto Rico, and pacify

Manila. A meager contingent of 25,000 before the war, the American army would expand rapidly into a mighty force of 100,000 in the summer of 1898, 70,000 serving outside the continental United States, 30,000 in the Philippines on the other side of the globe. At war's end its commanding officers found themselves in the uncommon role of colonial administrators in Cuba, Puerto Rico, and the Philippines. And in August 1898 President William McKinley would at last find the perfect administrator for this empire in Elihu Root, a corporation lawyer who became secretary of war after Alger became involved in a bitter political fight in his home state and was compelled to resign.[1]

The war brought impressive victories—Manila Bay, San Juan Hill, Santiago—but it also taught painful realities. One of the first myths shattered was the prewar image of craven Spaniard and noble Cuban. American troops landing at Daiquirí for the great assault against the Spaniards expected to be greeted wildly by their Cuban allies. Instead they were met by a ragtag guerrilla force, unkempt in appearance and darker in color than the drawings of Cuban rebels in New York newspapers. These wretches were less interested in camaraderie and battle tactics than in American rations. The Americans fed them but grew irritated when they refused to fight according to preconceived American notions of valiant warriors. This harsh judgment was in part explained by their tatterdemalion appearance. Grover Flint, who wrote a popular account of his wartime experience *(Marching with Gómez)*, attributed Cuban dishevelment to sacrifice, but many others, including Theodore Roosevelt, simply believed that Cubans would be of little use in a fight. American soldiers were similarly shocked when a Cuban squad, which had captured a Spanish spy, decapitated its prisoner.

If Cubans were inferior, as American soldiers came to believe, then it easily followed that Spaniards were superior—at least superior to Cubans. When Sherwood Anderson wrote that Spaniards had "dark cruel eyes" he imagined himself dispatching some evildoer in the glory of war and expressed a common prewar sentiment. But Americans serving in Cuba soon discovered that Spaniards could fight and fight bravely. At Las Guásimas the Rough Riders, who had landed contested at Daiquirí, encountered stubborn resistance and suffered seventy casualties. El Caney and San Juan Hill, probably the two most fiercely fought land battles of the campaign, swept away all notions of Spanish incompetence or cowardice in American minds. "No men of any nationality," Roosevelt said in a rare tribute to the Hispanic, "could have done better." When a group of American seamen tried to block the passageway to Santiago harbor, where the Spanish fleet was moored, by sinking an old collier in the channel, they were captured by one of Adm. Pascual Cervera's gunboats. The American commanders despaired of their fate but soon received a reassuring message from Cervera himself stating that all were well and would be fairly treated. Of this gesture Capt. Robley D. ("Fighting Bob") Evans observed: "Never [have I witnessed] a more courteous thing done in war."[2]

The second reality for which neither the War Department nor the army was prepared was the condition of the battlefield. Most Americans who went to Cuba had some vague knowledge about the island's climate and terrain—after all, the rebellion had been covered in detail by the large eastern newspapers—but they greatly underestimated the exacting toll tropical climate can take on men and matériel. Troops were either inadequately supplied or provided with useless equipment. And their medical treatment became a national scandal. Men could be ordered to march in step, but officers were hard pressed to convince the individual soldier that drinking water must be boiled, latrines constructed, and drainage channels dug. By midsummer, in the stifling heat and malarial atmosphere, the army that had won a rousing victory at El Caney and San Juan Hill had been devastated by sickness. In one regiment—that of the unforgettable Pvt. Charles Post—almost half of the nine hundred men were incapacitated. One by one the buglers came down sick, and there was no one to blow reveille or taps.[3] Elsewhere, the toll of diseased and disabled rose to alarming heights. When the Spanish surrendered Santiago, it was estimated, 90 percent of American soldiers were unable to continue fighting. The deposed secretary of war confirmed this grim statistic in his account of the war; 90 percent of American troops disembarking in New York, wrote Alger, were either ill or convalescent.[4]

Whatever the cost of the war to American soldiers, the physical toll on Cuba and its people was much greater. The years of struggle against Spanish rule and Spain's punitive retaliation had exacted a terrible price. Cuba had lost a tenth of its population, the census of 1899 revealed, a loss explained for the most part by rebel casualties and the harshness of Spain's counter-revolutionary measure, the *reconcentrado* program. The civilian population of the revolutionary eastern provinces had been herded into fortified towns in the garrisoned West where they had died of starvation and neglect. More ominous was the terrible sacrifice of Cuba's children: In 1899, in a population of 1.5 million, the island counted only 131,000 children four years old and under, 226,000 between five and nine.

Neither countryside nor town had been spared in the devastation. The acreage farmed plummeted to 0.9 million from the 1.3 million acres tilled in 1895. Some provinces, such as Havana and Matanzas, had been severely damaged; Pinar del Río, the westernmost province, cultivated more farmland in 1899 than in 1895, but its towns had been systematically burned in Antonio Maceo's western campaign. Where land was being farmed in 1899, hopelessly entangled laws made sale, transfer, or purchase difficult. Many of the large sugar plantations had been burned or could not operate; in Matanzas, center of Cuban sugar production in the nineteenth century, there were 434 mills in 1894, but five years later there were only 62. A similar precipitous drop in the number of mills occured in other provinces.[5] Two thirds of the island's wealth had been destroyed.

In June 1898 the American army had arrived as invader of Spanish domain; in the course of the war it had become conqueror of Cuba. Now, in 1899, despite a prewar congressional resolution disavowing any intention of annexing Cuban soil, American troops constituted an army of occupation.

In the debate over intervention, McKinley had declared his opposition to formal recognition of the Cuban republic. Thus, at war's end, the Cuban revolutionary junta, which had called for a free united Cuba in 1895, could rejoice in Spain's departure but faced an American army that intended to remain until the island was, in the official pronouncement, "pacified." During the war the people of Oriente province had elected a provisional government, composed mostly of rebel officers who organized an executive council, assessed taxes, and obtained supplies for the rebel army. Outside Oriente, however, the provisional government exercised little influence and was virtually ignored by the Americans. Its president, Bartolomé Masó, urged co-operation with the United States in the hope of obtaining American recognition. But the American government was of the view that Cubans were disunited. When the vice-president of the provisional government, Domingo Méndez Capote, arrived in Washington in May 1898 to ascertain American policy, he learned that Cuban and Spanish conservatives were already pressing the Americans to remain after the Spanish surrender. McKinley's intentions were likewise known from his special message to Congress: "To secure in the island the establishment of a stable government, capable of maintaining order and observing its international obligations insuring peace and tranquility and the security of its citizens as well as our own."[6] The genesis of the Platt Amendment of 1901, defining Cuba's "special relationship" to the United States, had appeared.

After the Spanish surrender, the War Department created a Division of Cuba and divided the island into seven military departments, corresponding to old Spanish jurisdictions; in mid-1899 it consolidated these into four—the city of Havana, Havana province and Pinar del Río, Matanzas and Santa Clara, Santiago and Puerto Principe, each headed by an American general. Inevitably there were allusions to the Reconstruction Acts dividing the South into five military districts after the Civil War. (One of the governors in Cuba was Fitzhugh Lee, a southerner, formerly American consul general in Havana.)

The most capable of the military governors was probably William Ludlow, governor of Havana, an engineer, who was sufficiently incensed at the wretched condition of the city that he advocated an American occupation "for a generation." But the departmental commander with the best political connections was Brig. Gen. Leonard Wood, a physician and career soldier, governor in Santiago, who instituted a regime of cleanliness in the city and meted out public whippings to citizens who violated sanitary regulations. Wood wrote detailed and perceptive reports on Cuban conditions for the secretary of war; his letters to the most influential of his friends, Theodore Roosevelt, were filled with savage comments on American mismanagement. One of Wood's aides published in the *North American Review* an equally strident condemnation of army misrule.

The commanding officer of these opinionated and occasionally troublesome proconsuls was Maj. Gen. John R. Brooke, a Union hero at Gettysburg and, in 1898, commander of the First Corps. In December 1898, while Cuban and American civilians quarreled about the island's future, McKinley appointed Brooke military governor but failed to give him precise instructions about American policy. The result was that Brooke ran the military government on a day-to-day basis, taking care of immediate problems by the most expedient course. He reestablished the civilian bureaucracy, reopened schools, collected revenue, and ordered the streets cleaned. In most cities the Spanish bureaucracy had ceased to function. In Havana, for example, the Spanish city officials had stopped burying the dead— leaving corpses in the street—and had stripped public offices of furniture and supplies. His relief measures probably kept the population from starving.[7]

But he failed to appreciate, as did Leonard Wood, that the American presence in Cuba was as much political as military. Brooke might dispense food to starving Cubans or reopen the schools, but he made the mistake of reappointing Spaniards to their old positions in the bureaucracy, thus angering the Cubans who had fought not only for an independent Cuba but also for political office in the new republic. By the summer of 1899 criticism of the military governor was widespread, even among his subordinates. Root had already become dissatisfied with Brooke's perfunctory reports; he was much impressed with the stern regimen of Wood in Santiago. In the backstairs gossip of the McKinley administration, Brooke's cause was severely damaged, and Brooke hurt himself by censuring Wood for refusing to share the revenues of Santiago with the other provincial commanders.

McKinley remained customarily aloof in this bickering, but by the end of the year it was obvious that the campaign against Brooke (which Brooke called "malicious and wicked") had worked. In December 1899 the president named Wood military governor of Cuba and instructed him to prepare the Cubans for independence.[8]

The official goal may have been the preparation of Cuba for independence, but Wood had uncommonly broad authority to accomplish that task. He was, wrote his biographer, "practically a free agent." Ecstatically optimistic about his task, he declared to the press a few weeks after his appointment that "success in Cuba is so easy that it would be a crime to fail."[9]

But governing in Santiago, where he ruled as virtual master over conquered Spaniard and war-weary Cuban, and ruling an entire country from Havana were quite different matters. He had already learned not to make Brooke's mistake of retaining the old Spanish bureaucracy. Cubans who took their places in the governmental machinery run by Wood now had a place, if not a sinecure. The problem was a gaggle of former rebel generals and political aspirants demanding more reward and power than Wood or the United States was willing to give. Gómez, the old Dominician, was offered what amounted to a sinecure for his acquiescence in behalf of the military government and haughtily refused. Most of the Cuban generals cynically believed that the American government intended to annex the island, despite the Teller Amendment and McKinley's—and Wood's—public disclaimers. The Cubans argued for universal manhood suffrage; Wood wanted an electoral code based on property holding as requirement for suffrage. When Gen. Rius Rivera, who served in the military government, proposed a plan for immediate independence, Wood peremptorily rejected it, and the Cuban resigned.

Wood attributed much of Cuban obstinance to the long years of Spanish rule and Cuban inexperience in democracy:

The great mass of public opinion [Wood wrote McKinley] is perfectly inert; especially is this true among the professional classes. The passive inactivity of one hundred and fifty years has settled over them and it is hard to get them out of old ruts and old grooves. . . .

For three months I have had commissions at work on laws, taxation, electoral law, etc., and after all this time the only result is the adoption of practically the original plans submitted by the Americans to the commissions as working models. . . . The people . . . know they are not ready for self-government and those who are honest make no attempt to disguise the fact. We are going ahead as fast as we can, but we are dealing with a race that has been going down for a hundred years and into which we have to infuse new life, new principles and new methods of doing things. This is not the work of a day or of a year, but of a longer period. We are much hampered by the lack of practical experience on the part of the really influential men and much tact has to be used to steer and divert them without offending and causing pain.[10]

Wood was already demonstrating the "practical" approach to nation building. He arose each morning at 5:30 and began a day of furious routine,

signing directives, giving orders, hearing complaints, and undertaking inspections of schools, hospitals, road construction, and public projects. He
would even investigate the routine operation of a municipal court. He ran
the military government like an efficient plantation owner with a show of
southern charm for his Cuban wards coupled with a Yankee sense of
organization and efficiency. He dined with the Cuban social elite and conversed with the lowliest *guajiro* (rural dweller) in the countryside. For sheer
intensity of commitment, Wood was unmatched by any Cuban executive
until Fidel Castro. Cubans who remembered the old three-hour workdays
under the Spanish now had to adjust to Wood's bureaucratic regime of 9:00
to 11:00, 12:00 to 5:00, six days a week. Wood's office ran on a twenty-four-
hour schedule, with the day-to-day business supervised by Frank Steinhart,
who later became U.S. consul and in 1908 took over Havana Electric
Railway.

The American military in Cuba was, by 1901, a skeletal force, its
numbers drastically reduced since Wood became military governor in December 1899. Following the war, the Americans had paid off the Cuban
rebels (at roughly seventy-five dollars per man) and created a Rural Guard,
presumably apolitical, that undertook the task of policing the countryside
and maintaining order in the towns. Though American officers occasionally
mediated disputes, American soldiers still in Cuba did little police work. An
army of occupation, Wood believed, increased Cuban apprehensiveness
about American intentions.

When Wood stepped down in May 1902 Cuba was not militarily occupied in the same way as, say, Germany after 1945, but it had already felt
the imprint of American ways and techniques, expressed through a military
regime and a stern-minded physician turned professional soldier. Mindful
of the biblical injunctions on cleanliness, Wood had proceeded to sanitize
the island's towns by strict regulations on garbage disposal (the Habaneros
had always thrown their refuse in front of the house), paving of streets, and
whitewashing of public places. Wood was convinced that filth explained
Cuba's epidemics of yellow fever, though an eccentric Cuban scientist (of
Scottish ancestry), Dr. Carlos Findlay, argued correctly that the culprit was
the mosquito. Wood's vigorous sanitary campaign nonetheless probably
helped to control another Cuban scourge, typhoid.

Preparation of Cuba for independence meant, of course, an educational
system worthy of a young republic. Brooke and Wood had inherited a
Spanish educational structure that had 541 primary schools and 400 private
academies, most of them run by clerics. Brooke used the Spanish model, but
Wood wanted the Cubans to have a "practical" education in civics, history,
science, and vocational training. The model curriculum, written by an
officer on the governor's staff, was patterned on the "Ohio Plan" and

emphasized preparation for citizenship and the acquisition of skills or the learning of a trade. Hispanic tradition was intentionally denigrated. The texts were translations of American books (modified to Cuban conditions), and the Cuban teachers, before entering their classes of six-to-fourteen-year-old students, were themselves drilled in American credos of instruction. School boards and superintendents, as in the United States, supervised the curriculum and instruction. At the head of Cuba's new educational system stood Alexis Frye, a driven pedagogue who frantically converted old barracks, warehouses, and unoccupied dwellings into 3,000 schools, with 3,500 instructors and 130,000 students. Wood and Frye had a falling-out over the inclusion of what Wood called "radical" methods in class instruction, but their collective energies inspired what seemed to be a great educational experiment. Yet the enthusiasm did not survive, and an investigation in 1906 showed that school population had actually dropped to 1899 levels.[11]

One concern, more than any other, dominated Leonard Wood's thoughts during his governorship of Cuba, and that was the future of the Cuban-American relationship. To him the solution to what some commentators called "our Cuban problem" was not military but political. America had promised not to annex Cuba but had dispatched a conquering army to its shores; it had annexed Puerto Rico and promptly begun demonstrating toward its Caribbean possession a salutary neglect. It had annexed the Philippines but had to wage a grisly military campaign against Filipinos in a guerrilla war that left some Americans, such as Mark Twain, who had supported the Cuban intervention, with feelings of remorse and even revulsion at American practice.

Within a year of Wood's appointment, the Cuban political system took democratic forms. The governor permitted the creation of political parties —three quickly appeared—and participation in local elections. In November 1900 the constitutional convention began its deliberations. From the outset the delegates seemed anxious about the future of the island's relations with the United States. When McKinley or Root or Wood spoke of Cuba, their comments were laced with references to its "special importance" or "strategic position" in the American geopolitical scheme. Cuba was vital and vulnerable—vulnerable to European machinations, a nineteenth-century American fear now made even more obvious by Germany's naval aspirations in the West Indies, and vulnerable within from political inexperience and financial uncertainty. By removing Spanish authority, Root argued, the United States had become responsible for stable government in Cuba. The war against Spain had been a "moral" crusade, the preservation of Cuba's independence a matter of American self-interest.[12]

America's guarantee of Cuban independence thus became the central feature of the Cuban-American relationship, the formal criteria spelled out in the Platt Amendment, an attachment to the Army Appropriation Act of 1901. The amendment embodied Wood's and Root's prescription for Cuba. The republic must maintain a low public debt, so as to prevent financial calamity or misuse of funds; avoid violating American rights in its treaty relations with other nations; grant the United States the right to intervene to protect American lives and property and enforce sanitary measures; and provide long-term naval leases to the United States.

When the Cuban convention got word of the Platt Amendment, a furious debate ensued as to American intentions. Cuban sovereignty was clearly violated, as the more radical delegates pointed out. A special commission delivered a formal protest to Wood, who castigated the group as ungrateful for American contributions to Cuba's welfare. Another delegation arrived in Washington to protest directly to McKinley and discovered that he had already signed the Platt Amendment into law. Even Henry Teller, whose name had been attached to the 1898 resolution forswearing any intention to annex Cuba, supported the amendment. Root himself, one of its coauthors, lavishly entertained the Cubans, then followed with a six-hour discussion about American rights under the Monroe Doctrine. The Platt Amendment would be narrowly interpreted, he told his guests, and Cuban sovereignty would not be violated.

The mollified Cubans returned to Havana with American reassurances and tried to modify the amendment before incorporating it into the Cuban Constitution, as the United States required. But Wood insisted that no alterations would be permitted and that American troops would remain until the amendment became a part of Cuba's fundamental law. Wood believed he understood the reason for Cuban fears. Cuban critics of the Platt Amendment, he wrote Root, "have attempted to make it appear that the intervention will take place at the whim of the officers occupying naval stations." The remark referred to the practice in which naval officers sometimes landed forces or even conducted negotiations without specific orders. The presumption in Wood's comment was that modern communication had made this practice unnecessary. "One thing you can be sure of," Wood concluded, "there will be no serious disturbance in Cuba."[13]

Wood went on to become governor of the Philippines, but he never achieved in that faraway American colony the triumphs that he had enjoyed as proconsul of Cuba. The army returned to Cuba in 1906 in a second tour of occupation, but Wood did not command it.

When American troops left Cuba in mid-1902, Theodore Roosevelt had been president for less than a year. He was to find new opportunities in the emerging Caribbean empire of the United States; to exploit them, he employed a military service with more experience than the army in policing the tropics—the navy.

2. TR and the Use of Force

In Roosevelt's thinking, using the navy to maintain an orderly empire was politically safer than dispatching an army to police unruly peoples. An occupying army, though more thorough than a naval landing force in its operation, especially in the countryside, not only brought painful reminders of the brutal crushing of the Filipino rebellion but precipitated criticisms that a republican America, now that it had imperial pretensions, was not at all reluctant to dispatch its soldiers to watch over its far-flung colonial subjects. And there was a more compelling reason for wielding American power in the Caribbean through the navy: It had a storied tradition, going all the way back to its beginnings, of policing the seas. Its officers could negotiate with local leaders—even princes or presidents—or they could "chastise" them for failing to protect foreign life and property.

After the Spanish-American War, the navy developed stronger interests in Caribbean affairs. In mid-1901 the General Board of the Navy, created in the preceding year to advise the secretary of the navy on long-range naval strategy and chaired by the war hero George Dewey, commented on America's hemispheric policy:

Whether the principle of the Monroe Doctrine, so far as it is the policy of this Government, covers all South America, including Patagonia and the Argentine, is not for the consideration of the General Board, but only the fact that the principles of strategy and the defects in our geographical position make it impracticable successfully to maintain naval control by armed force beyond the Amazon, unless present conditions are radically changed.[1]

This was an oblique reference to the navy's pursuit of more ships in the fleet and more bases in the West Indies. But the eminent naval strategists were less concerned with the possibilities of American intervention in some turbulent Caribbean republic than with a foreign threat to American security in the hemisphere. Naval planners were obsessed with German designs in the hemisphere and countered with energetic efforts to secure naval sites in the Caribbean Sea's insular eastern perimeter. The General Board's Atlantic Plan, which guided American naval thinking about the Caribbean

from about 1900 until World War I, assumed that Germany would challenge the Monroe Doctrine and that Great Britain, compelled in 1901 to
accept American dominance in the construction of an isthmian canal,
would remain neutral. It followed that German forces would probably
attack Culebra, the small island off eastern Puerto Rico, and other crucial
points in the West Indies. A few naval strategists, such as C.D. Sigsbee,
captain of the ill-fated *Maine* and subsequently chief of naval intelligence,
were convinced that Germany's Caribbean designs were merely a ploy and
that Kaiser Wilhelm's admirals were actually plotting an assault in Chesa-
peake Bay.[2]

But any successful German intrusion in the Caribbean would depend
heavily upon British cooperation—even a British alliance—and the neutrality of France and Russia. There were influential British political leaders who
wanted to end the nineteenth-century policy of splendid isolation and
looked to a German alliance. In 1902, when Germany made it clear that
it intended to punish the arrogant Venezuelan dictator, Cipriano Castro,
because his government had defaulted on its international obligations and
had abused foreign residents, Great Britain, whose citizens had also suffered
at Castro's hands, decided to join. Prominent American officials, including
President Theodore Roosevelt and Secretary of State John Hay, informed
the Europeans that wastrel Latin American governments must be taught to
pay their debts.

The German and British navies (joined ultimately by an Italian force)
blockaded the Venezuelan coast; they sank several Venezuelan gunboats
and bombarded the fort at Puerto Cabello. As the situation became more
serious, American newspapers expressed concern about German intentions.
Roosevelt, who in 1916 would boast about backing Germany down in this
crisis, reminded Europe that the American fleet was maneuvering in the
Caribbean, and the blockading countries acquiesced in arbitration.

The navy's (and especially Admiral Dewey's) obsession about ulterior
German motives in the Caribbean and its plans for the development of a
naval base at Culebra reinforced Roosevelt's 1916 account of this crisis.
From late 1901, when Germany threatened a naval demonstration against
Venezuela for its refusal to pay its international obligations, the navy's
designs for Culebra paralleled the growing international tensions in the
Caribbean. The following year, as Castro became more defiant toward his
European creditors, the General Board drew up a plan for the defense of
the Venezuelan coast, which called for mobilization of the fleet to head off
any German move to gain a foothold on the South American mainland.

Fortunately for Roosevelt's (and Dewey's) image as a tough defender
of the weaker Caribbean republics against the "German menace," the navy
carried out a major maneuver in the Caribbean in late 1902 and early 1903

(including the landing of a marine battalion on Culebra) almost simultaneous with the Anglo-German blockade of the Venezuela coast. Dewey himself was given command of the combined fleet—the Caribbean Squadron, consisting of four cruisers and two gunboats, and the North Atlantic Squadron of four battleships—and hoisted his four-star flag on the *Mayflower* on December 8, the same day Germany and Great Britain broke off relations with Castro.

The Caribbean Squadron had been created earlier in the year to protect "American interests" in the West Indies and along the Caribbean shores of South and Central America. Its function was as much political as military, explained the secretary of the navy: The squadron's presence would exert influence "in those regions where disorder would imperil the lives and property of our citizens" and would also promote "friendly relations with the people." While Dewey's ships sailed hesitantly toward the Venezuelan coast in this crisis, and indeed got as close as Trinidad, the only American warship maneuvering in Venezuelan waters was the *Marietta* of the Caribbean Squadron, dispatched by Dewey to the scene as observer vessel. The *Marietta* did more than observe: Its captain took on board Venezuelans captured by the blockading ships, delivered mail and diplomatic dispatches, and provided safe passage for diplomats throughout the crisis, maintaining, wrote the captain, a strict neutrality. His assessment of the crisis, which the American press rapidly played up as a dangerous German-American confrontation, reflected a gentlemanly respect for his German counterparts on the blockading vessels and a paternalistic disdain for the Venezuelans.[3]

On at least one occasion between 1902 and 1906 it was not the German peril but Roosevelt's opportunism and ambition that prompted him to use the navy in the Caribbean. In November 1903 the prompt dispatch of American warships to the isthmus and their preventing the Colombian government from suppressing the Panamanian rebellion assured the creation of another Latin American nation. Roosevelt's role in this drama brought down upon him the wrath of antiimperialists and even the criticism of some of his political admirers.

But for the navy there was only one important difference between its assignment in the Panamanian revolt of November 1903 and the service it had been providing for fifty years in guaranteeing a "tranquil" isthmian passage. Before 1903 American bluejackets and marines had been landed many times to protect the isthmian route and uphold Colombian sovereignty over it, the latter pledge having been made in an 1846 treaty between the United States and New Granada (as Colombia was then called). In 1903 the navy intervened in isthmian affairs to safeguard the isthmian route against menace *from* Colombia.

Years before the 1903 Panamanian revolution triumphed because the United States shielded it from Colombian retaliation, the navy had been policing the isthmian tropics. Despite the fact that the American government had signed in 1850 a major canal convention with the British providing for equality of treatment (and, presumably, of responsibility) in any transisthmian route, the American navy early took on the task of safeguarding the Panamanian route. In 1855 the Panama Railroad began transporting eager travelers headed for the California gold fields. Five years later the sloop *Saint Mary's,* cruising in the Bay of Panama, sent ashore one hundred bluejackets and marines to protect the railroad from what was officially declared an "insurrection." On two separate occasions in 1873 American forces landed from three warships of the Pacific Squadron at Panama City at the behest of foreign residents and an American consul frightened over the outbreak of fighting between rival political factions. Panamanian secessionists were continually plotting against Bogotá, even though the province was granted a virtually autonomous status within the Colombian federation.

In the most serious revolt of the nineteenth century, the Pedro Prestán uprising in 1885, insurgents destroyed considerable foreign property and even burned the American consulate at Colón. On this occasion the landing came on the Caribbean side of the isthmus. Six American warships with two thousand officers and men (including the entire Marine Corps of the east coast) under the command of Rear Adm. James E. Jouett—in numbers of men the most ambitious operation of American military forces on foreign soil between 1848 and 1898—crushed the revolt after a frantic Panama Railroad superintendent informed Jouett that Prestán's rebels had begun tearing up track. When it was over the American troops paraded in Cathedral Plaza in Panama City and left the task of cleaning up to the railroad and the meting out of punishment to captured rebels to loyal Colombians. In Colón officials ordered fifty-eight people—most of them, it was averred, innocent—shot by firing squad. Prestán himself, sporting a derby, was hanged before a huge throng on Front Street in Colón.

Two diverse personalities—Philippe Bunau-Varilla and Manuel Amador Guerrero, one an ardent Frenchman committed to his country's prestige in building the canal, the other an equally ardent Panamanian revolutionary—watched Jouett's forces handily restore order in the rebellious isthmus and remembered for years the authoritative presence of American warships.[4]

After the great victory over Spain, as American determination to construct an isthmian canal intensified and a great debate over where to build it—Panama or Nicaragua—was being waged among political factions in the

United States, the navy continued playing policeman in rebellious Panama. In 1899 Colombia was plunged into civil conflict—the Thousand-Day War —and the struggle soon extended to the Panamanian province. In late 1901, almost two years before the celebrated uprising of November 1903, Panamanian secessionists declared for independence. As in the Prestán affair of 1885, the powerful foreign community appealed for protection, and a French, a British, and four American warships arrived. The American vessels landed troops at both Panama City and Colón. One of the American officers, Capt. Thomas Perry of the *Iowa,* persuaded the warring leaders to negotiate a truce aboard the *Marietta.* The rebels agreed to surrender their arms, and a detachment of Marines protected the Panama Railroad.

But within six months the revolution was renewed. Once again an American warship from the Caribbean Squadron (the *Machias,* hastily arriving from the troubled waters of the Dominican Republic) anchored at Colón and sent a landing party ashore. As in 1901 the navy generally supported Colombian efforts to crush the rebellion, though American officers saw their principal task as one of maintaining the peace. Thus the captain of the *Machias* interceded between warring armies and arranged for the peaceable transfer of Bocas del Toro from one army to another in order to prevent its destruction. From the beginning, he wrote, "I made it clear that the 'New Regime' would not interfere with American businesses locally." Following nineteenth-century custom, he forbade the shelling of an unfortified town and during the transfer of authority sent marines and bluejackets to police the town, imposed an 8:45 P.M. curfew (signaled by a shot from the *Machias*), shut down the saloons, and ordered sentries to shoot "incendiaries and housebreakers." A fellow officer from another patrolling vessel summed up the navy's role along the vital isthmian passageway: "We will vigorously protect life, liberty, American and other peaceable employees."[5]

In the nineteenth century the navy's landings in Panama had almost always been directed at Panamanian secessionists whose rebellion against Colombian authority had been looked upon by American officers as threats to American and foreign interests. After 1901, when the United States gained exclusive rights to construct an isthmian canal in a treaty with Great Britain, naval officers patrolling in Panamanian waters increasingly became the peacemakers between rival Colombian factions, both of which constituted threats to the "isthmian neutrality" the American navy was treaty bound to guarantee.

In mid-1903, having committed the United States to the Panama route, Roosevelt watched furiously as Colombian nationalists bitterly assailed the canal treaty that Secretary of State John Hay had negotiated. When in a perfectly legal but impolitic move the Colombian assembly defeated the treaty, Roosevelt was prepared to invoke the treaty of 1846 and its special provision allowing the United States to maintain "isthmian neutrality" *against* Colombia.

The navy did not instigate the Panamanian revolt of November 1903, but it determined which side would win, as its force had been determining the outcome of isthmian battles for almost fifty years. The revolt was plotted by civilians, Panamanian conspirators abetted by Bunau-Varilla, who recognized what Roosevelt would do in the event of an isthmian uprising and had important contacts in Washington. Navy and army (the army, too, had isthmian interests) officers seemed to know less about the revolt than did Roosevelt. Two army intelligence officers who had been dispatched to assess isthmian political conditions reported to Roosevelt and found him well informed about Panamanian matters—so much so they gave up a fleeting thought of resigning their commissions in order to lead the revolt. And the commander of the *Nashville,* which arrived at Colón in the evening of November 2, was ill informed about the outbreak of hostilities. When Colombian forces arrived on November 3, he permitted them to land because the frantic cable ordering him to protect the isthmian route, as authorized by the 1846 treaty, *and* to prevent any disembarking of Colombian forces did not arrive until the following day.[6]

Once the *Nashville*'s commanding officer began receiving the terse orders spewing out from the Navy Department, he moved quickly to control the situation ashore. A small force of marines disembarked and took up a position at the railroad office. The Colombian troops who had landed from the *Cartagena* on the third, denied passage (the engineer demanded a ticket for each soldier) to Panama City to contest the revolution, far exceeded in number the American troops in the town. The railroad's engineer, J.B. Shaler, did provide transport for the Colombian commander to Panama City, promising his troops would soon follow. But the enterprising engineer was involved in the plot, and he "made sure no cars were available."[7]

Meanwhile, more American troops began arriving at Colón. The *Nashville* carried only a small landing contingent, fewer than fifty men, and its captain would have been hard put to deal with a much larger Colombian force had a clash erupted. He had also to consider the problems posed by the sizable American population in the town, most of whom had taken refuge in the railroad station. The local Colombian commander, incensed at the arrest of his superior across the isthmus, threatened to burn the town and kill every American in it unless he was released.

But on the evening of the fifth the American presence in Colón was suddenly strengthened by the arrival of a second American ship, the *Dixie,* sent also by a frantic navy telegram. It carried a battalion of marines under the command of Major John Lejeune. Ashore, the Colombian commander was soon quieted by a bribe of $8,000 (presumably a part of the $100,000 Bunau-Varilla was spending on behalf of the revolution) and a hasty arrangement of passage for his men on a British Royal Mail steamer anchored in port. In a driving rainstorm, Lejeune landed two companies of marines as the Colombian troops embarked for home, creating still another legend in the corps that the arrival of the marines had indeed saved the day.[8]

In 1911, while the debate over Roosevelt's actions was still raging, he boasted, "I took the Canal Zone."[9] But he could not have "taken" Panama without getting a favorable canal convention. He could not have gotten that without the Panamanian revolution, and the revolution would not have succeeded without the forceful role played by the American military at Colón.

In the aftermath of the revolt, the navy continued to perform a significant role in isthmian affairs. When the flagship of the Caribbean Squadron, the *Mayflower,* arrived, its commanding officer, J.B. Coghlan, reported that he planned to mediate between Panamanian and Colombian officials—in a move reminiscent of American military mediation in previous rebellions. By this time, of course, the American government had already recognized the de jure existence of Panama, and on November 18 Hay and Bunau-Varilla signed their canal convention. Neither Coghlan nor any American naval officer at Colón could have achieved a political reconciliation between Panama and Colombia. But Coghlan still had his orders. A special Colombian agent, Gen. Rafael Reyes, who had commanded the Colombian relief expedition in 1885, disembarked from a French steamer in late November and was offered the *Mayflower*'s hospitality but declined on the grounds he could not board a foreign war vessel. "General Reyes inquired very particularly as to the extent of the Zone in which our forces would prevent any landings of troops," a reference to the provision in the 1846 treaty that permitted the United States to protect the isthmian route. Coghlan replied: "I informed him it was the whole limits of the State of Panama."[10]

Roosevelt's almost single-minded ferocity in dealing with those "damned dagoes," as he unflatteringly referred to the Colombians who had rejected his canal treaty, and the urgency he exhibited in pursuing the Panamanian business belied his hesitant approach to the entire question of intervention in the internal affairs of troubled Caribbean republics. At heart he *was* the "reluctant imperialist." But he felt equally strongly about not permitting European nations, whose economic and political stake in Latin America remained high, to treat with improvident hemispheric governments without following American rules. It followed that these politically contentious and economically distraught societies also had to follow certain rules of conduct. And U.S. naval vessels in the Caribbean, commanded by old-school Anglo-Saxon officers with pronounced views about Caribbean cultures, were prepared to convey those rules, by persuasion if possible, by force if necessary.

One country whose external debts and internal political turmoil attracted Roosevelt's concern was the Dominican Republic. Freed from Haitian domination in 1844, it had been ruled successively by larcenous executives (one of whom, Buenaventura Báez, had signed a treaty of annexation with the Grant administration that even a nominally corruptible Senate refused to approve) or flamboyant despots like Ulíses Heureaux (nicknamed "Lílis") who dramatically improved the country's financial standing in European eyes. But Heureaux governed with such murderous intrigue (a Dominican story tells how he invited an enemy to dinner and after the exquisite meal declared, "Have a cigar. It will be your last. I'm about to have you shot") that he was gunned down on a dingy Moca street in 1899 by a political rival.[11]

After Heureaux's death the republic plunged back into debt and political turmoil. Heureaux had given the management of the republic's considerable external debt and collection of the customs over to an American concern, the San Domingo Improvement Company. His successor began harassing the company for funds to put down the conspiracies against him, arousing the concern of the State Department over the plight of an American business and the growing prospects of European retaliation to settle the republic's indebtedness. When in 1903 an arbitral commission declared in favor of the San Domingo Improvement Company, European claimants looked to the United States for similar assistance.

Roosevelt resolved to get a financial settlement that would satisfy the Dominican Republic's European creditors and prevent a dangerous confrontation like the Venezuelan crisis earlier. In pursuing a more aggressive policy toward the beleaguered republic he had the enthusiastic support of the navy.[12]

The navy had been interested in bases in Hispaniola—at Manzanillo on the northwest coast and at Samaná Bay on the eastern shore of the Dominican Republic—since the Civil War era. In the 1890s the United States had tried to secure a naval lease at Môle Saint-Nicolas on Haiti's north coast, but the effort had run afoul of Haitian suspicion of foreigners. Early in 1903 a team of naval officers, disguised as journalists, visited the island on a special mission for the Bureau of Navigation. They returned with an enthusiastic report of the potentiality for development of naval sites in the Dominican Republic. There they had revealed the nature of their mission to one of the republic's revolutionaries (and future president), Horacio Vásquez, patron of the Horacistas. Vásquez promised that on gaining power he would grant rights for a coaling station at Samaná.

In October 1903 the republic was plunged into a civil war by a revolt from the north. The leader of the rebellion, Gen. Carlos Morales, was an ex-priest and a disciple of Juan Isidro Jiménez, chief of the Jimenistas, a political faction that, along with the Horacistas, plotted against central authority. The government at first put up a determined resistance. In the capital, Santo Domingo, it mustered nine hundred troops (as against the four thousand Morales and his associates commanded) and reinforced the city walls with iron water pipes and barrels filled with stone, clay, and sand. Despite such desperate measures, the city capitulated after a brief fight, and the president and his cabinet escaped to a German warship in the harbor.

Morales declared himself chief executive and in so doing alienated Jiménez, who launched another revolution. By the end of the year the republic had plunged into another civil war, a condition that reinforced the contempt Roosevelt and American naval officers held for Dominican politics. In this second revolt, the lives and property of foreigners were endangered. In the Morales revolt, American, French, and Italian ships in the harbor of Santo Domingo had landed forces to protect their nationals. But Jiménez's authority existed primarily in the North, where the reach of Santo Domingo's presidents had rarely extended and where the rebels began systematically harassing foreigners and destroying foreign-owned property —killing livestock, burning cane fields, and interfering with the Clyde Line passenger and cargo vessels that operated on the north coast.

Throughout the agitation of 1903 ships of the South Atlantic Squadron patrolled Dominican waters, their commanders often interceding between insurgent leaders, American businesses, and commanders of European warships hovering off the capital. The commander of the U.S.S. *Atlanta* used his influence to assist a railroad construction firm that was losing workers to rebel bands, warning their leaders and the government: "It is unnecessary for me to call your attention to the importance of preserving law and order; whatever government may exist, and whoever may be in authority, will be held strictly accountable by the United States Government." And a few weeks later the American officer was vigorously arguing with the commander of the German vessel *Vineta,* which had participated in the Venezuelan blockade, who contended all the rebellious Dominican chieftains were criminals.

Naval officers circulated among Santo Domingo's "better" and "uneducated" classes, reporting that the former were "desirous" of American annexation and the latter took "for granted that the United States will take charge of affairs." And they also got to know the leaders of the most powerful factions. One American naval lieutenant spent several weeks with Vásquez's army and reported the Dominican leader's men to be "educated, polished, with a great deal of respect for the United States"—a rare tribute to Dominican capabilities. A more common sentiment among American officers characterized Dominican rebels as "ignorant, unreliable, uncivilized mobs."[13]

In early January 1904 Comdr. A.C. Dillingham of the *Detroit* landed contingents of marines at Puerto Plata and Sosúa, declaring, in typical nineteenth-century naval tradition, that fighting was forbidden in towns containing large numbers of foreign residents. A more serious incident took place in the capital itself. By the end of January fighting in the northern coastal towns had virtually ceased, and in Santo Domingo a shaky truce had been arranged between the Jimenistas and the government. On February 1 the truce was broken when rebels fired on a launch from the *Yankee,* an auxiliary cruiser, and killed an American seaman, J.C. Johnstown.

The South Atlantic Squadron, under the temporary command of Capt. Richard Wainwright of the *Newark,* was responsible for patrolling Dominican waters. Wainwright sailed for the capital, arriving eleven days after Johnstown's death, and discovered that the *Columbia,* which had preceded the *Newark* by four days, had already made contact with the insurgents to ensure the safety of foreign lives ashore and the safe docking of commercial vessels in port. A steamer, the *New York,* tried to dock on the eleventh under the protection of a launch clearly displaying the American flag. Both received rebel fire. The *Columbia*'s commander now decided to retaliate. Two battalions of shipboard marines and bluejackets from the *Columbia* and the *Newark* left for shore as the *Newark*'s guns blazed away at insurgent positions. The bombardment continued intermittently for more than an hour. In the evening the landing force returned to the two warships.[14]

The Dominican troubles of 1903–1904 and the limited military response are instructive in the history of the banana wars, not only for the choices taken but for the alternatives Roosevelt rejected. In a later era, under William Howard Taft, Woodrow Wilson, or even Calvin Coolidge, the severity of the revolution might have prompted a full-scale military intervention. But a military occupation of the Dominican Republic in 1904 was not seriously considered. Roosevelt was determined to prevent foreign intervention (a British warship had appeared in Dominican waters during these days), and the most expedient way of doing that was through the creation of a system whereby the republic could pay its foreign obligations. In 1904 the country's foreign debt was estimated at $32 million (some observers reckoned the figure at $40 million), two thirds owed to Europeans. Morales, harassed by impatient creditors and warring Jimenistas, looked to the United States for assistance. The idea of appointing Americans to collect the customs, which constituted probably 90 percent of the government's revenues, was as much a Dominican as an American proposal. If the American government appointed the customs collectors, it would have to protect them from foreigners and Dominican rebels, who had little to gain in a revolution if they knew they were not going to get their hands on the customs receipts. But in January 1904, when Morales's foreign minister descended on Washington beseeching aid, he was rebuffed. As Roosevelt explained,

I have been hoping and praying for three months that the Santo Domingans would behave so that I would not have to act in any way. I want to do nothing but what a policeman has to do in Santo Domingo. As for annexing the island, I have about the same desire to annex it as a gorged boa constrictor might have to swallow a porcupine wrong-end-to. Is that strong enough? I have asked for some of our people to go there because, after having refused for three months to do anything, the attitude of the Santo Domingans has become one of half chaotic war towards us. If I possibly can, I want to do nothing to them. If it is absolutely necessary to do something, then I want to do as little as possible. Their government has been bedeviling us to establish some kind of protectorate over the island, and take charge of their finances. We have been answering them that we could not possibly go into the subject now at all.[15]

But Morales persisted in his overtures. In the spring the Dominican president again offered Roosevelt control over the customhouses and was again turned down. It soon became obvious, however, that Roosevelt was changing his mind about American involvement in the beleaguered republic. On February 22, the day before Roosevelt wrote to J.B. Bishop of his determination "to do nothing to them" (the Dominicans), a special tribunal established under the Hague convention ruled that Venezuela must settle its foreign debt and pay *first* those nations that had laid the blockade of 1902. Roosevelt was severely shaken; the decision meant, he confided to an associate, that the international community sanctioned armed retaliation for nonpayment of foreign obligations—little consequence that a distinguished Argentine jurist, Luís M. Drago, declared at the same time that international law should not sanction the forcible collection of debts.

Hesitant to declare any drastic departure in policy before the November elections, Roosevelt waited until December before announcing, in his annual message, that "chronic wrongdoing . . . may . . . require intervention by some civilized nation, and in the Western Hemisphere the adherence of the United States, however reluctantly, in flagrant cases of wrongdoing or impotence, to the exercise of an international police power." The following month Commander Dillingham, the navy's most knowledgeable student of Dominican affairs and an avid promoter of a Dominican naval base, drew up a protocol with the Morales government. It provided for American management of all Dominican customhouses and a guarantee for the "territorial integrity" of the republic. The collectors would turn over 45 percent of receipts to Dominican officials; the remainder would be transferred to New York banks for disbursement to the republic's creditors.

Roosevelt viewed the customs treaty as political compromise; the Senate, suspicious of his foreign policy ventures, took one look at the clause guaranteeing Dominican sovereignty and adjourned without acting. But on the American warships circling the republic from early 1904 there was a firm conviction that the Dominican Republic was rapidly becoming "another Cuba" on the eve of American intervention. More than a year before he dutifully handed the customhouse protocol to the Dominican president, Dillingham had been maintaining law and order on the north coast. In January 1904, when Jiménez's rebels seized Puerto Plata, an old port on the sea lanes from Africa, Dillingham determined they must not hold the town. He landed three companies from the *Detroit* and the *Dallas* and ran them out, delivering an ultimatum to *both* Jiménez's and Morales's captains stating they could fight in the countryside and "show that they were capable of civilized methods."

To Dillingham and his naval colleagues policing off the coastal cities during the civil war, the insurgents and the government were expected to obey the same rules. When Morales's gunboats tried to blockade rebel-held ports and shut off the supply of munitions to the enemy, American commanders interfered on the grounds that not even the legitimate government of the country could blockade its own ports. The American minister complained to Secretary of State Hay: "It is a peculiar circumstance that in each of these late revolutions, we have invariably sided with the insurgents." But the navy was not "siding" with either faction as far as Dillingham was concerned; its ships were upholding the law, modified to meet local conditions: "International law," Dillingham responded, "can be applied here only so far as it suits the convenience of the United States Government."[16]

Roosevelt believed a satisfactory solution to the Dominican "problem" could be worked out without drastic commitments to the Dominicans or a confrontation with the European powers. His naval officers plying Dominican waters advocated increasingly forceful measures. "I doubt the feasibility of effecting a successful transfer of the custom-houses by personal influence, independently of an exhibition of naval power," wrote Rear Adm. Charles Sigsbee, who arrived on the scene in early 1905 to replace the more cautious Dillingham in dealing with the Dominican government.

The real problem lay in the failure of President Morales to control the North, especially the rebellious province of Monte Cristi and its revolutionary governor, Gen. Desiderio Arias. In October 1904 the United States, using as pretext the Dominican government's failure to make a regular payment in its settlement with the San Domingo Improvement Company, took charge of the customhouse at Puerto Plata, the main port on the north coast of the island. There was little trouble at Puerto Plata, but Monte Cristi, sixty-five miles to the west, also scheduled to get an American collector, proved defiant. Arias publicly condemned the Morales government and its acquiescence in American demands. Sigsbee preferred to let Morales take the lead in disciplining Arias but was prepared to chastise him ("I shall not hesitate to meet force with force") if Arias stood in the way of transferring the Monte Cristi customhouse to American control.

Though told explicitly by the Navy Department that he must not become involved in the civil conflict raging ashore, Sigsbee held a series of conferences aboard the *Newark* with Arias's representatives—Arias arrogantly refused to step aboard an American warship—from which emerged an agreement permitting one of Sigsbee's staff officers to take possession of the customhouse in Monte Cristi. Arias condemned the arrangement as unconstitutional, but Sigsbee went ahead, vowing to take all responsibility for his actions in the matter. The new customs collector, Lt. Edwards Leiper, took charge by demanding the local attendant produce the door keys while an angry Monte Cristi crowd gathered. As things turned out, only one Dominican employee quit, and Sigsbee proudly boasted to the secretary of the navy about the means he had employed to make Roosevelt's diplomacy work: "Now that we have peaceful possession of this customhouse, I shall regard further interference, on the part of authorities here, as forcible action against American interests, and I shall not fail to protect those interests after the usual methods employed in the West Indies."[17]

Thus, while Roosevelt was wrangling his *modus vivendi,* the executive agreement establishing the customs receivership until the Senate finally got around to approving the Dominican-American treaty in 1907, naval officers on duty in Dominican waters were talking about "preventing another Cuba." Roosevelt spoke about running the customhouses to assure that precious revenues would be used to satisfy claimants and not finance revolutions. His aggressively-minded sailors in the Caribbean recommended policing the ports in which the customhouses were located—Puerto Plata, Santo Domingo, Monte Cristi, Samaná, and Marcoris—in order "to establish a stable government on the island."[18]

But Roosevelt wanted—and got—a limited political solution to the Dominican problem, one that would satisfy the Senate and show his critics that he had no intention of annexing the Dominican Republic, that what he desired, as he had explained in early 1904, was for the Dominicans to "behave." And in the rule of Gen. Ramón Cáceres, who emerged from the civil commotion of 1905 as the dominant political figure in the troubled republic, Roosevelt believed he saw a prosperous peace in the Dominican future. But in the republic various rebellious factions seemed as ready as ever to renew the war. Seven American warships hovered in Dominican waters, ready to evacuate Americans.

Cáceres remained unwavering, however, and one by one crushed his opponents. In the process he received some unexpected assistance from an obscure American naval commander, who summoned a dozen rebellious generals to his ship and lectured them "on the evil effects of constant revolution in comparison with the peace and progress that would be enjoyed if Dominicans could only be persuaded to adopt American methods of settling their disputes."[19]

In the meantime Roosevelt was drawn again into the volatile world of Cuban politics, where a mere "chastisement" of the unruly, the punishment he had had the navy mete out to the Dominicans, would ultimately prove inadequate, and he would reluctantly choose an occupation army to deal with the situation.

3. The Second Cuban Intervention, 1906

Leonard Wood was only one of several influential Americans who believed that Cuba should be annexed, as Puerto Rico had been, developed by American capital, and then, once the economy reached a prosperous state, granted its independence. The "better classes of Cubans," Wood remarked on departing Havana in 1902, must certainly prefer annexation to the uncertainties of independence.

In 1902 Cuba was independent in name only. Even its new president, Don Tomás Estrada Palma, who purged American employees whenever possible and, wrote American consul general Frank Steinhart, seemed to "change everything that is American or that was done by Americans," never fully grasped the idea of independence.[1] Estrada thought in terms of dependence—dependence symbolized by the Platt Amendment and the Cuban-American commercial treaty. And then there were the droves of American entrepreneurs and investors who came to conquer the tropics. Frank Steinhart, a holdover from the Wood regime, was one. Percival Farquhar, who came in 1898 with a grand scheme for electrifying Havana's tramways, was another. He turned eventually to the massive task of building a railway from Havana to Santiago. Other ambitious adventurers began developing the Isle of Pines (which the American government regarded as separate territory until 1925) and even built a town named McKinley. The banana emperor, Minor Keith, who founded United Fruit Company in 1899, bought 200,000 acres on Nipe Bay for a trifling $400,000. By 1902 Cuba was assuming the classic characteristics of a marketplace economy. The American stake, calculated at $50 million in 1895 by Secretary of State Richard Olney, already had reached $100 million by the time of Wood's departure.[2]

Militarily Cuba was an appendage of American territory. The U.S. Navy, which looked to the Caribbean and especially to Cuba for new naval sites, had proposed a list of four sites on the island (Santiago, Guantánamo, Nipe Bay, and Havana); the Platt Amendment obligated the Cubans to provide them. When the Cubans protested, Roosevelt told Hay to be insistent on the issue. Not only must Cuba provide naval leases but, Roosevelt argued, the sites would be developed within the next few years. Wood himself had preferred Santiago as the site of the major American naval base in Cuba. Guantánamo, by its proximity to the Windward Passage, was the most strategically located of the four sites. Navy admirals added Havana to their list because they considered the capital a principal target of enemy assault and, frankly, because Havana would be the most probable spot for landing American troops if the United States again intervened on Cuban soil. But the prospect of an American naval base in Havana aroused the most intense Cuban objections, and Estrada found in Roosevelt a sympathetic listener. Frustrated, the navy's General Board now watched as Roosevelt relinquished its plans for a Havana base, substituting for it a site at Bahía Honda (west of the capital) but retaining the proposal for a long-term lease at Guantánamo. The arrangement was incorporated into the 1903 Cuban-American treaty. Ultimately the navy gave up on making Bahía Honda into a base; it was left, thus, with Guantánamo, strategically placed but vulnerable to attack.[3]

But the driving force behind the 1906 Cuban intervention was not the navy—despite its ambitions for Cuban bases—or the powerful American economic community in Havana. The occupation of Cuba came about because of the breakdown of Cuba's political system and Roosevelt's frustration in dealing with the island's political crisis.

Estrada Palma became president in 1902 under auspicious circumstances. But he ruled with an administrative machinery created by Americans and under a constitution modeled closely on that of the United States. The party system only vaguely resembled that of the United States, however, and the parties themselves—the Republicans and National Liberals—tended to be dominated by former rebel generals who were constantly intriguing. In the 1904 elections for the Cuban congress there occurred sporadic violence, and when the legislative assembly convened the following year the Liberals, who charged the opposition with fraud, refused to participate and thus prevented a quorum.

By this time everyone was gearing for the presidential election to determine who would succeed Don Tomás. The Liberals put forth a popular ex-general, José Miguel Gómez, former governor of Santa Clara province; the Republicans, now calling themselves the Moderates, had no one to offer except the avuncular Estrada himself. Though party leaders differed on a few issues—the Liberals, for example, advocated immediate abandonment of the Platt Amendment; the Moderates, eventual abrogation—their principal dispute was over who should get "twenty millions of the treasury."[4] As the electoral campaign got underway, there was once again random violence. It quickly became apparent that the Rural Guard and the police were going to ensure Estrada's victory. When the president's reelection was assured, Goméz descended on New York, declaring that the United States "has a direct responsibility concerning what is going on in Cuba." The American government, he went on, should intervene and guarantee a fair election, which would demonstrate that "eighty percent of the Cuban people were Liberal."[5]

But by the spring of 1906 the Liberals realized that the United States was not going to guarantee a fair election and resolved to act quickly, to "seek justice somewhere else," as one former rebel general announced. In August the conspirators declared against the government, in the Spanish tradition of denunciation of central authority, and laid plans for the rebellion and seizure of the railway Farquhar had constructed. Another former general, Mario Menocal, a sugar baron, arrived in the capital on September 8 offering his services as mediator, but Estrada refused to negotiate until the rebels put down their arms. Even as Estrada and Menocal talked, the rebels were already stealing horses and issuing manifestos. Random fighting erupted. After Menocal departed, Estrada sent a frantic message to the American government via Steinhart requesting two warships, one at Havana and the other at Cienfuegos. The Cuban government, he declared, could no longer guarantee the safety of foreign property.

The Liberals had a force of twenty-four thousand; the government could rely on only the three thousand of the Rural Guard. More importantly, it had no regular army to crush the uprising.[6]

Cuba had fallen, to use Roosevelt's contemptuous phrase, "into the insurrectionary habit." The old Cuban president, using emergency measures under the 1901 constitution, issued sweeping decrees suspending certain civic liberties and increasing the size of the Rural Guard. "The Government has made many arrests," the American chargé d'affaires reported, "and seems to be acting with energy and determination." Former generals in the war against Spanish rule trooped into Havana to offer their services, but the number of war heroes in the rebel camp disheartened Estrada. Even the loyalty of the Rural Guard was questioned. In one engagement, a detachment sent to deal with insurrectionists joined the enemy.[7]

Late summer found Roosevelt vacationing at Oyster Bay. He was not surprised at the dreary turn of events in Cuba. "What I dreaded has come to pass in the shape of a revolt," he wrote the British historian George Otto Trevelyan. What must be prevented was not only the loss of life and property but, more importantly, "the creation of a revolutionary habit." He would not be stampeded into ill-advised measures, he informed Trevelyan:

In confidence I tell you that I have just been notified by the Cuban Government that they intend to ask us forcibly to intervene in the course of this week, and I have sent them a most emphatic protest against their doing so. . . . On the one hand we can not permanently see Cuba a prey to misrule and anarchy; on the other hand I loathe the thought of assuming any control over the island such as we have over Puerto Rico and the Philippines.[8]

But a few days later Roosevelt sent a brief message in cipher to Assistant Secretary of State Robert Bacon ordering the navy to dispatch more ships "at once" with as many marines "as possible" to Cuban waters. He followed with a soothing letter to the Cuban minister to the United States, Gonzalo de Quesada, who once had served in the Cuban junta in New York, expressing his sorrow over the "menace" to Cuba's "peace, prosperity, and independence" and the "evil of anarchy, into which civil war and revolutionary disturbances will surely throw her." Roosevelt mixed caution with determination. Cuban independence could be jeopardized if the Cuban people "show their inability to continue in their path of peaceful and orderly progress." "Life, property, and individual liberty," principles the United States had guaranteed to the island in the Platt Amendment, were imperiled, Roosevelt said, and he would not "shirk" his duty in defending them. He closed the letter with an announcement of his decision to send a special delegation, headed by Secretary of War William Howard Taft and Bacon, who were departing shortly for Havana to resolve the Cuban crisis.[9]

An admiral of the U.S. Navy took one look at Roosevelt's recommendation for as many marines "as possible" for Cuban duty and politely told Bacon that bluejackets performed as well as marines and could be more easily assembled. The admiral could have two thousand bluejackets in the Cuban capital in five days; a marine force took much longer to ready. On the day Roosevelt sent his ominous analysis of Cuban affairs to the Cuban minister, the *Denver* and *Marietta* were already landing bluejackets on Cuban soil. The *Marietta*'s commander, William F. Fullam, was contemptuous of Cubans and determined to protect American property owners harassed by Cuban rebels. Fullam had received desperate pleas from American planters around Cienfuegos; protecting their interests, he believed, constituted part of his duty.

With similar attentiveness to his role as policeman in the tropics, Comdr. J. C. Colwell of the *Denver*, anchored in Havana harbor during the political turbulence of mid-September, acted in accord with long-standing naval practice in Caribbean waters. Invited ashore by Steinhart, he donned civilian clothes and accompanied by the American chargé, called on a "nervous" Estrada. After a brief conversation he concluded that the Cuban president was not only "nervous" but also "extremely unpopular," making it relatively easy for the rebels to take the city. When Estrada confessed he

could not guarantee protection to American lives and interests, the chargé
turned to Colwell and asked how long it would take to land his men from
the *Denver.* "Half an hour," replied Colwell. By 4:30 P.M. of the same day
(September 13) of his visit with the beleaguered Cuban president, Colwell
had landed a battalion of bluejackets and marines, two Colt machine guns,
and one three-inch artillery piece in Havana. Sensing a dramatic shift in
American policy, rebel generals now descended upon him with a litany of
grievances.

But by late evening the American chargé, who had accompanied the
forceful naval officer in a call upon the Cuban executive earlier in the day,
came by with a telegram from Bacon stating that no troops were to be
landed. Colwell's only response was that the telegram bore the date September
12 and took no cognizance of the events of the following day. Accord-
ingly, he could not return his men to the *Denver* but assured the chargé he
would take "all responsibility." The following day, "finding the city quiet,"
Colwell ordered his force back to the ship. Explaining his actions of the
thirteenth, which technically violated State Department policy and Bacon's
directive, Colwell wrote that he had been fulfilling an obligation as policeman in a disorderly society protecting the lives and interests of Americans:
"Having received no instruction, I do not know the policy of my Government with respect to Cuba, nor the effect of my actions in Havana upon that
policy; but I do know that the immediate effect of my landing . . . was to
prevent the occupation of Havana that night [September 13] by the rebels
with probably much disorder."[10] Thus when Taft and Bacon arrived they
found that the American navy had preceded them.

The special mission that had been entrusted to him was not the high
moment in the illustrious public career of William Howard Taft. He had
served his country in another tropical place, the Philippines, where American soldiers, who called themselves "goddamns," civilized "gugus," as
American troops referred to Filipino rebels, with a Krag rifle. Taft had
declared he would treat Filipinos as "little brown brothers." He did not
make a similar declaration about Cubans. He arrived in Havana aboard an
American warship on September 19, armed with Roosevelt's instructions
to mediate the Cuban crisis but knowing that the president had virtually
resolved upon occupation. Just about every major faction in the country
wanted some form of American intervention: the Liberals, who were gam-
bling the Americans would intervene only long enough to guarantee a free
election, which of course the Liberals would win; the Moderates, who
believed a brief military intervention might save Estrada Palma; the foreign
community of Europeans, mostly British, Spanish, and German, who feared
the ravages of a civil war and who looked to the Americans to keep order
in the Caribbean.

A limited intervention had of course occurred before Taft arrived. The *Denver* had posted a detachment of bluejackets and marines in the Plaza de Armas in the capital, and the aggressive Fullam of the *Marietta* had sent two officers and thirty-four bluejackets ashore at Cienfuegos to protect the Soledad Sugar Company, an American concern, from assault by rebel forces. The action had been taken, Fullam boasted, "in accordance with my orders to protect American interests." The *Marietta*'s protective shield covered only Cienfuegos and the immediate surrounding area, however, and he reluctantly declined to send troops when rebels burned the Hormiguero Central Company estate, also American-owned, because it was "too far away to be protected by the limited force at my disposal."

Fullam was contemptuous of the rebels who were trying to provoke American intervention. "Nine-tenths of the revolutionaries are negroes, and they are not under good discipline."[11] He was arrogantly assertive about his mission in Cuban waters: "The rebels must be made to understand," he wrote a junior officer on duty ashore, "that you will fire upon them if they come within range and menace you or do any damage to American property." When the chargé in Havana questioned his readiness to dispatch troops ashore without specific orders from Washington, Fullam snapped, "I feel that we did right. We were sent here to protect American interests . . . ; we gave [help] to the best of our ability."[12]

Taft began his labors with a dreary analysis of Estrada's position; the president had only the woefully inadequate Rural Guard to protect the government against an enemy eight times larger. If the United States intervened to prop up Estrada, he told Roosevelt disconsolately, then "we should be fighting the whole Cuban population."[13] There might be hope for compromise with the Liberals, he believed. A few days after his arrival the genial emissary sat down with several insurgent generals and discussed their grievances. He came away from the meeting with misgivings though not without hope:

What is needed here, as in the Philippines and elsewhere in the tropics, in dealing with people like this, is patience, but the trouble lies in the irresponsible character of the men in arms, who, although they represent a great majority of the people in their cause, are themselves, many of them, lawless persons of no particular standing in time of peace, and whose motive for continuing in arms is very strong because of the importance that they enjoy [in] such conditions while peace means to them [something] which they hate most—work. Still, we will work along.[14]

When Taft talked about landing more troops, Roosevelt approved, but the president desperately wanted to avoid using the word "intervention." He was already pondering action much more consequential than the limited

intervention of more bluejackets or marines. As Estrada's cause faltered and
the rebels threatened to expand hostilities, he contemplated the mechanics
of another Cuban occupation, using the army, which, after all, had had the
responsibility of governing the island for four years after the war with Spain.
And it had performed a peace-keeping role in the Philippines.

But the latter experience had left some Americans with unpleasant
memories. Pacification of the Filipino rebels had become a grisly business,
and one army officer, Frederick Funston (whom Roosevelt briefly considered for command in Cuba) had scandalized Victorian America with his
rapacious campaign against the Filipinos. Some outspoken army officers,
anticipating Cuban occupation, expressed doubts about pacifying the island
in a prolonged campaign in which the army would have to resort to the
tactics that "Butcher" Weyler, the despised Spanish general, had introduced in his counterrevolutionary campaign in Cuba in 1896—the *reconcentrado* and the *trocha*—measures that brutalized the civilian populace,
aroused American indignation, and materially contributed to American
intervention.[15]

In his history of the second Cuban occupation, Allan Millett argues
persuasively that Roosevelt's hesitancy and maneuvering contributed to
Cuban uncertainty, encouraged the insurgents to prolong the war, and
ultimately compelled the president to accept occupation of the island. By
permitting limited interventions from the *Denver* and *Marietta,* which were
charged with protecting American interests ashore, Roosevelt was in fact
undermining his repeated profession to solve the Cuban crisis peacefully,
"to put an end to anarchy without necessitating a reoccupation of the island
by our own troops."[16] But, ultimately, a military solution for Cuba's ills was
Roosevelt's answer.

For one thing, the American navy was already broadening its responsibilities in Cuban affairs. In the south of the island, around Cienfuegos,
Commander Fullam extended his protective shield to include the Cuban
Central Railroad stations at Cienfuegos, Palmira, and Hormiguero—necessary measures, Fullam wrote, for the protection of "American and British
interests." In the nineteenth century it was not uncommon for naval commanders patrolling off disturbed areas to declare towns "neutral zones" and
forbid fighting in them. Determined to prevent either government or rebel
troops from using the railroad, Fullam dispatched a small force ashore to
Palmira. There the American had a nervous encounter with about 350
insurgents who had ridden into town bent on stopping Estrada's forces from
using the railroad. Fullam announced that both groups were denied its use.
He blocked the street in front of the station with sentries and ordered two
Colt machine guns readied on an adjacent platform. The rebels "seemed
pleased" with his peremptory action; they traveled by horse, so Fullam's

action favored their cause. An hour after the Americans arrived, the rebels left town. Fullam met later with the local government commander who, Fullam boasted in his report, volunteered to serve under his command.[17]

Had Estrada been as cooperative with the Americans as his commander in Palmira, Taft's mission would have been much easier. The major issue, Taft wrote the Cuban president in a supercilious letter, was the widespread fraud in the 1905 elections. The law under which the election had been held was defective; therefore, Estrada's election was fraudulent, as the rebels charged. The sensible solution called for the resignation of Estrada's cabi-net, which the Liberal Alfredo Zayas had suggested, and the appointment of nonpartisan members. This would be followed by new elections for the National Assembly and, in time, a reformed judiciary and new municipal codes. In short, the electoral and judicial flaws embedded in the 1901 constitution would be excised.

The plan depended on Estrada's staying on as caretaker executive until a temporary replacement could be found. But Estrada refused to accommo-date the American emissary until the rebels laid down their arms. Neither Roosevelt nor Taft had counted on the obstinacy of this old man who had spent twenty years in the United States and had often spoken pathetically about "teaching his people" the glories of American-style democracy. Es-trada's intransigence, which modern Cuban historians interpret as national-istic ardor, upset Taft's plans. Hearing about Estrada's sulkiness and refusal to "act like a patriot," Roosevelt too became more determined to do some-thing. Just as he had reacted angrily in 1903 when those "damned dagoes" in Bogotá destroyed his canal treaty with Colombia, he grew furious with the Cubans. But he had resolved not to be rushed into a large-scale military involvement in the island. The United States could not take the "place of his [Estrada's] unpopular government and face all the likelihood of a long drawn out and very destructive guerrilla warfare." And, on September 28, he alluded to the attitude of the American people to Caribbean intervention: "I think it would be a misfortune for us to undertake to form a provisional government if there was a fair chance of obtaining peace by according to the Cubans themselves to form their own provisional government. Remem-ber that we have to do not only what is best for the island, but what we can get public sentiment in this country to support."[18]

But everything hinged on Estrada's cooperative spirit. On September 25 Roosevelt had sent the Cuban executive a special plea to abide by Taft's plan. But three days later, Estrada and his vice-president appeared in the assembly and, after a moving speech by the president, resigned. Outside, a marine detachment hurried to protect the millions in the national treasury, which were, wrote a contemporary, the real prize in the battle between the Moderates and Liberals. Estrada's party followers immediately departed with him. He would not permit a Moderate to form a provisional government.

Thus Cuba no longer had a government. Taft now assumed extraordinary powers. The day after Estrada resigned, he declared a provisional government in the name of the president of the United States, who was still talking about a reconciliation of the Cuban crisis! Two thousand marines disembarked from American battleships and went to a place outside the city called Columbia.

The second Cuban occupation had begun.[19]

4. Cuba Occupied

The intervention and the creation of a provisional government in 1906 left a bitter legacy among Cubans. Denied the right to be arbiters of their own destiny by Taft's proclamation, they were ruled for the next twenty-nine months by an American civil service bureaucrat and a coterie of American soldiers.

But Cubans themselves had done much to bring on this calamity. The Liberal insurrectionists, who never proved Don Tomás Estrada Palma was anything but an aged, competent administrator, had been so bent on making José Miguel Gómez president of the republic that they risked civil war and American intervention. They plundered the countryside, stole horses, and seized the funds of municipal treasuries from the towns they pretended to defend. Around Guantánamo, where American property interests were large, wrote one naval officer, local officials, presumably loyal to the government, were aiding the rebellion. Even the ordinarily complaisant Taft was taken aback by their rapacity. In early September a Liberal general in Santa Clara declared that either the central government demonstrate "justice" or his forces would commence operations aimed at provoking American intervention. "The properties which we will commence to destroy," he added ominously, "will be those of American citizens."[1]

The pleas for intervention from foreign property owners and businessmen, European governments alert to the dangers to their countrymen in Cuba, and the old Spanish element that had remained on the island were ultimately grounded in one seemingly irrefutable argument: The Cuban government could not provide law and order.

What he wanted for the island, Roosevelt informed Congress in December 1906, was "that it shall prosper morally and materially" in order that "Cubans ... shall be able to preserve order among themselves and therefore ... preserve their independence."[2] It sounded transparent, but Roosevelt had expressed similar sentiments in his private correspondence.

To achieve order and tranquillity Cuba now had a provisional government created by the authority Roosevelt had vested in his faithful secretary of war. Cuba's new proconsuls were American army officers, as in 1900, but in 1906 their superior was no stern medical missionary bent on bringing civilization to the tropics but a former real estate tycoon and country lawyer from the prairie town of Lincoln, Nebraska—Charles Magoon. In 1899 Magoon had come east and met William McKinley, who was then looking for someone with legal skills to assist the military governors of newly conquered Cuba who were striving to reconcile abstruse Spanish law and American rules. Magoon soon joined the Bureau of Insular Affairs of the War Department, which was the closest American equivalent to a colonial office. In 1904 he arrived in Panama as counsel of the Isthmian Canal Commission but provided a more effective service in reconciling Panamanian nationalists smarting at American arrogance on the isthmus. Even his friends regarded Magoon as dull and unimaginative, but his labors caught the attention of important persons. Roosevelt had been earnestly pressed to return Wood to his old fiefdom in Havana, but Magoon's civilian status better suited the president's strategy of persuading wary Europeans and a suspicious Senate that the provisional government was not a military authority. Roosevelt was also apparently convinced that Magoon, who had gotten along with Panamanians, would make friends in Cuba. In this case, lamentably, the president's judgment proved embarrassingly wrong. Cubans admired and certainly respected Leonard Wood; Magoon, they believed, was a vulture and a leech.[3]

Magoon hardly conformed to the Cuban image of him as the Yankee exploiter in the tropics. He was, like Taft, inclined to go along in order to get along. His favorite pastimes were eating and riding in an automobile. His most reprehensible action, Cuban historians have bitterly observed, was the dissemination of patronage to Liberal wrongdoers who pilfered the treasury that Don Tomás had so carefully accumulated. So savage have been the Cuban assessments of Magoon, wrote Hugh Thomas in his magisterial history of the island, that Cubans blame the graft and corruption of Magoon's successors on the despoilment of his administration, though the evidence overwhelmingly confirms that Magoon was an honest man.

Magoon retained some of Estrada's appointees in the civil service, but when vacancies occurred he deferred to a committee composed of prominent Liberals, who of course recommended their own followers for the posts. The Liberals had initiated the civil war to enjoy the fruits of office; Magoon's tutelage fulfilled the quest. In his own administrative staff, Magoon kept the heads of departments from his Cuban predecessor, appointing an American military officer as aide to each. In 1908, he enacted a civil service law, but by then it was already apparent that American rule was coming to an end, and the Liberals who anticipated taking over were not disposed to abide by its provisions. Cuban bureaucrats did not learn graft under Magoon; they were quite capable of learning that art without American guidance.

Magoon's administrative record was marred, too, by decisions that may be regarded as errors of judgment rather than personal wrongdoing. He let out public works contracts to American firms and arranged payment by issuing bonds on the provisional government in the amount of $16.5 million, considered by the most critical Cuban assessments of the occupation as a financial burden for his successors. The work was left uncompleted when the occupation ended, and the State Department applied considerable pressure to the republic to honor the contracts. One of the representatives of the company guaranteeing the loan, Speyer and Company of New York, was Charles Taft, brother of the president. In another instance, Magoon drew criticism by his close association with Frank Steinhart, former U.S. consul in Havana, who resigned his post to assume the directorship of Havana Electric, one of the earliest and one of the most despised foreign concerns in pre-Castro Cuba. Steinhart succeeded in Cuba, it was rumored, because of his relationship with Magoon. One American official, Col. Enoch Crowder, the governor's secretary of justice, remarked years later that Steinhart "virtually controlled Magoon and was the invisible government."[4]

Magoon's image as a dull but competent bureaucrat gave the occupation a civilian patina, but it was the participation of the American military that provided the litmus test of the American impact on Cuban life. Before Magoon arrived in Havana to take over his new duties, Taft had appointed four army officers to advise the secretaries of five government departments; among them was Crowder, who played a vital role in drafting a Cuban electoral code during the occupation and, many years later as American emissary to Cuba, virtually determined the selection of the republic's president. After Magoon took charge, still more army officers were brought in to staff the occupation's bureaucracy. Lt. Col. Robert Bullard and Capt. James Ryan became Magoon's aides; Maj. Francis Kernan and Capt. George Reid served on the Cuban Claims Commission, which plunged into the nightmarish tangle of claims for losses in the insurrection; and eight more army officers served as special advisors to the Rural Guard. By the last months of Magoon's rule, the occupation had almost sixty American officers serving in a political, medical, legal, or technical capacity.[5] Thus the occupation of Cuba represented civilian rule only in the imagination of Americans who could not easily accept another military rule over the island. Even the War Department found the official title, Army of Cuban Pacification (which Roosevelt had chosen in an effort to avoid using "occupation"), somewhat curious phraseology.

The pacification of the island began appropriately with disarming the rebel population, a measure the Americans had used in the Philippines and would employ on other occasions when venturing into the Caribbean. To carry out this assignment, Taft had none other than a hero of the war with Spain and the Filipino insurrection, Frederick Funston, a gruff, adventurous Kansan who had joined the Cuban rebels months before American intervention and, later, had captured the Filipino rebel, Emilio Aguinaldo. Funston spoke passable Spanish and presumably could negotiate with the rebels for the surrender of their rifles, for which the Americans were willing to pay, and settle accounts over the large numbers of horses stolen by the insurgents during the civil war.

Funston's handling of the stolen-horse problem probably cost him the appointment as the senior American officer in Cuba. Taft devoutly believed that stolen property should be restored to the rightful owner and issued an order to this end, but he permitted the surrendering rebel to retain his mount until the legal owner turned up. Funston botched the translation of Taft's directive, leaving the impression among the insurgents that they could keep their horses and the government would reimburse the owners. One suffering property holder, Edwin Atkins, proprietor of Soledad plantation, eventually recovered only forty dollars per animal for horses worth two hundred dollars each. Taft was furious, and Funston was sent back to the States. The military establishment now rallied to his defense. It was widely believed in army circles, said the *Army and Navy Journal,* that Funston had been relieved because of his "unpopularity with some of the unscrupulous but . . . influential leaders of the insurrectionary party."

Disarming the rebels fell to the marine contingent, commanded by the "pacifier" of Samar in the Filipino war, Littleton Waller Tazewell Waller, Sr. For the first time in the banana wars, the marines got the assignment of disarming "natives," and the lesson was not lost on them. The marines left Havana in a "drizzling rain," wrote one of Waller's officers, William Upshur, commanding a company assigned to collect rebel arms in Pinar del Río. There the marines disarmed rebel *and* government troops. "The whole thing is exactly like Richard Harding Davis' description of a revolution," wrote Upshur. The surrendering rebels were a "dirty rabble of Negroes armed with every type of antiquated weapon." For every eight or so men, he wrote contemptuously, there is a general. Cubans, he wrote his Virginia father, "are harmless. . . . If you could only see these 'spiketys' our detachment could clear the island of them in a jiffy." His father doubtless understood Upshur's racial characterizations of Cubans: "We have a steady stream of generals filing in and out of the quartel all the time and the government side is nearly as bad. . . . I have to meet these people with the major so that I shake hands with the Nigger Generals, with great gusto— there's nothing else to do."[6]

American officers generally viewed Cuban politics as imperfect, if not always corrupt, and argued persuasively for a prolonged occupation. A generation of American tutelage might be required. The republic had failed, they believed, because of Cuban inability to live with the system created under Wood's aegis. The esteemed Cuban thinker José Enrique Varona might say that, if Cubans could not make their own laws for their own needs, provide their own protection, and respect their own institutions, then no expansion of the meaning of the Platt Amendment would be useful. But American military men had only to cite what was to them a more meaningful statistic: the number of property owners who had wanted American intervention and hoped for a long occupation. Robert Bullard, who traversed the island gathering material for reports to Magoon, was not surpised to hear property owners in Camaguey assert "that there is nothing for Cuba but the government of the United States."[7]

Thus Magoon might write ecstatically about American morale, the "commendable interest" of American soldiers "in their duties," and the cultural benefits from the "mingling" of American and Cuban soldiers, but American troops ordinarily considered their role as protectors of private property menaced by civil disturbance. Where opinion on the subject of the occupation—or, more precisely, on how long it should last—was sought, it almost always came from proprietors of sugar plantations or mills more dependent than other elements on the American presence. From the beginning of the provisional government rumors of imminent American withdrawal circulated, followed by warnings from planters, businessmen, and bankers of another "reign of insurrection." As one officer grimly observed, "The cessation of American control . . . will result in another insurrection in six months . . . , extending to partisan action, destruction of property, and general turbulence."[8]

The experience of Bullard in Cuba illustrated the frustrations of American soldiery in the Caribbean. Bullard had been deeply influenced by the reform movement within the army (as had Leonard Wood), which called for a more professional service to meet the needs of an imperial power and, imperatively, an officer corps prepared for modern war. Given the reason Roosevelt had acquiesced in the intervention—to tutor the Cubans in the art of good government—Bullard expected a challenging assignment. As special advisor to Magoon, he plunged into his role as proconsul with the zeal of a dedicated medical missionary dispatched to a faraway land to heal his fellowman. He roamed the island, cajoling the rebels to throw down their weapons and take up honest work; but, instead of a yeoman citizenry eager to start rebuilding the republic, he found bickering Cubans interested only in personal gain. In a philosophical mood, he began writing incisive articles on Cuban education and culture that were, in the words of his biographer, "intelligent comments upon Cuban life." They were also by implication critical of Magoon's rule, which estranged Bullard and almost brought about his censure. (At one point Bullard rushed about Havana buying up every copy of the *North American Review*, which contained an article Magoon found offensive.)[9]

Bullard left Cuba deeply disillusioned about the prospects for reformed societies in the tropics. He wrote bitterly, "The Cuban public permitted Mr. [Estrada] Palma's government to do nothing. They show the same obstructiveness whenever the U.S. Provisional Government attempts to move in any matter, even a matter that tends to advance public business. . . . The proposition eternal . . . is do nothing; it's wrong in Cuba to do things."[10]

The American proconsuls in Cuba were also obsessed with the preservation of public order, and they set about to create institutions that maintained public tranquillity. In the first Cuban republic public order had been guaranteed by the Rural Guard, a makeshift force of some five thousand scattered about Cuba in 250 posts. Its function was to police the countryside, deal with banditry, and perform routine police work in the towns. In the civil war of 1906, the guard's ineffectiveness in handling the Liberal insurgency had, in the view of American observers, contributed heavily to the fall of Estrada's government. When the provisional government was established, Magoon decided to revitalize the guard by assigning American army officers to advise it.

At first the American plan focused on reviving guard morale, which had collapsed during the civil war, doubling the existing force of five thousand, and dispersing the enlarged force about the republic in a more sensible pattern. Special training schools for new recruits opened in Havana and three other cities, and an energetic effort to purge the organization of "political elements" followed.

In the course of applying these reforms, the American proconsuls encountered resistance from virtually every organized political faction in the country. Conservatives feared a political army; the Liberals opposed any armed force whose political values varied from their own. In the months of haggling, the Liberals eventually prevailed on Magoon to scrap the original plan and substitute for it a more ambitious scheme for a permanent army. On April 4, 1908, after a searching examination by the Advisory Law Commission, Magoon announced creation of the Armed Forces of Cuba, composed of the militia, the Rural Guard, and a permanent army. With some modification, the plan represented the handiwork of a gaggle of Liberal politicians.

Thus was created an institution that was ultimately politicized and became a curse for twentieth-century Cuba. It is perhaps ironic, wrote Millett in his study of the occupation, that American officers were more perceptive than their Cuban contemporaries in recognizing the drain a permanent army would place on the Cuban treasury and the danger it posed for the civil liberties of the Cuban people. Their fears appeared justified with the announcement that the head of the newly created force was Gen. Faustino Guerra, who had figured prominently in the insurrection against Estrada.[11]

"The Americans created an army," a cynical Cuban saying of the Magoon years goes, "then they held an election." Though the elections for the new Cuban president did indeed follow the promulgation of the law creating the Armed Forces, politicking began as early as the fall of 1907. From the beginning it seemed clear the Liberals, enjoying at last the luxury of an American-held election which they had clamored for in 1905, would triumph. But in the provincial and municipal elections of August 1908, held under the law devised by Crowder and the Advisory Law Commission, Conservatives won a smashing victory. Three months later, however, in the presidential contest, the Liberals elevated one of the heroes of the 1906 rebellion, Jóse Miguel Gómez, into the Cuban executive office. Affable, generous, Gómez personified the Cuban politician who knew how to treat his friends. He always wore a broad grin beneath a huge Panama hat; the Cuban people loved him and wished him well. Escorting Magoon to the dock for his return to the United States aboard an American battleship, he declared, "Once again we are completely free."[12]

In 1909 Cuba was no longer the wasted society Wood had presided over in 1900. But the American proconsuls of the Magoon years departed with misgivings about the island's future. "The U.S. will have to go back," wrote Bullard ruefully on leaving; "It is only a question of time."[13] He had in mind another occupation similar to that of 1906. That would not be repeated in Cuba's relations with the United States, but another military intervention occurred three years after Bullard and his comrades departed Havana.

The Cuban trouble of 1912, the "colored revolt," had its origins in the latent Negro frustrations after the war for independence. In the Magoon years, a former insurgent in the struggle against Spain, Juan Masó Parra, plotted the overthrow of the occupation government and the eradication of foreign-owned property. The wildest rumors held that the conspirators were planning to eradicate the entire foreign population. Masó Parra and his cohorts were arrested in August 1907 before any violence broke out, but American intelligence officers closely monitored Negro political activity. Among the American (and conservative Cuban) residents the fear of a Negro revolt persisted.[14]

The uprising of 1912 was thus in several ways an outgrowth of similar discontent among Cuban Negroes who felt abused and alienated from national life. Historically the Cubans had accommodated the African into the social fabric; Negroes, in fact, had composed an important element in the rebel army and produced a general for the army, Antonio Maceo. But after the rebellion Cuban Negroes were virtually excluded from the republic's new political organizations. When he became president, Gómez gave them government jobs, but as members of the Rural Guard and army they were forbidden to participate in politics. In desperation they organized their own party, the Independent Party of Color, and in May 1912 raised the standard of revolt against the government. The agitated Gómez quickly mobilized the army and crushed the revolt everywhere except in Oriente. Secretary of State Philander C. Knox dispatched grim warnings to Gómez about protecting American lives and property. When the Cuban army failed to stifle the revolt in Oriente, Knox sent another message to the Cuban government stating that an American force would be landed, declaring that the measure was not "intervention."

On May 31 a marine force went ashore at Daiquirí, where the American invaders had landed in 1898. Its mission was the protection of the sugar mills and mines in the valley stretching inland from Guantánamo Bay. The force was a part of a hastily assembled provisional brigade under the command of Col. Lincoln Karmany. It included Lt. Col. John Lejeune, whose marines had performed a similar function at Panama in November 1903. (On this occasion the landing party had considerable difficulty getting the heavy equipment ashore in the choppy Cuban waters. One young marine officer, Alexander A. Vandegrift, recalled years later his vivid impressions on seeing the hulks of three sunken Spanish ships in the water as his detachment landed.) Their principal activity ashore was routine patrol of the mines and the mills of the Guantánamo Sugar Company.[15]

The American experience in Cuba in the age of Roosevelt ultimately proved a precursor of the American experience in other parts of the Caribbean. In late summer 1912, when the marines finally returned from eastern Cuba, Roosevelt had already plunged into the American presidential campaign. The reasons for the occupation of 1906 were now only dimly etched in his mind. He may have gloomily concluded in early 1909 that the imperial administration of another culture was of limited success and that, as he had speculated in 1906, the American people were reluctant to accept prolonged military intervention in other societies, even those so strategically important as Cuba.[16] But the American military departed Cuba frustrated but not disillusioned over its efforts. It had in the span of a decade ruled the island on two occasions and had directly participated not only in the creation of the new republic but in the revision of its fundamental political and military structure. What failures had occurred, the imperial proconsuls believed, lay not with the institutions the Americans had brought but with the Cubans themselves. For the American military the Cuban experience was no deterrent to future military intervention in the tropics.

Teach Them to Elect Good Men

5. Nicaraguan Menace

In 1907, as American soldiers guarded the Cuban treasury, patrolled the dirt paths traversing the Cuban interior, and laid out grand designs for the island's political rehabilitation, Theodore Roosevelt seemed more concerned with the volatile world of Central American politics. A generation of Americans whose knowledge of the isthmus usually amounted to a much-slanted story of Roosevelt's "taking" of Panama in 1903—a debate still raging in 1907 as the Senate pondered the Dominican-American customs receivership treaty—and a passing acquaintance of Central American geography now observed the president and his creative secretary of state, Elihu Root, as they labored to sort out the tangled affairs of the isthmian republics. At stake, in order of importance, were the security of the future Panama Canal (which ultimately rested on stability throughout the isthmus, the State Department argued), the American presence in Nicaragua (represented by a significant American population at Bluefields on the eastern coast and the continuing American interest in a Nicaraguan canal), and Roosevelt's obvious desire to play the role of peacemaker among the perpetually warring Central Americans.

Though Central America was terra incognita to most Americans of Roosevelt's generation, their forebears had been going there—or going across the isthmus—since the late 1820s. The Central American Federation, fashioned in 1824 by isthmian founding fathers who dreamed of a united Central America, emulated the American federal republic. In the same era, a small group of American entrepreneurs, encouraged by the John Quincy Adams administration, founded an isthmian canal company. Adams's successors were also interested in canal diplomacy and dispatched agents to the area, but the United States played a minor role in Central American affairs until about 1845. (Of the eleven agents sent to the isthmus between 1829 and 1845, only four ever arrived; one of them spent most of his time studying Mayan ruins, and another, after a year or so of fruitless negotiations, returned home and killed himself.) The principal foreign presence was symbolically represented by the British consul, Frederick Chatfield, Esq., who played the Guatemalans and Costa Ricans against the Nicaraguans, Salvadorans, and Hondurans. When the federation fell apart in the late 1830s (largely because of Guatemalan disaffection), the federalists blamed its demise on British machinations. Nicaraguans especially resented the British presence in a vast Indian reserve in the eastern portion of the country called the Mosquitía, which became by midcentury a virtual British protectorate.

Following a diplomatic clash in the late 1840s, the United States and Britain signed in 1850 a major treaty—the Clayton-Bulwer convention—neutralizing any transisthmian passageway and prohibiting future expansion of British territory. In the following decade the isthmian routes attracted Americans from the east and south making their way to the California gold fields. One route lay across the Panamanian jungle, traversed in 1855 by a railroad that carried prospectors, adventurers, and wayfarers and their "missy ladies" from Colón (or Aspinwall, as Americans called the town) to Panama City. Ultimately, the Panama route proved more popular, even though it cut through a pestilential jungle, where it was customary to measure the annual rainfall in feet. Farther west, at the mouth of the San Juan River, lay another route that began at a ramshackle village (San Juan del Norte, renamed Greytown after its capture by an Anglo-Mosquito army in January 1848), followed the river into the Nicaraguan interior until it reached the lakes (Nicaragua and Managua), and culminated in an overland journey to the Pacific shore.

The prospect of lucrative profits in the isthmian routes naturally attracted every kind of entrepreneur, adventurer, and soldier of fortune. Colón and San Juan del Norte particularly were heavily populated with foreigners. San Juan was virtually an outpost of the British Empire, a collection of crude huts and saloons and a few petty British officials. When one had the temerity to levy port charges against a vessel belonging to Cornelius Vanderbilt, a power in transisthmian commerce, he incurred the wrath of the American navy. In 1854, an American naval officer, Capt. George Hollins of the U.S.S. *Cyane,* disgusted over the treatment of Vanderbilt and other Americans in Greytown, gave the inhabitants a two-hour warning and then burned the town.

A few years later, in the midst of a fratricidal Nicaraguan civil war, a southern gentleman with delicate features and haunting eyes, William Walker, landed at Realejo on the Pacific coast with fifty-seven "immortals." Within a year, his force controlled the country, largely because Walker quickly realized the strategic importance of the isthmian route and gained domination over it. In 1856 Walker declared himself president of Nicaragua and won the admiration of Americans, though not recognition by the American government. The following year a coalition of Central American armies, historically disunited unless imperiled by a common enemy, brought Walker down but not before his cause had electrified a generation of American adventurers, mostly southern, who dreamed of tropical empire. Walker surrendered to an American naval officer, returned home to a thunderous welcome, and wrote a book about his Nicaraguan escapades. In 1860, while attempting another invasion, he was captured by a British man-of-war whose captain turned him over to a Honduran firing squad.

After the Civil War, there was renewed interest in isthmian canal projects; in 1867 and 1884 two different administrations negotiated canal conventions with Nicaragua, and in 1872 President Grant appointed an Interoceanic Canal Commission. In the following decade the French undertook their herculean effort to cut a canal across the Panamanian isthmus, and American attention was diverted from Nicaragua until the 1890s. In 1895, the year of a major Anglo-American confrontation over the British Guiana–Venezuela boundary, the Nicaraguan president threw a British consul out of the port of Corinto and so infuriated London that a detachment of British troops occupied the town for a week. President Grover Cleveland, who railed against the British menace in Guiana, arranged a settlement by helping the Nicaraguans raise the £75,000 indemnity the British demanded, but Nicaragua had the satisfaction of destroying the remnants of British dominion in the Mosquitía.[1]

After the turn of the century, the navy regularly patrolled the Caribbean coastline of the isthmus, demonstrating special concern for the American population living in the small port towns cut off from the interior capitals by vast jungle lowlands. Greytown was probably the best known of such ports in the nineteenth century, but in the early years of the twentieth century it was surpassed in importance by Bluefields, a town of about four thousand on Nicaragua's eastern coast. Here lived a sizable foreign population of Americans and English-speaking Negroes whose commercial and political connections lay with the United States or Britain and who evinced little concern for the authority of Nicaraguan chief executives in Managua. Together with Puerto Cabezas and a few towns on the Honduran coast, Bluefields was a major center of operations for banana companies, lumber interests, and gold mining. American residents, periodically threatened by revolution or chafing under what they considered arbitrary authority of a local official, felt only too keenly the need for an occasional landing of bluejackets or marines.

Excepting Costa Rica, whose Europeanized leaders tended to remain aloof from their fractious neighbors, the republics seemed perpetually at war with each other. Guatemala, ruled from 1900 by the despotic Manuel Estrada Cabrera, who ruthlessly modernized the economy with Indian slave labor, had been the most formidable of the republics in the nineteenth century, but its influence had been largely supplanted in the 1890s by Nicaragua, ruled after 1893 by the mercurial Liberal José Santos Zelaya.

Both forceful, autocratic leaders, they were mortal enemies. Estrada Cabrera had managed to convince American observers that he was an enlightened progressive desperately striving to bring Guatemala into the modern age. Zelaya, a rotund man with an avuncular bearing, gained a fierce reputation by his thorough chastisement of his Conservative enemies. Americans disliked him because of his practice of granting lucrative business concessions to his cronies, his meddling in the internal affairs of his neighbors, and his sometimes crudely expressed nationalism. (According to legend he once told a Peruvian protesting his expulsion from Nicaragua, "Appeal by all means! When I ridicule the United States, laugh at Germany, and spit on England, what do you suppose I care for your beggarly little Peru?")[2] The canal route ultimately chosen by the American government came about in some respects because Zelaya refused to deliver the vast concessions Americans demanded in the Canal Zone. Infuriated over the selection of Panama, Zelaya allegedly threatened to negotiate concessions with the Japanese.

In each of the republics, revolutionaries plotted against governments and sought sanctuary across the border. The Guatemalan president believed his enemies used Honduran and Salvadoran soil to plot against him. In June 1906, Tomás Regalado, El Salvador's mercurial secretary of war, who hated Estrada Cabrera, got drunk and led an invasion of Guatemala. In the assault Regalado was killed, and, though Honduras entered the conflict as El Salvador's ally, American officials arranged a truce aboard the U.S.S. *Marblehead.*

The next year Zelaya invaded Honduras, which shares a border with Guatemala, El Salvador, and Nicaragua and was thus a staging area for revolutions. Zelaya had granted favors to concessionaires on the Honduran border and required a friendly government in Tegucigalpa. He resented also Estrada Cabrera's meddling in Honduran affairs. When Miguel Dávila, his erstwhile Honduran ally, began a revolt, Zelaya sensed an opportunity to bring down President Manuel Bonilla and help to install Dávila in power. At one point Secretary of State Root, fresh from his triumphant appearance at the Rio de Janeiro meeting of the Pan-American Conference, was on the verge of mediating the conflict, but Zelaya refused to participate in the proposed peace talks, arguing that the United States had no right to interfere in Central American affairs.

Zelaya's army swept through Honduras and on March 18, 1907, defeated Bonilla's force and its Salvadoran allies in the battle of Namasigüe, where the use of machine guns inflicted such heavy casualties that it earned the ghastly distinction as the bloodiest in history in terms of losses for the length of battle time.[3] In the course of the war American vessels patrolled the Honduran coast and, in accordance with nineteenth-century naval custom, forbade the shelling of coastal towns containing sizable numbers of foreign residents. One American officer, William F. Fullam of the *Marietta,* who had performed a similar policing of the southern Cuban coast during the civil war of 1906, arrogantly declared to a Zelayista general: "If bombardments of coast towns are to be resorted to during the frequent wars and revolutions in Central American states, the mercantile and commercial interests of all foreigners will be absolutely insecure in the future."[4]

Four years earlier Zelaya's meddling in Honduran affairs had stimulated the patrolling Caribbean Squadron to look after American interests on the north coast. On that occasion the captain of one warship in the squadron, the *Panther,* recognizing the de facto control of northern Honduras by rebels, had actually asked the permission of the insurgent leader to land American troops to guard the consulate at Puerto Cortés. Now, in the troubles of 1907, Fullam and the *Marietta* performed a similar policing of the long Central American coastline from Puerto Limón, Costa Rica, northward along the isolated Nicaraguan coast, dotted with ports populated by foreigners continually complaining of Zelaya's harassment, to Cabo Gracias a Dios at the northeastern bulge of the isthmus and from there along the banana route of the northern Honduran ports.

In these patrols Fullam revealed once more his contemptuous disdain for local authority. Hearing that Zelaya's governor in Bluefields had been "harassing" American business, he collared the American consul and stormed into the governor's residence, lecturing the stunned Nicaraguan in such forceful language that the Zelayista functionary had to scurry out for a glass of water. A month later (March 1907) the *Marietta* was cruising the stormy Honduran coastline. When the invading Nicaraguan army routed the local Honduran force from La Ceiba, one of the banana ports on the north coast, Fullam sent a ten-man shore party to police the town, issuing a proclamation that required, among other things, the closing of every saloon in La Ceiba. For his Honduran proclamation Fullam was "mildly censured" by Root, who was laboriously striving to bring peace to the troubled isthmus through a series of multilateral treaties.

Fullam, of course, was unapologetic. The duties of American naval vessels patrolling Caribbean waters long antedated Elihu Root's legalistic schemes for isthmian tranquility. "Treaties between [the Central American countries]," Fullam wrote, "will not suffice." The thing to do was to send the Nicaraguans back into their own country. After the contretemps with the State Department, he continued patrolling the Honduran port towns, the ever-vigilant policeman on duty in the tropics. On one occasion, in Chaloma, he dispatched a shore party of twenty bluejackets and ten marines, armed with two Colt guns, to *investigate* the arrest of a Spanish subject by a local commandant who had personally pledged to Fullam that foreigners would receive the full protection of the law. If culpable, the commandant, Fullam told the shore party, was himself to be arrested and brought to Puerto Cortés and punished for committing such an "outrage."

Neither Roosevelt nor Root contemplated intervening in local affairs to the extent Fullam and his fellow officers did in the coastal towns of the isthmus. Fullam displayed little reticence in undertaking such actions; a successor in the isthmian patrol, Comdr. John Hood of the *Tacoma,* did request more precise instructions and was informed by the secretary of the navy: "The vessels stationed in Caribbean waters are there for the purpose of protecting the interests of Americans in those countries in which revolutions and insurrections are frequent."[5]

Both State and Navy agreed that Zelaya's meddlesomeness in the internal affairs of Nicaragua's neighbors, especially Honduras, explained isthmian troubles, but they were of different minds—and certainly of different methods—when it came to dealing with the "Nicaraguan menace." Root was a lawyer who thought in terms of rules and regulations that even the factious Central Americans ought to agree on if they were ever going to have real peace among themselves. Fullam and his generation of naval officers patrolling the long Caribbean coastline of Central America, where foreigners had taken up residence and gone into business, were more concerned about protecting American citizens and their property from the strife of national wars, begun in remote capitals in the interior, that often afflicted them. Root believed the United States must be the judge of the behavior of Central America's states; Fullam and his fellow officers argued that the United States must be the policeman, the guarantor of law and order, along the turbulent Central American coast.

And in 1907 Root achieved his goal of presiding over a Central American Peace Conference in Washington. Even Zelaya, chastened when he learned that neither the United States nor Mexico, cosponsors of the conference, supported his policies, dispatched a representative. Delegates from the five republics negotiated treaties guaranteeing isthmian tranquillity. In the general treaty of peace and amity they established a Central American Court to settle disputes, declared that national territory could not be used as a staging area for revolutionary movements, and proclaimed the neutrality of Honduras, the most abused of the five republics, whose territory was constantly being tramped over by revolutionaries and whose governments were continually assailed by its neighbors. In a second treaty, the conferees pledged to withhold diplomatic recognition from any government obtaining power by revolution unless the people of the nation gave it constitutional approbation.[6]

For Root the treaties represented the high point of Central American idealism. He even undertook a press campaign to publicize the treaties, and Andrew Carnegie donated funds for building the Central American Court in Costa Rica.

Yet before the end of the year the isthmus was plunged into another commotion involving, as always, Honduras. Root had received news that Estrada Cabrera in Guatemala was aiding a filibustering expedition organized by Lee Christmas, a former railroad engineer who had departed penniless from New Orleans in the fall of 1894 but who had become a *general de brigada* in Honduras. Christmas had thrown in with Manuel Bonilla, the Honduran politico whose forces had been utterly routed at Namasigüe by Zelaya's troops.[7] It was widely believed in the State Department that Christmas was working for United Fruit Company, which had ambitious plans for expanding its operations in Honduras. In July 1908 Christmas landed on Honduras's north coast; at the same time another expedition entered the country from El Salvador. Their goal was the overthrow of Miguel Dávila, the Honduran president and Zelaya's sometime political ally. But in the midst of the invasion the Central American Court, after a dramatic appeal by Honduras, interposed, demanding that the belligerents submit to arbitration. Root was heartened and at one point even considered backing the court's decision with military force. But before he could act the invasion collapsed.

A few months later, Root left office, convinced that his treaty system would maintain the peace. He never anticipated that the United States, determined to rid the isthmus of Zelaya, would be the destroyer of his creation.[8]

In Managua, Zelaya was unfailingly courteous to the American minister, John Gardner Coolidge, an experienced diplomat, even as Coolidge characterized Zelaya and his Liberal allies as reckless military adventurers who plunged Nicaragua into one affray after another. The Conservatives, long identified with the old commercial center of Granada, were composed of wealthier elements who considered themselves the republic's natural aristocracy. Their resistance to Spanish colonial administration in León carried over into the republican era, when León became a Liberal city, and produced the bitter political rivalries of the nineteenth century. The Conservatives suffered particularly after Zelaya took over in 1893, for he took away much of their commerce and banished the more defiant from the country. Coolidge argued that Zelaya had survived only because he had the apparent support of the United States. Upon his return from Managua to Washington, he recommended that the United States show its displeasure with the Nicaraguan leader by delaying the naming of a new minister. The new secretary of state, Philander C. Knox, a former Pittsburgh corporation lawyer and banker with ambitious economic schemes for Central America, decided to follow his advice.[9]

In October 1909 a group of conspirators at Bluefields, led by the governor of Bluefields province, Juan J. Estrada, declared against Zelaya and openly solicited aid from the American residents in the town. Most Americans in eastern Nicaragua had bitter feelings toward Zelaya; his favored concessionaires, particularly the Bluefields Steamship Company, which had antagonized the banana planters in the region, had cut heavily into their business. The American consul, Thomas Moffat, proved unfailingly helpful and was unabashedly prorebel. An American naval officer, Rear Adm. W. W. Kimball, who led a naval expedition to Nicaragua when the revolt erupted, characterized Moffat as Estrada's agent.[10] For two months before the rebellion broke out, Moffat went about town every evening spreading stories that American naval officers wanted the local residents to get rid of Zelaya. Rumor had it that sometime during the first week of October Moffat was awakened in the dead of night by a mysterious voice outside his window saying the revolt would begin on the ninth with the seizure of the Bluff, a promontory that controlled the entrance to Bluefields harbor. The uprising began just that way.[11]

American residents were ecstatic. Prosperity, they now believed, was imminent, because the rebels controlled the Bluff and the town and Zelaya's hated customs officials would be removed. Estrada happily announced his government would "recognize" the United States if Moffat would recipro-cate, but the State Department dispatched an admonitory message to the impetuous consul that his duty was to look after American interests and remain neutral. Estrada had another ally, however: Adolfo Díaz, secretary of La Luz and Los Angeles Mining Company, who was a reliable source of funds for the rebel leader. Small, always impeccably groomed, Díaz was virtually unknown to the State Department in the fall of 1909, but he would become, three years later, "our Nicaraguan."[12]

Zelaya was undismayed and unafraid. He immediately began raising an army. Plunging into the thicket of eastern Nicaragua, he ordered the arrest of suspected rebel sympathizers and thus destroyed a plot for an uprising in the interior towns. A loyalist naval force steamed down the San Juan River to invade Bluefields. On the way Zelaya's troops captured two Ameri-cans, Lee Roy Cannon and Leonard Groce, professional dynamiters laying charges in the river. Zelaya had both executed, but not before Moffat tried vainly to obtain their release and the condemned wrote plaintive letters to their next of kin. Hearing of the executions, Knox wrathfully described Zelaya as "a blot upon the history of Nicaragua."[13]

Though the State Department pursued a blatantly anti-Zelaya course during the troubles of 1909–10, the navy's role in the Bluefields rebellion generally followed the traditional pattern of looking out for the safety and well-being of the town's American population. When Estrada went looking for adherents in the summer of 1909, he sought out the vocally anti-Zelayista American consul, requesting the "disinterested moral support of the United States" and "financial aid to the amount of fifty thousand dollars and two thousand rifles." Moffat was unabashedly enthusiastic about the rebellion, but the commander of the U.S.S. *Tacoma,* patrolling off Bluefields, while acknowledging that the situation ashore was bad, reported that the presence of the ship was "distasteful" to both sides. Several months later, in December 1909, when Estrada's cause faltered under Zelaya's counterattack, the *Des Moines,* having taken up *Tacoma*'s position, dispatched a landing party ashore to seize the wireless and telephone station, close the bars, protect the lives and property of Americans, and, the commanding officer declared, "disarm [the] soldiers of both sides."

It was several months later, when the rebellion was on the verge of being snuffed out by Zelaya's encircling army, that Estrada told the American consul he could not defend the town and that once it fell Zelaya's troops would loot it. Moffat frantically cabled for marines.[14]

On May 27, 1910, Mrs. Smedley Butler and her two children, Snooks and Smedley, Jr., had left their quarters at Camp Elliot in the Canal Zone to take the train to Panama City for a day of shopping. When they returned late in the day, Mrs. Butler found a note from her husband saying he had left for Nicaragua.

Maj. Smedley Butler had been a marine since the Spanish-American War and had participated in the sack of Peking after American and European troops had crushed the Boxer Rebellion. An angular man with a prominent nose, he had already earned the reputation of being the corps' most flamboyant officer and could have posed for Marine Corps recruiting posters. Butler had in fact returned from Nicaragua, where he had accompanied the Kimball reconnoitering expedition and, as part of his assignment, had "traveled the length of the Nicaraguan railroad" to survey the countryside from Corinto to Granada. Now he was returning with 250 officers and men to police Bluefields, which he called the "jumping off place of the world." Butler arrived in Bluefields—he described the town to his mother as a pleasant place reminiscent of New England villages—afire with his new assignment of protecting Americans and other foreigners in the town. Rear Admiral Kimball had earlier alarmed Bluefields' American entrepreneurs ("concession-hunters" who were backing the revolution for profit, Kimball called them) by posting about town a notice declaring that the American military in Nicaragua would not protect any "so-called American interest that as a matter of fact has no existence in law or in right." One of the American residents had angrily responded: "Then what are we going to get when the Revolution we are backing wins out?"[15]

At first Butler had little regard for Nicaraguans. In Corinto, as a member of Admiral Kimball's expedition, he looked upon them as combative, spending too much time in "scrapping," which meant the United States would have to be in the country for a long time. Nor did he have much use for the Americans financing the rebellion to protect their investments. Over the next two years he came to know and even admire several Nicaraguans, especially in Granada, which awarded him a citation and a gold medal for his conduct in the campaign of 1912.

In Bluefields his days were normally spent in playing the role of town policeman, issuing sweeping sanitary regulations—all garbage, he decreed, must be buried at least two feet underground—or fuming over having to protect Estrada, whose revolution was protected by the American prohibition against fighting within the city limits. When Butler arrived, Estrada's position was weak. The rebel chieftain was down to only 350 men and facing an army that numbered at least 1,500. The regular Nicaraguan army was unable to get at Estrada, Butler complained, because the United States supported the revolution. Butler grew furious over his role as protector of Estrada and the entrepreneurs and soldiers of fortune drifting about town, as he characterized Bluefields' American citizens.

Butler could not readily understand the State Department's position in this affair, but as he explained to his father, a powerful Pennsylvania congressman, he recognized that his duty was to police Nicaragua.[16]

6. The Nicaraguan War, 1910-1912

Philander C. Knox's bitter condemnation of José Santos Zelaya, which one Nicaraguan historian called virtually a declaration of war,[1] had widespread repercussions. President Porfirio Díaz of Mexico, Roosevelt's ally in the 1907 treaty system for the troubled Central American isthmus, looked with disbelief at Taft's and Knox's persecution of the outspoken Nicaraguan leader. Zelaya was certainly meddlesome, Díaz knew; but he also served as counterweight to the Mexican's old adversary, Estrada Cabrera of Guatemala, who Díaz feared might reassert Guatemalan influence in Central American affairs. And Knox's declaration that Juan J. Estrada's revolution had the broad support of the Nicaraguan people was demonstrably absurd. But in the realities of isthmian politics it was equally apparent that either Zelaya or Knox must yield—and it was not going to be Knox.

So Díaz pushed for a compromise whereby Zelaya would resign, thus placating the Americans, and yield his place to another Liberal. Actually, Díaz had already been moving ahead with such a plan when Knox denounced Zelaya. The mercurial Nicaraguan president seemed willing to go along and announced that his choice as successor was Dr. José Madriz, a former anti-Zelayista then serving on the Central American Court. Knox, however, declared Zelaya a bandit and refused to have anything to do with the scheme. Politically exhausted, Zelaya sensed he was beaten. The revolution in Bluefields could not be crushed as long as the navy and marines controlled the town and permitted Estrada Cabrera of Guatemala to supply the rebels.[2] Naming Madriz as his successor, Zelaya abruptly resigned and left Nicaragua aboard a Mexican warship, his hasty departure greatly facilitated by Rear Adm. W. W. Kimball.

The Kimball Expeditionary Force, backed up by an impressive squadron of nine American warships in Nicaraguan waters, had arrived at Corinto, the republic's most important west coast port, in early December 1909. Zelaya was then in his last days of power, his reputation as liberal ruler sullied throughout the hemisphere by Knox's character assassination. His army had been prevented from mopping up Estrada's rebels in Bluefields by an American naval force sworn to keep the town off limits to fighting. Unlike the faraway observers of Nicaragua's violent politics, Kimball was not unqualifiedly anti-Zelaya or pro-Estrada, as was the secretary of state. He helped Zelaya get out of the country because he believed Zelaya's life was in danger if he remained, and he witnessed the enthusiastic reception given to Madriz—Zelaya's putative disciple, according to State Department analyses—in Corinto, where wild followers escorted their hero to the local hotel and listened as Madriz decreed the release of all political prisoners.

As far as Knox was concerned, Madriz was a Zelayista, and the hortatory instructions of the secretary of state left no doubt that he considered Nicaragua a battleground between two competing forces (Madriz's and Estrada's) which should fight it out. Kimball's on-the-scene reports should have been sufficient to convince the American government that press commentary about Madriz's perfidy was exaggerated and that Americans living in Nicaragua favored Estrada because he had promised them concessions and privileges. Estrada, Kimball wrote, wanted to be another Zelaya.[3]

Madriz took up where Zelaya had left off in the struggle to suppress the Bluefields rebellion. His ships patrolled the access to the bay, and his troops retook the Bluff and the customhouse. But local American naval commanders undermined Madriz's cause by declaring that Nicaraguan officials could no longer clear vessels into Bluefields harbor. Incoming ships began hoisting the American flag, and arms shipments from Guatemala, which Madriz's ships had virtually stopped, soon revived.

Inspired by the apparent American commitment to their cause, the rebels launched a counterattack. In the summer of 1910 they pressed toward the capital. In August Madriz resigned and, as had Zelaya, fled the country. Juan J. Estrada was now proclaimed president. Determined, apparently, to satisfy the American prescription for Nicaragua's financial rehabilitation, he appealed for diplomatic recognition, declaring his commitment to new elections and a thorough restructuring of the national economy. This was precisely the kind of talk Knox liked to hear.

Nicaragua's political salvation, Knox believed, rested undeniably upon its financial rehabilitation. He had, after all, the apparent success of the Dominican Republic, which had been strife-ridden and indebted until 1905 when Theodore Roosevelt's customs receivership had been installed, to serve as example. Taft and Knox envisaged a similar scheme for Nicaragua and indeed for Nicaragua's financially troubled neighbors. Political stability might thus be achieved, as the expression went, by "dollars instead of bullets," and the United States could achieve its goal of a stable Caribbean without resort to armed intervention or military occupation. Roosevelt had observed before the establishment of the Cuban provisional government in 1906 that the American people were reluctant to support prolonged military involvement in other countries.[4]

A secondary and equally salutary result of "dollar diplomacy" would be the undermining of European financial strength in Latin America. The British were the historic creditors of Central American governments; Honduras alone, it was estimated, owed British creditors some £17 million in interest on its accumulated obligations from the previous century. The British minister to Central America, Sir Lionel Carden, proposed renegotiation of the debt, with Honduras pledging its railway system (a portion of which was currently leased to the American promoter Washington Valentine) as collateral. Furious over British machinations in Central America, Taft and Knox killed the scheme.[5]

But control of Nicaragua's finances offered the key to American success, and Knox avidly pursued an adjustment with that country. The first task, he believed, was ridding the country of Zelayista influence. Zelaya had been opposed to foreign meddling in isthmian affairs; his followers, presumably, felt the same way. When Estrada asked for assistance in procuring a loan from American bankers, Knox insisted on the removal of Zelayistas from the Nicaraguan government. To assure that none of the exiled dictator's followers would obtain power, the secretary of state dispatched an emissary to Managua, Thomas Dawson (who would become the first chief of the new Latin American division in the State Department), to prepare Nicaraguans for new elections. The Dawson agreements, which the American agent compelled Estrada, Adolfo Díaz, and Generals Emiliano Chamorro and Luís Mena to sign, broke up Zelaya's monopolies, established a claims commission to compensate foreign residents for losses in the civil war, and provided for American supervision of a customs receivership created on the Dominican model. It was agreed, finally, that Estrada would become president and Díaz vice-president.[6]

His work done, Dawson left Managua and American affairs in the custody of the American minister. His agreement with Nicaraguan leaders soon came asunder. Estrada suspected his secretary of war, General Mena, and General Chamorro, who had mysteriously departed for Honduras, of plotting a rebellion. The president, believing himself surrounded by enemies, began drinking heavily. He declared the republic could be saved only by the creation of an American protectorate. Desperate, he threw Mena in jail and tried to disseminate arms to Managua's Liberals, but the army defied his orders. Late in the evening of May 8, 1911, Estrada appeared at the American legation, intoxicated, accompanied by Díaz. After a thorough counseling, he resigned the following day and, like Zelaya and Madriz, fled the country.[7]

Nicaragua's destiny was now in the hands of the elegant, compliant former functionary of a Bluefields mining company, Adolfo Díaz.

Díaz proved even more unctuous than Estrada in cultivating American goodwill. A month following Estrada's hasty departure, Nicaragua's new chief executive signed a treaty with the United States permitting the republic to negotiate (subject to State Department approval) a loan with private American banks. The United States would establish a customs receivership and guarantee repayment of the loan. The Senate was already considering a similar convention negotiated with a shaky political regime in Honduras, but it had run into unexpected opposition from Democrats on the Foreign Relations Committee. Undismayed at criticism that his financial schemes for Central America were creating undesirable political obligations, Taft sent the Nicaraguan treaty to the Senate with his enthusiastic endorsement. But Congress adjourned before the upper chamber could pass on either convention.

The success of dollar diplomacy rested of course on the willingness of private investors, convinced that their loans would be secured by American supervision of isthmian politics, to invest in the tropics. As the Nicaraguan and Honduran treaties languished in the Senate, several companies (Speyer and Company, Brown Brothers, and J. and W. Seligman) responded favorably to Nicaragua's desperate request for funds. Speyer and Company offered to take $15 million in Nicaraguan bonds at 5 percent interest. The treaty with Nicaragua anticipated much greater involvement, however; the banks were also expected to assist the republic in developing its railroads, stabilizing its currency, and setting up a national bank. Even as the Senate pondered the Nicaraguan and Honduran treaties, a consortium of banks loaned Díaz's financially plagued government $1 million, stipulating that the money would be repaid from customs receipts.

In March 1912 Nicaragua's National Assembly, acting on the advice of two American economists, reorganized the money system, and in December Col. Clifford D. Ham became collector of Nicaraguan customs. Six months later, the National Bank of Nicaragua began operations. America's purpose, Knox explained to a Toledo audience, was a noble one:

In Central America the [Taft] administration seeks to substitute dollars for bullets by arranging, through American bankers, loans for the rehabilitation of the finances of Nicaragua and Honduras. The conventions with those countries . . . will take the customs houses out of politics so that every ambitious revolutionist shall not seize them to squander the resources of his country to impose himself as dictator. By this policy we shall help the people of these rich countries to enjoy prosperity instead of almost incessant revolution and devastation. *We shall do a noble work.* [8]

But already Nicaragua had plunged into another crisis, one that Americans believed had come about because of unscrupulous politicians but that in fact had resulted from the nationalistic pride that even the unscrupulous are motivated to defend.

Adolfo Díaz was in Knox's estimation a "good man." The Nicaraguan leader wanted financial and political stability for his country. But in every agreement with his American tutors his strength at home deteriorated. General Mena, his secretary of war, declaring the president was selling out the nation to New York bankers, organized a following in the National Assembly. By some clever maneuvering he got the assembly to write a new constitution providing for, among other things, his own succession to the presidency. Díaz desperately appealed for American assistance, and Knox wrote an angry note warning that the general's behavior violated the Dawson agreements.

A furor erupted in Managua. Knox wanted the American minister, George Weitzel, to chastise the Nicaraguan secretary of war personally. The secretary of state now decided to imitate his illustrious predecessor, Elihu Root, who had visited Latin America in 1906, by undertaking a goodwill tour of his own. He arrived in Managua on March 5, 1912, as rumors of his assassination were noised about the capital. Díaz was the model of hospitality. He thoughtfully jailed a hundred demonstrators and censored anti-American press commentary. Knox spoke before the National Assembly, which was heavily anti-American, and even suffered the sarcastic references to American meddling in national affairs from the pro-Mena assemblyman who introduced him. Knox delivered a solemn pledge that the United States had no territorial ambitions south of the Rio Grande and promptly departed the city.[9]

The moment he was gone the bickering resumed, confirming in Weitzel's mind that Managua's anti-American politicians were only opportunists. Mena was the most dangerous of them, the American minister wrote. The ambitious secretary of war began stashing arms at strategic locations around Managua and moved munitions to Granada, where they were stored in an old church that had been converted into an arsenal. By threat and intimidation Mena got control over the district chiefs of Nicaragua's political departments and in countless other ways undermined loyalty to Díaz. When the general brought 150 new recruits into the Managua garrison in late July, Díaz reacted forcefully. A Mena contingent, dispatched to seize La Loma, a fortified hill strategically guarding the city, was driven off by soldiers loyal to the president. Another assault soon followed in Las Limas, a cluster of military barracks, but once again a loyalist force, commanded by General Chamorro, repelled the attackers.

Díaz seemed to be winning on every front, but his own confidence had virtually dissolved. He was determined to fire Mena, but he wanted Weitzel to deliver the message. So the American minister drove in a furious rainstorm to obtain Mena's resignation. He found the shaken secretary of war in his office (which, Weitzel found out later, was connected to a nearby barracks by a secret tunnel). Hearing Mena's disjointed account of humiliation at Díaz's hands, Weitzel got a letter of resignation. He promised only to ask the president for protection for Mena and his family. To celebrate his triumphant mediation, Weitzel even planned a dinner at the legation for Díaz and other Nicaraguan notables. It would be a fitting occasion for announcing Mena's replacement. But, as the party sat down at the dinner table, the lights went out. An anxious Weitzel shortly received a telephone call from Chamorro telling him that Mena, joined by the police, had suddenly departed Managua. On the way, the secretary of war had shut off the electricity to the capital.

A few days later Knox wrote President Taft to explain that Mena was in open rebellion and that his troops threatened the American-owned railway running from Corinto to Granada. The Nicaraguan foreign office, he continued, desired American intervention to protect American lives and property. F. M. Huntington Wilson, the assistant secretary of state and an architect of dollar diplomacy, noting the disruption caused by Mena's coup, put it more succinctly: "We must eliminate influence of these elements."[10]

The administration that sought to substitute dollars for bullets to achieve isthmian peace now turned increasingly in the summer of 1912 to a military solution of the Nicaraguan crisis. In the first week of August, Mena's forces broadened the war by capturing the steamers on Lakes Managua and Nicaragua. Since the steamers belonged to the railroad company that was currently under American management, Mena had directly threatened American property. Weitzel cabled for American troops to protect the legation, and one hundred bluejackets landed from the *Annapolis*. The rebels launched an attack on Managua, subjecting the capital to a four-hour bombardment. Americans and other foreign nationals sought refuge in the Hotel Lupón, which received several direct hits from rebel artillery. On August 15 Smedley Butler arrived with the Panama battalion of 354 marines.

Within the State Department the newly created Latin American division, searching for an appropriate historical analogue to these events, compared the Nicaraguan outburst with the Boxer Rebellion, the attack on foreign legations in China in 1900 that had been ruthlessly suppressed by American and European troops. Huntington Wilson, the resourceful assistant secretary of state, recommended dispatching the Tenth Infantry of the army to the isthmus, but both army and navy high commanders objected, arguing that the Nicaraguan troubles could better be resolved by marines and bluejackets.[11]

The commander of American forces during the Nicaraguan intervention of 1912 was a navy rear admiral of aristocratic bearing, W.H.H.

Southerland, who supervised operations ashore (occasionally from the rear car of a train) and along the western Nicaraguan coast. He had at his disposal six ships—*Justin, Cleveland, Colorado, Denver, Annapolis,* and *California,* flagship of the squadron. The *Denver,* after landing its marines and bluejackets at Corinto, sailed for San Juan del Sur, where on the morning of August 30 a detachment disembarked and took positions near the American consulate. Meanwhile the *California* sailed for Panama to pick up another marine force, the First Provisional Regiment of 750 marines under the command of a squat, popular marine officer, Col. Joseph H. ("Uncle Joe") Pendleton. On September 4, Pendleton's regiment arrived at Corinto. The United States now had more than a thousand marines and bluejackets in the Central American republic, as Wilson had forecasted a week before. Their immediate goal, Admiral Southerland wired, was the securing of the railway from Corinto to Managua.[12]

Control of the railroad was vital because there were pockets of rebel and government forces sniping at one another along the 150-mile route. As the line ran inland from Corinto, it turned abruptly southeastward toward León, festering with rebel sympathizers, skirted Lake Managua, and continued to the capital and then on to Masaya, also a rebel stronghold. From Masaya the line ran eastward until it reached Granada on Lake Nicaragua.

Marine units held various points along the route, but as of early September they had not established control of the entire line. In one engagement a detachment of fifty bluejackets and twenty-five marines had set out by rail from Managua to report on conditions in the capital to the commander of the *Denver.* In León the train was "captured" by a mob that so frightened the American commander that he leaped from the car, leaving behind his cap and personal belongings, and the Americans had to return on foot, led by their humiliated commander riding a borrowed horse. About thirty miles out of Managua the officer called Butler, asking permission to take passage on the wood train that called regularly at towns along the route. Butler went down to the Managua depot at 4:00 A.M. to meet the retreating force. He spied the officer, wearing a straw hat, sitting atop the woodpile behind the locomotive. For Butler it was a humiliating moment, mitigated only by the fact that the commander was a naval officer. The sailors in the detachment memorialized the event with a ditty called "Walkemback's Retirement":

> Walkemback, never mind the engine.
> Walkemback, to hell with the train.
> Walkemback, never mind the checkbook.
> So we walked 'em back to Managua in
> The pouring-down rain.

Government troops slain by rebels at León, August 19, 1912. The man lying with his head near the board in the foreground is Harvey Dodd, a member of the Mississippi state bar, son of a prominent Mississippi lawyer. *National Archives*

Determined to avenge the insult, Butler raced to the American legation and laid out a scheme for retaking the train in León to his senior officer, who was relaxed in blue silk pajamas and sipping Scotch and mineral water. Told that his plan was too risky, Butler shot back to his quarters and wrote a stinging complaint in which he pointed out that the reputation of the United States in Nicaragua was at stake. He threatened to resign and tell the world his reasons. This time his senior reacted favorably, and Butler got together a force of one hundred and commandeered another train. The attackers made their way back to León slowly, however, stopping to rebuild culverts and repair track that the rebels had ripped from the ties but unthinkingly abandoned nearby.

Arriving in León, Butler's expeditionary force was almost caught in a fierce battle between rebel and government troops. In this affray, Díaz's soldiers got the worse of it; their commander, trying to escape from the city, formed his men in a column, but rebel snipers on the rooftops systematically picked them off. Before the government troops had moved six blocks, Butler recounted, the entire force of seven hundred men and horses had been wiped out. Butler got his own force through the town with his customary bluff and theatrics. A rebel general who came aboard the train determined to arrest him was in turn threatened and disarmed.[13]

One week after the "breakthrough" to Corinto, Butler was back in Managua. Exhausted from his expedition, he came down with a fever and tossed in bed for days with a temperature of 104 degrees. Despite his illness, he was determined to get on with his next task, which was the opening of the rail line southward to Granada. In order to obtain permission to get out of bed, he chewed on ice to lower his body temperature.

The Granada-bound detachment left the capital with Butler in command, propped up in his railway car, still running a high fever. About fifteen miles out, near Masaya, the line passed between two hills, Barranca and Coyotepe, which had been taken by rebels and fortified with artillery. As the train crept along, a rebel shell exploded in a nearby field; two hundred yards down the track, a second shell, this one much closer; another quarter mile, a third explosion along the track. Butler stopped the train, grabbed his adjutant and a Spanish-speaking sergeant and headed for the rebel position. He demanded to see the rebel commander in Masaya, Gen. B.F. Zeledón, Mena's chief lieutenant. The Americans were disarmed and had to sit on the track under a fierce sun for what seemed like hours waiting for Zeledón's reply. Blindfolded, they were led to Zeledón himself, who appeared on horseback. Butler cursed his predicament, refusing to discuss anything with the Nicaraguan until he dismounted. Speaking through his interpreter, Butler declared: "General, you can't fight along the railroad. I'm giving you your chance to move away and take your revolution elsewhere."

This was the forceful rhetoric of the consummate banana warrior. Zeledón, noticeably impressed, seemed ready to capitulate on the spot, but the sergeant blurted out something about an American admiral in Nicaragua, and Zeledón suddenly refused to do any more negotiating with Butler. Crestfallen, Butler returned to the capital and checked into the camp hospital, where he soothed his wounded pride with quinine and limeade. Returning to Coyotepe, he met Southerland, who had just negotiated an agreement with Zeledón giving the marines safe passage to Masaya and the surrender of Coyotepe and Barranca.

By the provisions of Zeledón's capitulation, Masaya, the next town down the line, should have been traversed with no incident. But Butler was taking no chances. He had no faith in Zeledón or in his "surrender." The Americans arrived in the town after dark, having exhausted themselves in getting the locomotive and cars over the 3.5-degree grade outside Masaya, a task made more difficult because a band of Nicaraguans had soaked the tracks with milkweed. The engine wheels had begun spinning furiously, and four hundred men were required to push the train up the incline. The track ran along the main street through the center of town. Butler was determined to get through without attracting undue attention and press on to Granada. But at the depot a crowd had gathered, shouting and waving an enormous white flag. Disregarding this sign of peaceful intention, Butler kept the train moving slowly, the darkness ahead dimly illuminated by a man holding a lantern from the locomotive. Suddenly Butler spied a horseman racing down the track, firing wildly. He jumped off to give chase. By this time the train had halted and was suddenly assaulted by 150 armed horseman, firing from both sides. Snipers opened up from houses along the street. Butler yelled at the engineer to start the train again, but he had crawled underneath his seat when the shooting began. Butler roused him from his hiding place, and the train crept forward, shots ricocheting from the cab and the houses. "It was a gorgeous spectacle," Butler remembered. "A sheet of fire was spitting into the darkness on both sides of the road. Four hundred Marine rifles were popping with tongues of flame, the sixteen machine guns were rattling out a staccato beat, the engines were screaming and puffing—all in one narrow little street."[14]

The entire battle lasted less than half an hour. Afterward, Butler got an apologetic note from Zeledón, borne by four envoys. At Butler's insistence they surrendered three Americans who had fallen into rebel hands during the fighting. Five days later, the Americans finally arrived in Granada, though the city lay only fifteen miles from Masaya. Butler's eyes were so bloodshot from fever and lack of sleep that the marines serving under him nicknamed their commander "Old Gimlet Eye."

Nicaragua, 1912. *Above:* Overturned train. *Below:* Marines clearing railroad track. *National Archives*

Savoring victory, Butler now sent a stern warning to Mena stating that he intended to secure the railroad line "with or without your permission." Professing neutrality in the civil war, he warned Zeledón, Mena's subordinate, that any rebel firing would cause a prompt American military response with artillery and machine guns. He appended a list of other requirements that both sides in the conflict must observe: no bombardment of fortified towns; no acts of "barbarous" warfare in areas garrisoned by American troops; no transport of troops or munitions on the railroad; and respect for American lives and property.[15]

On September 22 Mena capitulated. He agreed to turn over to Butler all the railroad rolling stock, telegraphs, and even the steamers operating on the lakes. He further pledged that his troops would not molest American troops, citizens, or property. Three days later Mena himself surrendered, requesting permission to leave the country, a concession Díaz quickly granted. But Zeledón had repudiated his earlier agreement, and Butler soon learned that the rebel Nicaraguan was still holding Coyotepe and Barranca, the two hills guarding Masaya.[16]

The battle of Coyotepe hill proved to be the fiercest contest the marines fought in the 1912 Nicaraguan intervention. This operation was under the command of Butler's superior, Uncle Joe Pendleton, the marine commander in Nicaragua, who waited until early October before moving against Zeledón's troops. On October 2 he sent the Nicaraguan chieftain a demand to surrender; when it was rejected, he authorized Butler to open fire with artillery against Coyotepe and Barranca at eight o'clock the following morning. The shelling from the American artillery continued through the day of October 3, with no response from Zeledón's guns. That night Butler camped in a small house on a nearby coffee plantation, his men stretching out on the concrete floors where the coffee beans were spread to dry.

Coyotepe, where Zeledón's main force was dug in, was scarred by ravines and trenches dug by rebel soldiers. At its crest the Nicaraguans had placed artillery and machine guns. These commanded the distant approaches and the valley between the two hills but could not easily be directed against an adversary lodged at its own base. At 3:30 A.M. on the fourth, Butler's 250 marines began moving toward Coyotepe. Marching silently in the night, holding hands so as to lose no one in the pitch-black darkness, they made their way to its base. The plan was for Butler's marines to move up the hill from the southeast base at daybreak, with Pendleton's force of 600 marines and detachment of bluejackets, who had been awakened at 1:00 A.M., advancing from the east. The battle lasted less than half an hour. Pendleton watched intensely through his field glasses as shots from the Springfield '03s hit the trench tops with deadly accuracy, killing twenty-seven Nicaraguans. At the summit the attackers seized the rebel artillery and began firing across the valley against Zeledón's men atop Barrancas, sending the Nicaraguans scurrying for cover.

With Mena's ignominious departure—he had been aggravated with a severe case of dysentery at the time of his surrender—and Zeledón's defeat at Coyotepe, there was little solidarity in the rebel cause. General Chamorro, who had remained loyal to Díaz throughout the civil war, took Masaya in a battle in which Zeledón was killed. An American expedition dispatched to clear out the last elements of resistance in León, center of the Liberal cause, received rebel fire, and three marines died before the rebels were routed.[17]

The "ladies of Granada," citadel of Conservative faith, presented Admiral Southerland with a memorial expressing "the desire that our elder sister, the great Republic of the United States, so wise, so powerful, will bring to us permanently the benefits which all her sons enjoy throughout all her vast and peaceful domain."[18] The accolade figured prominently in Southerland's official report. But in León a poetic contributor to the Liberal press castigated "the blond pigs of Pennsylvania [Butler's home state] advancing on our garden of beauty."[19] In mid-October Pendleton commanded a mounted expedition of marines and bluejackets over mountainous terrain to Matagalpa (where his troops swam lazily in the Matagalpa River) in order "to impress the people of all classes . . . that the United States does not intend longer to tolerate Central American revolutions." And in every town they occupied the marines distributed Red Cross relief supplies.[20]

The marines counted thirty-seven casualties in the 1912 Nicaraguan intervention out of a force of eleven hundred; Nicaraguans suffered more than a thousand casualties in the civil war. But the Dawson agreements were enforced; Old Gimlet Eye and Uncle Joe had upheld them. In November the long-awaited elections were held. Prominent Conservatives urged Chamorro, now a war hero, to announce for office, but he astutely checked with Weitzel, the American minister, who politely told him that his candidacy violated the Dawson agreements. Nicaragua needed civilian rule, Weitzel averred, and Chamorro withdrew in favor of Díaz.

In a few weeks the marines and bluejackets departed for Corinto and the ships of the American naval force in Nicaraguan waters, leaving behind in Managua a legation guard of one hundred marines, symbolic reminder of the American military presence in the republic. Before sailing from Corinto, Admiral Southerland honored the president at a dignified reception aboard his flagship, the U.S.S. *California.* [21]

The Nicaraguan intervention of 1912 was an ominous precedent for American policy, not only in Central America but elsewhere in the Caribbean and in Mexico, where a few years later a professedly antiimperialist

American president would dispatch a force several times larger than that commanded by Rear Admiral Southerland in Nicaragua to "teach them to elect good men." Failing in its mediatory role in the arcane and unpredictable world of isthmian politics, the American government sought to direct its influence largely through financial channels in a vain effort to wean the fragile Central American economy from its European sources. When that effort ran afoul of isthmian nationalist sentiment, its only recourse was a military one, using bluejackets and marines, who had for years patrolled the isolated port towns of the Caribbean coast, to intervene directly in western Nicaragua, ousting the anti-American elements Zelaya had commanded and installing political leaders sympathetic to American aims. The bluejackets and marines brought an imposed peace to Nicaragua for fifteen years, but the presence of American military power did little to instruct the Nicaraguans in the American ritual of electing "good men."

7. The Mexican Crisis

In March 1913, when he became the twenty-eighth president of the United States, Woodrow Wilson gave every indication of a more cordial relationship with Latin America. He despised the imperialism of his age. He had criticized the interventionist policies of his Republican predecessors and looked upon the regular naval patrols of the Central American and Mexican coasts, which Taft and Knox had stepped up, as manifestations of gunboat diplomacy. Privately confessing the limitations of his knowledge of foreign affairs (though he was the best-informed president on that subject since John Quincy Adams), he was sufficiently alert to America's role in the Caribbean since the Spanish-American War to issue a polite condemnation of dollar diplomacy. His secretary of state, William Jennings Bryan, was even more fervently outspoken against the machinations of private American capital in the tropics. The outgoing team of Taft and Knox, anticipating a reversal of their Caribbean policies, feared that Wilson's rhetoric might touch off revolutionary explosions throughout the area.

Manifestly, a new era in inter-American relations had arrived. But Wilson turned out to be the greatest interventionist of all in the internal affairs of the Latin American republics. His Mexican policy alone would earn him the badge of infamy among hemispheric critics of the United States.

The Mexican republic that Wilson so desperately sought to reform commemorated in September 1910 the centenary of the *grito de Dolores,* the ringing of church bells in the village of Guadalupe signaling the revolution against Spanish rule. In the nineteenth century, the republic had been governed by savants and opportunists; by statesmen with visions of a peaceful society, where politics would be infused with reason; and by despots who ruled in the tradition of central authority inherited from the Spanish monarchy. American observers considered Mexico an arrogant nation misruled by such unscrupulous leaders as the "crimson jester," Antonio López de Santa Anna, until the republic lost almost half of its territory in war with the United States. After that, many Americans, notably rising Republicans like Abraham Lincoln, thought of their neighbor as a ravaged society, wasted by internecine civil war or preyed upon by European interlopers. The one

figure of nineteenth-century Mexico who conveyed a statesmanlike image
was Benito Juárez, who in the 1850s fought the power of the church and
military and in 1867 overthrew Maximilian's monarchy. Yet Juárez, for all
his dedication to political ideals Americans cherished, remained essentially
an inscrutable Zapotec Indian with suspicion of anything foreign and har-
bored deep distrust of the rambunctious republic to the north.

Juárez, at least, made Mexico the example of a republic that threw off
its European trappings. One of his lieutenants in the antimonarchial struggle, Porfirio Díaz, who became president in 1876, presented to the world
a stable, prosperous republic. He began by convincing a skeptical American
government that the border between the two countries must be secured
against marauders, so that the American army would not have to cross the
Rio Grande to chase cattle thieves, Indians, or bandits. Resisting American
pressures to send patrols into the wastelands of northern Mexico, Díaz
started policing it with *rurales,* who kept the peace and earned Díaz American plaudits.

In the 1880s, as he centralized his authority, Díaz opened the country
to speculators, engineers, and promoters of all stripes. Mexico would be
modernized with foreign technology and talent. The republic joined the list
of "civilized" nations on the gold standard. Its foreign trade jumped
markedly; its exports diversified. And its economic ties to the United States
multiplied: In 1872, when Juárez died, Americans purchased 36 percent of
Mexican exports; by 1890, 75 percent. American capital and technology
poured into mining, railroading, and oil exploration. The American presence was fittingly symbolized in 1881 when the New York legislature incorporated the Mexican Southern Railroad and named Ulysses S. Grant as its
first president.

And Díaz patronizingly protected the foreigner, removing legal obstacles to foreign concerns and assuring a ready supply of unskilled labor for
their use. Privilege went to foreigners to such degrees that it was commonly
observed that Mexico was the parent of aliens and the stepparent of Mexicans. By 1910, fully 75 percent of the mines and 50 percent of the oil fields
belonged to Americans.[1]

After 1900, as his power became more entrenched, Díaz grew increasingly apprehensive about the large American presence in Mexico. His Central American gestures on behalf of Zelaya were in part aimed at offsetting
American influence, and he provided concessions to British oil interests as
a way of countering the enormous amount of American capital invested in
Mexican petroleum.

But it was not American capital that brought Díaz down eight months
after the 1910 celebration. As he aged, he became mellower; his associates,
uncertain about the succession, began maneuvering furiously behind the

scenes. They became even more frantic after Díaz declared in 1908 in a famous interview with an American journalist, James Creelman, that he had guided Mexico into the twentieth century and the nation was now ready for democracy. His retirement would coincide with the centennial in 1910. In the aftermath of the interview with Creelman there was a flurry of political activity. New parties appeared, and angry voices, silenced by Díaz for thirty years, spoke harshly against the political system the dictator had created.

Taken aback by the rising opposition, Díaz recanted his retirement pledge and announced he would seek reelection. It was even argued that he had granted the Creelman interview only to assuage his foreign critics. His political machine hastily prepared for new elections. Díaz did not campaign, but his running mate did and was rudely received wherever he journeyed. Yet there was no one to lead the opposition.

The man who eventually toppled Díaz was an improbable leader. Francisco Madero stood only five feet, two inches tall, sported neatly trimmed brown whiskers, and spoke in a falsetto voice. He shunned liquor, ate only vegetables, and practiced spiritualism. Scion of a wealthy landowning family in the northern state of Coahuila, he had been an obscure hacendado until 1908, when he published a slim volume, *The Presidential Succession of 1910,* which called for an honest ballot and a single presidential term— in other words, "no bossism." The book was essentially an exercise in nineteenth-century political liberalism, glossing over Mexico's profound economic inequities, but it made Madero a folk hero and a presidential contender. He gloriously toured the republic and even obtained an interview with Don Porfirio himself.

But as Madero's reputation grew, Díaz became alarmed about his influence and, using a convenient law prohibiting incitement, had Madero jailed. In the centennial celebration in September, which was supposed to be a glorification of the eighty-year-old president, there was a violent pro-Madero demonstration. Two weeks later, Díaz's reelection was declared.

Madero, however, had been bailed out of San Luís de Potosí prison and taken refuge in Texas, where he declared the elections fraudulent, proclaimed a revolution, and named himself as president of Mexico. Crossing the river into Mexico to launch the armed struggle, he almost quit the fight when in the first engagements with Díaz's troops his forces got the worst of it. He was on the verge of forsaking everything and had in fact reentered the United States when he received news of continuing anti-Díaz unrest in the North, fomented by Pascual Orozco and a cattle rustler turned revolutionary, Pancho Villa; and in Morelos, south of the capital, by a bronze Indian with deep-socketed eyes, Emiliano Zapata, whose followers were taking over the sugar plantations.

The dictator may have been confused by what seemed to be contradictory American responses. Safe in the United States, Madero plotted against Díaz but scrupulously avoided any action that might be construed as a violation of American neutrality laws. Díaz even dispatched agents to the United States to prod the American government to arrest Madero. Taft, by nature a social conservative, sympathized with Díaz's predicament but registered his concern about the revolt by stepping up American naval activity off the Mexican coast and mobilizing 20,000 troops on the Texas border, actions that alarmed Díaz as to the possibilities of an American intervention. Taft had no such intention, but shifting American policy in the final months of Díaz's rule confused the Mexican government and made him uneasy.

In several battles Díaz's forces, led by an officer corps riddled with corruption and inner strife, were beaten by the rebels. Following the loss of Ciudad Juárez in May 1911, a battle the residents of El Paso watched from their rooftops, Díaz fled the country. He died penniless in Paris four years later, convinced to the end he had given Mexico enlightened rule. In October, after the most honest election in the history of the republic, Francisco Madero became president of Mexico.[2]

Madero had become only the head of government, not the leader of a nation. He ruled with a gaggle of generals of putative loyalty, some of them holdovers from the Díaz era. And in the vast reaches of the North and in the Indian states to the south the violence continued. In December 1911 there was a revolt in Nuevo León and another in Veracruz in October 1912, the first staged by the opportunist Bernardo Reyes, the second by Felix Díaz, nephew of the deposed dictator. Both were arrested but escaped execution through the personal intervention of Madero himself. In Morelos, Zapata, whose Plan de Ayala with its direct, radical solution for agrarian reform frightened Madero, defied the president's authority.

And there was another problem for Madero, though he was slow to recognize it: the continual intrigue carried on by the American ambassador, Henry Lane Wilson. A small man with penetrating eyes and a notorious temper, Wilson was considered the dean of the diplomatic corps in Mexico City. He had served in diplomatic posts in Chile and Belgium before taking up his duties in Mexico in 1910. Thus he had witnessed the last days of Don Porfirio's rule and the tumultuous events that swept Madero into power. The powerful American colony in the country liked Wilson because he protected their interests. Though the ambassador had on occasion complained about Díaz's treatment of American activities in Mexico, his assessment of Madero, both privately and officially, was unhesitatingly condemnatory. Mexico, he believed, was unready for democracy; Madero, thus, must disabuse himself of his silly liberal notions and govern firmly.

Madero ruled, Wilson wrote, from day to day, barely surviving; his failure to govern authoritatively, in the tradition of Díaz, lay in the president's character, his "disordered intellect" and "dangerous form of lunancy."[3]

In February 1913, when the president got wind of a plot among his generals to free Reyes and Felix Díaz and overthrow the government, Madero discounted it, a lapse that foretold his undoing. On the ninth, the revolt—what Mexicans call the *decena trágica* (the ten tragic days)—was put into action. Reyes was killed in the ensuing fighting, but Díaz captured the Ciudadela, the government arsenal. Madero entrusted the defense of the government—and his life—to a man who had previously saved the president but who would now betray him.

Victoriano Huerta, who would become Woodrow Wilson's nemesis, was a more probable leader for the strife-ridden country than the man he would betray. Huerta had the blank stare of the Indian and the awkward gait of a soldier who had spent too many years in the saddle. Madero might persuade with appeals to intellect; Huerta spoke emotionally, waving his arms and beating his chest to convey a thought. His oratorical powers alone would have made him an appealing figure to a revolutionary generation obsessed with the mass leader, but he had another quality that Woodrow Wilson's America, convinced that he was a craven murderer, never appreciated: a daring, almost reckless bravery. Huerta cared little for his own safety and even less for the lives of others. Once, it was said, hearing a mob outside his hotel screaming for his death, Huerta went to the door and announced his presence.

Now, in February 1913, bound to defend Madero's government, Huerta would strike a bargain with Felix Díaz. In this sordid episode Huerta and Díaz would consummate another deal—this one with Henry Lane Wilson. In the fight for Mexico City, the ambassador had turned the American embassy, a fortresslike structure located at the juncture of two major thoroughfares only a short distance from the battle zone, into a refugee encampment. Wilson was convinced Madero was doomed, and he made no secret of his views. His duty, he believed, was to hasten the inevitable and thus spare further bloodshed. He called in the British, Spanish, and German ministers, whose nationals, along with those Wilson represented, constituted the most influential segments of the foreign community in the capital, and laid out a plan for ending the strife. Under Wilson's prodding, the ministers publicly called for a cease-fire, then, when Madero rejected it, a curtailment of the fighting to a specified portion of the city.

Wilson pressed for Madero's resignation. When the president haughtily refused, the ambassador, enraged, wired the State Department a bitterly critical assessment of the situation. On February 16 Wilson received word from Huerta himself that Madero's rule might be shortly ended, news that lifted the ambassador's spirits. Two days later Huerta personally arrested Madero, addressing him in the final encounter as "Señor ex-presidente." Wilson moved quickly. He knew that both Huerta and Díaz wanted to be president and that their inevitable rivalry would only make for more trouble. So he hastily arranged a meeting between them in the embassy. There, with the American ambassador contentedly looking on, the two generals negotiated what Mexicans consider an alliance as odious as the Nazi-Soviet nonaggression pact on the eve of Poland's dismemberment in 1939—the Pact of the Embassy. Huerta would become provisional president, and Díaz would have a major role in the selection of the cabinet. Shortly afterward, Wilson wrote a boastful account of his role in the crisis and his success in restoring peace to the capital.

The deposed president and his vice-president, Pino Suárez, were still prisoners in the National Palace. Madero's family feared for his life, and his mother beseeched Wilson to intercede. But Wilson reacted perfunctorily, seemingly unapprehensive about Madero's safety and presuming, as did others, that he would probably be sent into exile. On February 22, Huerta and an official entourage of the new regime appeared at the Washington's Birthday party at the American embassy. Later in the evening, two cars with three guards in each sped away from the palace with the former president and vice-president of Mexico. Arriving at the rear of the penitentiary, the guards removed their prisoners from the cars and, using the glare of the headlights to aim, shot and killed them.[4]

The official explanation of the deaths held that Madero and Suárez had perished in the cross fire between their guards and a band determined to rescue them. The American press was uniformly suspicious, however; some newspapers were already referring to the "murder" of one Mexican president by his successor. Denying any wrongdoing, Huerta privately lamented that he had done only what Madero had urged him to do to Felix Díaz. Ambassador Wilson, recovering from the initial shock of the killings, recommended prompt recognition of Huerta's government. But Taft and Knox hesitated, awaiting a satisfactory response on the settlement of an increasing number of claims with Mexico. Clearly, they would have moved on the ambassador's strong recommendation, but before matters could be settled and Huerta recognized, Woodrow Wilson was inaugurated.

The new American president already had a reputation for stern views and a personality that brooked little criticism, especially if the critic failed to grasp the truth as it was revealed to him. Much has been made of Wilson's puritanical bent of mind and its impact on his Mexican policy. He certainly believed Huerta to be an "immoral" man, and his refusal to grant Huerta's government the diplomatic recognition so earnestly championed by the ambassador (and the British minister to Mexico) rested in part on his own conviction that Huerta was a murderer. But Wilson's assessment of the Mexican situation in spring 1913 went much deeper than his revulsion toward Huerta. He intended to influence the course of Mexican history, to educate the Mexican people, who, he believed, deserved a better society and certainly a more decent leader than the hawk-nosed general now claiming that distinction.

The policy that evolved would be called "watchful waiting," political pressure reinforced by the military presence of the United States in the Gulf of Mexico and along the long Texas-Mexico border. An American Naval force had been patrolling the Mexican coast since the fall of Díaz two years before, and the General Board of the Navy was continually updating its basic Mexican war plan, which had been drafted several years before Díaz's overthrow and called for the occupation of Veracruz and several other ports. Across the broad Gulf, at Guantánamo, a marine brigade readied for an invasion of Mexico. Army planners also figured prominently in preparations for conflict with Mexico; indeed, the Army War College advanced an ambitious proposal that anticipated not only the landing of forces at Veracruz but an assault against the capital (as Winfield Scott had done in 1847 during the Mexican War) and the occupation of large areas in northern Mexico.[5]

A week after the inauguration, Secretary of State Bryan, reflecting the sentiments expressed by Wilson in a major address, declared that the United States would not recognize a government that did not rule with the consent of the governed. The administration would in fact extend recognition to new regimes in Peru and China that failed to meet that test, but it was readily apparent that the principle applied to Mexico. Wilson could not manipulate the Peruvian and Chinese situations; manifestly, he believed he could influence what happened next door in Mexico.

Distrusting the American ambassador but unable to replace him because such a move would imply recognition for Huerta's government, Wilson sent a journalist, William Bayard Hale, as special emissary to Mexico, the first of almost a dozen executive agents the president sent there. Hale was to report on conditions and, specifically, to check out the persistent reports about the role of Ambassador Wilson in the tragic ten days of February. Hale arrived to find an embassy halfheartedly pressing Wilson's conditions for recognition: new elections and Huerta's pledge that he would not be a candidate. If these were met, Wilson offered to mediate between Huerta and his numerous enemies. Hale's report on the Mexican situation also included an indictment of Henry Lane Wilson's role in Madero's ouster and death. The ambassador was ordered home for consultation and, back in Washington, dismissed from the diplomatic service, convinced to the end that the origins of America's troubles in Mexico lay in the refusal to recognize Huerta.[6]

Late summer 1913 found another Wilsonian emissary in Mexico, John Lind, former governor of Minnesota, who had been sharply critical of Henry Lane Wilson. Lind knew little Spanish and was notoriously anti-Catholic, but he was a political crony of Bryan's and enjoyed the president's confidence because he had no Mexican connections and was therefore, in Wilson's mind, objective. The United States, Lind was informed, was slowing its arms shipments to Mexico—arms Huerta used to fight his enemies—and increasing its political pressure. Lind's mission was to convince the Mexican leader that these actions did not constitute intervention and that the crisis could be resolved if Huerta accepted mediation (which would mean recognizing the belligerent status of the rebels), established a provisional government (which meant forsaking power himself), and held a new election (which Huerta already planned to do). Huerta insisted on recognition as the initial step in the reconciliation. Elections were held in October, but the circumstances were so irregular as to invite Wilson's condemnation.

Wilson renewed his campaign to purify the Mexican political house. Furious over the recognition of Huerta by several European governments, he declared, in a major speech in Mobile, Alabama, that Latin America must free itself from European economic intrusion. Boldly he announced, "The United States will never again seek one additional foot of territory by conquest."[7] The British were the first to comply. Sometime later the president got an agreement that, in exchange for his support for equal tolls in the Panama Canal, scheduled to open in 1914, London would adhere to his Mexican policy. There was another demand for Huerta's retirement, reinforced by a delegation of European diplomats in Mexico City delivering a special appeal to Huerta to step down.

Huerta now faced an even more ominous threat in the North in the person of Venustiano Carranza, an aging patriarchal general with a full beard who had proclaimed himself chief of the Constitutionalist revolution. Carranza had his own emissary in Washington, Luís Cabrera, who enthusiastically promoted the Constitutionalist cause with detailed reports on Mexican social and economic conditions. Pleading for American recognition, the Constitutionalists were rebuffed, but they did get something just as beneficial—a lifting of the arms embargo that had been imposed following the failure of Lind's mission.[8]

To reinforce his diplomatic pressures on Mexico, Woodrow Wilson had at his command a powerful naval force patrolling Mexico's Gulf coast. The most impressive aggregation of warships cruised off Veracruz; their commander, Rear Adm. Frank Friday Fletcher, remained alert throughout the uncertain days of 1913 to the problem of seizing Mexico's most vital port, an assignment made more dangerously probable by the president's unrelenting pressures on a government the United States steadfastly refused to recognize as legitimate.

Fletcher had been in Mexican waters long enough to realize that the situation in the country was infinitely more complicated when viewed at close range. The General Board's war plan for taking Veracruz seemed precise enough; the problem lay in the execution of the plan, as any intelligent military tactician realized. A short time after Madero's murder, when feelings ashore were running strong, he wrote to Adm. Charles Badger, commanding the Atlantic Fleet: "It would be quite unfortunate if we had to land against the consent of the [Mexican] authorities. The temper of the people is such that it would undoubtedly result in war." In a calculated move to convince port authorities of the firepower at his disposal—and the hopelessness of Mexican defenses against it—Fletcher invited Veracruz's military and civilian leaders aboard the *Vermont*, his flagship.

Convinced of his military superiority—he was already considering the use of bombs and machine-gun-bearing planes to frighten the Veracruzanos from the city in order to avoid a general bombardment from the big guns of his ships—Fletcher was perplexed about the course his civilian commander in chief was pursuing. Huerta cannot quell his enemies, Fletcher observed in late August, but if he falls (and Woodrow Wilson had declared he must fall) the country will be plunged into further anarchy. A junior officer on his staff, assigned to assess the political situation in Mexico in early summer, had arrived at conclusions markedly different from those of the president. The "chaotic conditions" in Mexico, the report said, would continue "unless there is some radical change in the attitude of the United States Government." The only hope for a stable Mexico was Huerta's survival; the only hope for his survival was American recognition *and* American financial, diplomatic, and "if necessary" military support to a man the president of the United States devoutly believed was a murderer.

But a rear admiral in the United States Navy did not make policy for Woodrow Wilson. Fletcher dutifully sent the report to the secretary of the navy and resumed his "watchful waiting" on the Mexican coast. There was, however, a naval tradition he intended to uphold; when in November a Constitutionalist force pressed against "virtually undefended" Tampico, Fletcher informed the Constitutionalist commander: "I shall safeguard American and foreign lives and their non-military property from the effects of [your] attack."[9]

In the same month the secretary of state informed the American chargé d'affaires in Mexico, Nelson O'Shaughnessy, that a special message had been sent to representatives of other nations, excepting Mexico and, inexplicably, Turkey. Entitled simply "Our Purposes in Mexico," it read in part:

Usurpations like that of General Huerta menace the peace and development of America as nothing else could. . . . It is the purpose of the United States therefore to discredit and defeat such usurpations whenever they occur. The present policy of the Government of the United States is to isolate General Huerta entirely; to cut him off from foreign sympathy and aid from domestic credit, whether moral or material, and to force him out.

O'Shaughnessy read the message carefully, noting its deliberate directness, its lack of nuance, its moralistic tone. Huerta was a menace to democracy and decency; if he would not voluntarily step down for the good of his country and of Western civilization, then, as Bryan put it, "it will become the duty of the United States to use less peaceful means to put him out."[10] This was uncommonly forceful language coming from a man with a pacifist reputation, but O'Shaughnessy realized that behind those stern words stood an equally determined Woodrow Wilson. The chargé was a cultivated man with European tastes and disposition, a Republican heritage, and powerful connections with Theodore Roosevelt, more than enough to make him suspect to Wilson or Bryan and probably enough to result in his dismissal were it not for the president's predicament of being unable to name a new ambassador. O'Shaughnessy and his sophisticated wife, who would later write a revealing memoir of their Mexican sojourn, moved easily among the Huertistas, and Huerta himself exhibited a noticeable fondness for the chargé.[11]

But in spring 1914 O'Shaughnessy's personal contacts in the Mexican government seemed of little utility. The president of the United States, personally directing American policy toward Mexico, had resolved on a course from which there would be little deviation and no retreat. By political pressure and adroit maneuvering he had brought the British government, until now suspicious of his assault on Huerta, to a point of acquiescence in his leadership. Yet in a curious way Wilson clung to the belief that he was resisting intervention. In a press conference on February 26, 1914, alluding to rumors of marines being dispatched to Mexico, the president called the story "nothing but yarns." (In fact, a marine mobile regiment had been dispatched to Pensacola in late 1913 for possible deployment in Mexico.) When a reporter brought up the Nicaraguan involvement of 1912, which along with the Boxer Rebellion served as historical analogue to the current trouble with Mexico, Wilson expressed ignorance about the reasons for the intervention. To a reminder that James Buchanan had recommended to Congress in 1859 the passage of a law authorizing the president to use military force in Mexico during a time of civil war in that country, Wilson responded: "I saw that message. It was just like saying, 'We will come in under arms, but please consider this just a polite call.' " Asked if the present situation with Mexico warranted such a step, Wilson snapped, "We could go through the motions, but it would be war all the same."[12]

Responding to a letter from his secretary of war, Lindley Garrison, who strongly advocated intervention as the only recourse in Mexico, Wilson declared:

We shall have no right at any time to intervene in Mexico to determine the way in which the Mexicans are to settle their own affairs. . . . There are in my judgment no conceivable circumstances which would make it right for us to direct by force or by threat of force the internal processes of what is a profound revolution, a revolution as profound as that which occurred in France.[13]

But in the fall of 1913 Wilson had informed the secretary of the British ambassador to the United States: "I am going to teach the South American republics to elect good men!"[14]

Wilson was not going to commit the first act, however; Huerta would have to do something so despicable, so outrageous, and something that would be such an affront to the laws of nations and proper international behavior that American retaliation would be manifestly justifiable. Huerta's internal strength in March 1914 was ebbing on every front. In the South the Zapatistas carried on their struggle for agrarian reform virtually oblivious to the presence of federal authority. Three Constitutionalist armies advanced from the north: one toward Monterey and Tampico; a second aimed at Torreón, center of the Mexican cotton kingdom; and a third on the west coast. Late in the month, Pancho Villa's army routed the federals from Torreón and opened the path toward the capital itself. Though Villa was soon defying Carranza himself, creating a rift in the Constitutionalist cause, Huerta seemed to be in the worst shape of all. He could not last much longer as Mexico's "pretender," and Wilson knew it.[15]

Yet, surprisingly, the incident that would precipitate American action occurred not by Huerta's hand or even by Wilson's but by an unthinking Huertista officer in Tampico and a zealous rear admiral in the American navy.

In the nineteenth century Tampico had been a typically somnolent Mexican fishing village. But oil had been discovered in the region, and the town had grown rapidly into a small city of 30,000 with a sizable foreign population and a prosperity symbolized by the mushrooming oil refineries and warehouses of Standard Oil, National Petroleum, and other companies.[16] The American inhabitants, second in importance in the country to the American colony in the capital, knew only too well that the Constitutionalists wanted to take this rich prize from Huerta's forces.

The American residents of Tampico were continually reassured by another powerful force, United States naval vessels, part of a constantly changing number of ships of the Atlantic Fleet patrolling the Mexican Gulf coast. In command of the Fifth Division, which anchored in Tampico, was Rear Adm. Henry T. Mayo, a veteran of forty years who had languished in the ranks until the previous year, when Josephus Daniels, Wilson's secretary of the navy, impressed with his administrative abilities, made him his personal aide and quickly promoted him to rear admiral. Owing to difficulties of communication with the naval station in Key West (and in keeping with the nineteenth-century tradition allowing a ship's commander considerable latitude in his decisions), Mayo had the authority to act on his own judgment in an emergency, though in unusual circumstances he was expected to communicate through Rear Admiral Fletcher, commander of the Fourth Division at Veracruz. Some of the vessels in the American force, such as the *Florida,* Fletcher's flagship, had the latest radio communications equipment, but even these had a range of only two or three hundred miles. In a crisis, then, Mayo must use his "best judgment," as George Dewey had done at Manila Bay in 1898, and consult Washington later.[17]

On April 9 a party of seamen from the *Dolphin,* one of Mayo's ships anchored at Tampico, was arrested by a Huertista officer and marched through the city. The Americans had arrived at the dock in a whaleboat to purchase gasoline from a German civilian who had heard about the difficulties the Dolphin's officers were having in procuring supplies and had offered to sell them several cans he had stored in his warehouse. The boat had docked less than a hundred yards from a bridge heavily guarded by federal forces and, though the Americans were flying their flag, they had been arrested by a nervous Mexican officer for trespassing into that part of the city without special permission. As soon as the military governor of the city, Morelos Zaragoza, learned of the arrest, he apologized, explaining that the arresting soldiers were members of the state guard, uninformed in the rules of war, and ordered the immediate release of the American prisoners.

The whaleboat's crew had been detained little more than an hour, and no one in the American party seemed dissatisfied with Zaragoza's oral apology. But Admiral Mayo considered the incident a grievous insult not only to his command but to the United States. Without consulting Fletcher or, indeed, anything but his own conscience, he dispatched a brisk note to Zaragoza stating that the Mexican commander's apology was insufficient. A proper response, he wrote, demanded a written apology, the hoisting of the American flag at a prominent spot in Tampico, and the firing of a twenty-one-gun salute by Mexican troops.

At the time of the Tampico incident Wilson was vacationing in West Virginia. Information reached him in piecemeal fashion, but the first skeletal outline of the affair aroused his fury at the Mexican government and especially at Huerta, who, the president believed, was somehow culpable. At each stage of evaluation within the American bureaucracy, military and civilian, the Mexican commander's actions appeared more heinous and Mayo's demands more justifiable. Fletcher, on learning of Mayo's response, had of course upheld his fellow officer, even to the point of adding that the situation warranted retaliatory action, perhaps the seizure of a Mexican gunboat.[18]

O'Shaughnessy, still functioning as American chargé in the capital, tried as delicately as possible to negotiate a satisfactory settlement. But in less than a week the Tampico incident was transformed into something far more ominous than a stupid mistake by an obscure Mexican official. Huerta's minister of foreign relations now explained that Tampico had been, after all, under siege by rebels (who, he added gratuitously, were equipped with weapons procured from the United States), and precipitate actions there by federal officers were understandable. The Mexican minister even suggested a plausible solution to the crisis: a salute to the *Dolphin* by a Mexican gunboat or battery followed by a salute to the Mexican flag by the Dolphin's guns. The entire incident, he explained, had provoked an outburst of Mexican chauvinism among all classes.[19]

But an American salute of the Mexican flag would have meant recognition of Huerta's "illegal" government. The president actually believed the incident at Tampico was, by itself, trivial and so stated to a delegation from the House and Senate Foreign Affairs and Foreign Relations committees. The real issue was the "studied and planned exhibitions of ill-will and contempt for the American government on the part of Huerta."[20] Col. Edward House, Wilson's confidant and advisor on matters of state, alluded to another problem that helped explain why the Tampico affair had generated a war crisis. Until recently naval commanders had been allowed to use their good judgment in such situations; Mayo had had that authority at Tampico. But the rear admiral also had contact with Fletcher at Veracruz, who could relay messages to Washington. Mayo should have used the wireless, House wrote, for modern communication had done away with a commander's reliance on his own judgment. "Such things were as obsolete as the duelling code."[21]

Among the patrolling naval forces off the Mexican coast in April 1914 there was a ominous urgency about reports from the situation ashore and Washington's reaction to them. A determination to "do something," even if it meant a military response to what the president of the United States informally called a "trivial" incident, seemed to be the only justifiable recourse. Aboard the *Prairie,* which had transported the weary marine mobile regiment from Pensacola after arduous navy maneuvers at Culebra to Veracruz, news of the Tampico incident interrupted the dreary routine of shipboard life in Mexican waters. Expectation of American retaliation for the "insult of the flag" relieved the boredom. Frederick Delano, the mobile regiment's adjutant wrote ecstatically: "Chance we may go to Tampico and stir things up a bit—I hope we do, for this is no end monotonous and all hands are sick of it."[22]

8. Veracruz

In February 1913 an American naval officer, assessing the probable resistance to American intervention in Mexico, observed that the turbulent political conditions in that country would probably prevent a successful Mexican defense of Veracruz. The inability to hold the port against an attack, he went on, would dictate withdrawal of Mexican forces into the interior, out of reach of a naval bombardment, to hold off an American advance on Mexico City. Concluding on an ominous note, he warned: "Pride or blind sense of duty may lead to attempted defense against landing."[1]

Now, in the uncertain days after the Tampico incident and Huerta's haughty defiance of Admiral Mayo's demand, the "pride" and "blind sense of duty" seemed a more appropriate characterization of the mood in Washington than of that in Mexico City. Huerta had not only defied an American admiral; he had committed an unforgivable injury to the United States, its president, and its people. The issue at hand was the nature of the retaliation and the place of execution.

Tampico, site of the incident that had precipitated the crisis, suddenly became the object of feverish planning by Mayo and his staff. Just as quickly, it was ruled out as a favorable target for military assault when it was pointed out that sandbars prevented the larger ships from entering the Pánuco River and smaller craft from landing on the beaches. And there were other drawbacks to a Tampico operation. The federals, if attacked by foreign invaders, might possibly receive support from the Constitutionalist army advancing on the city. Mayo even considered a naval barrage to avenge the insult but rejected that alternative because Tampico possessed no fortifications and international law forbade bombardments of unfortified towns. And, more importantly, the seizure of Tampico would not topple Huerta.[2]

But Veracruz was another matter. As Mexico's principal port, it was vital economically and even politically to Huerta's cause. Moreover, as Wilson revealed in a press release on April 15, there had been an "incident" in Veracruz, one in the lengthening list of Huerta's abuses. A mail orderly from the *Minnesota,* which had sailed down the coast from Tampico, had been arrested by federal soldiers who had mistaken the American seaman for a Mexican deserter whose picture adorned the wall of the local post office. An interpreter was finally brought in, and the matter was cleared up in a short time. The report of the arrest by the American consul, William W. Canada, hopelessly confused the details so as to make the entire affair appear as another of the dictator's affronts, one carried out by a nameless Mexican functionary. The president could have read an accurate version of the story in the *New York World* of April 12, which correctly interpreted the arrest as inconsequential, a view later sustained by Admiral Fletcher's official investigation. But there had been still another injustice. On April 11, a petty bureaucrat in Huerta's censor's office had delayed transmission of a coded dispatch from Bryan to the embassy. O'Shaughnessy, expecting a message, called the telegraph operator and learned of the delay. Edith O'Shaughnessy appropriately characterized this "incident" as "less than nothing."[3]

But Wilson had already made up his mind. It mattered little that O'Shaughnessy, for the first time in his otherwise undistinguished career, was performing a notable role in his unceasing appeals to Huerta to bend, at least a little, to the president's demands. Huerta seemed as adamant as Wilson. He would salute the American flag *if* an American warship off Tampico would simultaneously return the honor. When an ecstatic Bryan brought the news to the president, the crisis momentarily appeared to take a turn for the better, but within a day Wilson rejected the proposal of simultaneous salutes as woefully unsuitable for the injury to the American flag. As commander in chief he was already massing an invasion army on Mexico's borders and had ordered the Atlantic Fleet to reinforce Mayo and Fletcher in the western Gulf.

That weekend (April 18–19) two seemingly unrelated messages clicked off the telegraph receiver at the State Department. One came from O'Shaughnessy in the Mexican capital, saying that Mexican guns at Tampico would salute the American flag and would fire *first* if there was a promise to return the salute from Mayo's warships. But the concession was so worded that acceptance implied recognition of Huerta's government, something Wilson had repeatedly rejected. The second telegram arrived from Canada in Veracruz early on Sunday. It reported the unloading of a steamer laden with ammunition and almost casually mentioned the expected arrival of another vessel, the *Ypiranga* (which Canada misspelled *Ipiranga,* causing confusion among State Department clerks trying to locate its registry), carrying 250 machine guns and 15 million rounds of ammunition.[4]

This news galvanized the State and Navy departments into action. Fletcher must move promptly at Veracruz to intercept the *Ypiranga*'s cargo and prevent the munitions from getting into Huerta's hands. Wilson had left for West Virginia on the afternoon of April 18 to bring his ailing wife back to Washington, but the General Board of the Navy had met in emergency session that morning and would convene again the following day, Sunday, to debate the growing list of recommendations on Mexico, ranging from some kind of reprisal at Tampico to a much larger operation, a landing at Veracruz coupled with an army invasion across the Rio Grande. By late Sunday, the various proposals had been set aside in favor of a limited operation at Veracruz to take the wharf and customhouse and intercept the *Ypiranga*'s arms. Hastily dispatched orders went out to Mayo at Tampico to sail for Veracruz to reinforce Fletcher, compelling Mayo to abandon the American colony in Tampico to the inevitable wrath of the Mexican population.[5]

Wilson did not return to Washington until early Monday, April 20. He breakfasted with his family and spent the rest of the morning shaping his special address on the Mexican situation, scheduled for delivery that afternoon before a joint session of Congress. The message was essentially a summing-up of the accumulated grievances against Huerta. In the initial draft, Wilson had written that the incident "was of no great importance" but scratched out these words and replaced them with "the incident cannot be regarded as a trivial one." The seizure of Veracruz offered the best course for retaliation and, he was assured, could be undertaken without significant loss of life. The action he recommended was not a declaration of war but one that would in fact obviate an armed conflict of much more dangerous proportions. America was not making war on Mexico or its people, the president said, repeating the distinction he had continually been making during the past year. Mexicans could settle their internal affairs without outside interference.[6]

The House of Representatives, more sensitive to the noticeably belligerent mood in the country, speedily passed the resolution "justifying" rather than "authorizing" the president's use of force against Mexico, but the Senate debated the measure well into the evening and adjourned without taking action. By the time the upper house finally rendered its approval, American troops were already ashore at Veracruz.

That night Wilson was awakened by a courier with another telegram from Canada. The vessel the consul had alluded to in his previous report was indeed the *Ypiranga*. Fletcher must land as quickly as possible.

Founded by another conqueror, Hernán Cortés, in 1519, Veracruz had historically been the objective of Mexican invaders. With Mount Orizaba as backdrop, the city offered the viewer from the sea a panorama of pastel buildings, imposing monuments, and graceful plazas flourishing with palms. On arriving, however, the visitor was immediately engulfed by the overpowering stench from garbage littering the streets and wharves and the sight of milling vultures thronging the waterfront. The *zopilotes* were pro-

tected from human menace by a city ordinance, for these disgusting birds
constituted the municipality's only reliable sanitary brigade. At the garbage
dumps they were joined in the feasting by packs of stray mongrels. Admiral
Fletcher's objective, the customhouse, stood along the waterfront with most
of Veracruz's other important public buildings—the Terminal Station, cable and telegraph offices, post office, and power plant—and the Naval
Academy, a quadrangle of two-story barracks.

The admiral's staff had drawn up a tentative plan for a landing a week
before, on April 13, when Fletcher organized a naval brigade divided into
a marine regiment under Lt. Col. Wendell C. Neville, commanding the
mobile regiment that had arrived aboard the *Prairie* from Pensacola, and
a seamen's regiment under Lt. Comdr. Allen Buchanan of the *Florida.*
All told, Fletcher could count on a landing force of more than a thousand men and fifty-two officers from the *Florida* and its sister ship, the
Utah. The landing parties would be put aboard whaleboats and towed by
motor launch to pier 4, where the large oceangoing vessels regularly
docked.

But Fletcher had not anticipated having to land on such short notice.
Taking the customhouse would not be such a formidable task, provided of
course he could be assured that there would be no resistance. He did not
want to commit his forces until the *Ypiranga* docked; if warned, the ship
carrying the arms and munitions Fletcher had to intercept might suddenly
alter course and put in at another Mexican port. But Fletcher now had
another worry, as it turned out, an overriding one—the weather. Storms
blew up quickly in the western Gulf, and Veracruz often lay in their path.
And on this gray morning the weather seemed to worsen with every
minute's delay. In a storm, none of the launches could be sent into the inner
harbor. About nine o'clock in the morning, detecting a sudden shift in the
wind, Fletcher decided to send his landing party ashore.[7]

The landing had not been unexpected by Veracruz's defenders. The
local Mexican commander, Gen. Gustavo Maass, a comical figure with a
brush mustache who bore a vague resemblance to Kaiser Wilhelm II of
Germany, in an informal conversation with Canada had confessed the
hopelessness of holding Veracruz against an American occupation. The
guns of Admiral Fletcher's warships, Maass had said, could easily destroy
the city of 40,000 within a few hours. Dutifully Canada had relayed this
sentiment to his superiors. Peering through his field glasses from the roof
of the American consulate, he watched with an inner reassurance as the
launches pulled away from the *Florida* with their trailing convoy of bluejackets and marines. Having anticipated what was now happening, he had
already warned American residents in Veracruz to take passage on the
steamers *Mexico* and *Esperanza,* tied up at the pier. At 9:30 an American

naval officer, Capt. Henry Huse, had appeared at the consulate to say that
the landing would commence about eleven o'clock. Canada was instructed
to inform Maass by telephone that the landing party intended to seize the
customhouse, telegraph and cable offices, and the railroad yard, where three
locomotives stood ready to take the *Ypiranga*'s cargo and other vital supplies into the interior. The landing force would not fire if not fired upon,
Huse stated.

A few minutes after eleven, as the *Florida*'s regiments were towed past
a British man-of-war (whose seamen cried out, "Give 'em hell, Yanks, give
'em hell"), Canada left his observation post to call Maass. Hearing the news
of the invading Yankees, the general exclaimed, "No, it cannot be!" Canada
made a second call, to the port collector, who also expressed amazement
at what was happening and demanded time to close his office and rush home
to his family, and a third to Veracruz's police chief, who calmly pledged
to assist in maintaining order, a commitment, Canada wrote in his official
report in August, that was not kept. The first shot fired at the Americans
came from the weapon of a white-uniformed street-corner policeman.[8]

The *Florida*'s contingent had no way of knowing that General Maass
had already made preparations for a fight. Maass had anticipated that his
superiors in Mexico City would probably order him to withdraw with his
force to Tejería, a small town on the railroad about ten miles from Veracruz.
But he had also surmised that he must put up some show of resistance to
give himself time to evacuate and to make a gesture of defiance of the
invaders, for national honor and his own reputation. Addressing his men
in patriotic language, he declared that anyone who wished could volunteer
to go down to the wharf and resist the invaders. He also ordered the release
and arming of the *rayados* (literally, "striped ones") of La Galera military
prison.

Robert Murray, one of the dozens of foreign journalists in Veracruz,
joined a crowd of curious Mexicans and Americans at the waterfront watching the boatloads of marines and bluejackets plow through the choppy
waters toward pier 4. It was a "show," Murray recalled years later, executed
in a routine manner. Murray had hastened down to the wharf to give
warning to the Americans after spying dozens of Mexican civilians and
soldiers, some armed with two and three rifles and laden with cartridge
belts, scurrying from house to house, looking for cover. Frantically he tried
to shout an alarm to the approaching launches.[9]

Disembarking, the *Florida*'s landing force, cheered by the Americans
in the onlooking crowd, stepped briskly up the concrete steps to the wharf,
regrouped, and divided. One regiment, under Neville, moved out to take the
cable office, power plant, railway yard and station house. Neville was experienced in this kind of activity; he had been taking towns in the Philippines,

China, and the Caribbean since the turn of the century. Perched once more on the consulate roof, Canada spied a carriage with three Mexicans and a machine gun racing into the railway yard. They quickly unloaded the gun and gave every indication of using it, but Neville's contingent occupied the yard and station without incident. The Mexican locomotives, however, had already gone, and the marines found no one in charge inside the station. The cable office was also taken without any firing, though the squad dispatched to seize it had to stop at the consulate and ask for directions.

The seamen's regiment, under Lt. Richard Wainwright, Jr., had the principal assignment—the seizure of the customhouse—which turned out to be more hazardous. During the landings Maass's volunteers, the *rayados*, and ordinary Veracruzanos who joined them, had been scurrying up to rooftops or nestling behind windows and watching the bluejackets and marines organize and move out along the waterfront. Some of the Mexicans had invaded the Hotel Diligencia, a favorite of the American tourists, and the Municipal Palace. One group of the newly created resistance had even lugged a one-pounder artillery piece to the top of the lighthouse. The advance unit moving toward the customhouse got within one block of its objective when the first shot was fired. The shot signaled a barrage of rifle fire from what seemed to be every direction. Atop the Hotel Terminal, American guests who had joined the naval signalmen at the outset dashed downstairs to their rooms. The most concentrated firing seemed to be coming from the lighthouse, the Hotel Oriente, the customs warehouse, and the Naval Academy. A few rounds quickly silenced the artillery piece in the lighthouse. In the yard of the academy a young Mexican naval artillery officer, José Azueta, son of the Mexican commodore, directed a machine gun crew raking the pier with fire. A boatswain's mate replied with several rounds at the Mexicans, hitting Azueta, who managed enough strength to inspire the others to continue firing. When their leader lapsed into unconsciousness, they carried him inside. Azueta died later from his wounds and was immortalized as one of Veracruz's most valiant defenders.[10]

In the city and on Fletcher's ships there was understandable confusion. At the street corners along the waterfront squads of marines and bluejackets hurried about, looking anxiously for Mexican snipers. No sooner would one be silenced by American fire, it seemed, than another three or four would commence shooting. The planning undertaken by Fletcher and his staff for what was supposed to be a relatively simple operation was being frustrated by countless unknown Mexicans lodged in the houses, hotels, and public buildings of Veracruz.

Assessing the day's events, Fletcher decided to increase his forces ashore. The *Utah* had spent most of the morning of April 21 preparing to get underway for Puerto México, 125 miles south of Veracruz, to intercept

Huerta's arms shipment if the *Ypiranga* changed course for that port. But by early afternoon it was clear that the *Utah*'s contingents were needed to assist the units pinned down in the city. One of the relief companies, commanded by Ens. Paul Foster of the *Utah,* arrived to find that the seamen's regiment had at last entered the customhouse but was still receiving fire from snipers on the roof. Foster sent reinforcements to clear the roof and another group to take the warehouse next door. They were barred from entry by two enormous iron doors but broke through by picking up railroad rails and using them as battering rams.[11]

By midafternoon of the first day, the invaders had taken the customhouse, their original objective, and the surrounding area but not the Plaza Constitución or the Naval Academy. The cadets of the academy, emulating the *niños heróicos* of Chapultepec of 1847 who had perished defending the Mexican capital against the American army of Winfield Scott, had sniped at the *Utah*'s launches as they came ashore and were continuing to rake the waterfront with fire. Fletcher was in a quandary: He did not want to carry the fight into Veracruz's streets and houses, nor did he wish to use his big guns in a bombardment. Three picket launches carrying one-pounders had set out from pier 4 in an effort to silence the Naval Academy snipers but had been struck several times by rifle fire and the one-pounder artillery piece the cadets were using. To protect the launches, the *Chester* had opened up with its three-pounder guns against the academy.

Even during all this furious shooting, American authorities ashore were still trying to negotiate. Captain Huse and Canada vainly searched all afternoon for Veracruz's mayor who, they believed, might be able to call off the city's volunteer defenders. They finally located him at home, barricaded in his bathroom. Mindful, apparently, of an 1862 federal law prohibiting Mexican public servants from aiding an invader (which had been passed when the French sent an army into the Mexican interior), the mayor denied responsibility for the actions of the citizenry and graciously deferred to the chief of police. But the American searchers found the police station abandoned.[12]

During the melee ashore, the *Ypiranga* suddenly appeared in the outer harbor. It was immediately boarded by an American naval officer explaining what was happening in the port. The ship's papers revealed that the arms cargo had actually been purchased in New York, but Huerta's agents had cleverly routed the arms through Hamburg, Germany, to avoid the American embargo. Ordering the *Ypiranga* to remain within gun range of the *Utah,* Fletcher dispatched a hasty cable to Washington, explaining his decision and noting the day's troubles. The admiral's casualties at this point were two dead and twenty wounded. Wilson was deeply shaken by the news of American losses; and Bryan now had to explain to the German ambassa-

dor that Fletcher had exceeded his instructions. The *Ypiranga* was technically free to sail from Veracruz with or without its cargo. In the curious
aftermath of this incident, the *Ypiranga*'s captain chose to remain at Veracruz for several days. After taking on refugees and other supplies, the ship
sailed for Tampico and Mobile, then, mysteriously, for Puerto México,
where its lethal cargo, the putative reason for Fletcher's invasion, was
unloaded into Huerta's hands.[13]

As darkness fell on Veracruz, the sniping died down. Within the city
there was now greater alarm over the activities of wandering *rayados,* the
released prisoners from the military stockade, who invaded houses, assaulted Veracruzanas, and committed numerous robberies. Fletcher had no
intention of withdrawing to pier 4; rather, he was determined to augment
his forces ashore. At the power station, American soldiers kept electric
lights on, illuminating the broad expanse of the waterfront. After midnight
the *Chester*'s captain, exhibiting some tricky maneuvering, brought his ship
into the inner harbor and landed another contingent of marines (including
the perennial banana warrior Smedley Butler) and bluejackets. A few hours
later Vice-Adm. Charles Badger's warships, which had been racing to
Veracruz, finally arrived.

Fletcher had no way of knowing it, but a significant portion of his
organized resistance in the city had already departed. In the early evening
Commodore Azueta, who had delivered an emotional appeal to the Naval
Academy cadets earlier that day, received orders from General Maass to
withdraw to Tejería. Azueta was determined to march out of Veracruz, but
the entry to the academy was covered by American guns, so the cadets
chopped a hole through the rear wall. They assembled outside, out of view
of the Americans, and marched through the streets, picking up another
group of volunteers on the way, and finally reached Tejería about midnight.
As Fletcher and Badger pored over their assault plans in the early hours
of the morning of April 22, their opposition ashore consisted only of disorganized bands of snipers.

At daybreak, launches from Badger's ships began docking at pier 4,
discharging more marines and bluejackets. Fletcher now surmised that
Veracruz lacked any organized resistance. The task at hand, then, was
clearing out the snipers, aroused by daybreak, still lodged in the houses and
on the hotel rooftops. Naively, Fletcher persisted in the belief he could find
a cooperative Mexican official to assist in maintaining order. One of the
arriving regiments, under Capt. E. A. Anderson, convinced that the wharf
was now safe, began marching toward the Naval Academy. Anderson was
something of a legend in the navy (he wore a West Indies medal with five
bars), but he had never fought a land engagement. Though warned about
Mexican fire by an aide, he refused to send scouts ahead. As the front

companies made the turn on Calle Francisco Canal, the entire regiment was suddenly raked with fire. There was utter confusion. At the rear of the column men began shooting aimlessly ahead, narrowly missing their comrades in the advance units racing for cover. Hastily determining that the fire came from the Naval Academy, Anderson signaled the ships in the harbor. There commenced a furious barrage from the guns of the *San Francisco* and the *Chester,* which pummeled the academy for five minutes. This second, more devastating, shelling completely demolished the inside of the building and was unnecessary, for Azueta and the corps had already departed. The firing from the academy on this morning may have been the work of a few stragglers or *rayados.* Jack London, arriving in Veracruz to report on the occupation, visited the academy and assessed the destruction under the gaze of buzzards perched on the blown-out window sills. The inside of the structure was a mass of crumbled plaster and smashed furnishings. Some of the shells had plunged completely through the outer structure, flown across the patio, and exploded in the rooms on the other side of the quadrangle. "Such," mused London, "is the efficiency of twentieth century war machinery."[14]

The Americans spent most of the second day clearing the hotels and houses of snipers. Ens. Paul Foster with a company of bluejackets from the *Utah* took the Municipal Palace on the plaza. From the tower of the municipal building the Americans were able to open up on the remaining snipers atop the Hotel Diligencia, while a squad of marines, who had a reputation for being more proficient in breaking down doors, burst through the entrance. Inside they found American women tourists tending Mexican wounded. As the fighting moved into the city, Mexican women and younger men occasionally picked up weapons and began firing randomly. Several of the women, on close inspection, turned out to be men who neglected to pull their pants' legs above the hemline. Some of the bluejackets, nervous under more than a day of sniping, even fired at their fellow American invaders. Frederick ("Dopey") Wise, whose marine unit did not get ashore until the major buildings had been taken, went from door to door, vainly searching for snipers. Wise's men found none, but they were pinned down under withering fire from American bluejackets atop the Hotel Diligencia who had mistaken Wise's outfit for the enemy! Traditional rivals for the glory in such imperial ventures, the marines and bluejackets seemed to maintain their rivalry even when fighting for the same thing.[15]

In a city swept with fear of bombardment or sacking by the invader, it was understandable why Veracruzanos behaved the way they did during the first days of the occupation. And it was equally understandable why the bluejackets and marines, assigned by their government with the simple task of taking a customhouse, should grow increasingly apprehensive and then

vengeful when their comrades died from snipers' bullets. The seizure of the
city had produced war's tragicomic moments. Most of the American invaders had never been in combat. One marine, whose unit burst into the Hotel
México, came face to face with a terrified Mexican gesticulating wildly and
gibbering in Spanish. The marine froze until the lieutenant bellowed,
"Shoot him!" He recalled: "I was standing . . . so close . . . that I couldn't
raise my gun to my shoulder. But I put it up as far as I could and fired.
The bullet struck him right in the heart, and I remember that he stared at
me in surprise and then he fell back—dead. It was the first man I had ever
shot and I felt mighty queer."[16] In another instance of defiance of the
invaders, a bald Veracruzano, casually reading a newspaper on his second-
story veranda, abruptly jumped to his feet, pointed a revolver in the general
direction of several American soldiers, and fired. He then sat down and
resumed reading. After the man repeated this several times, a bluejacket
shot him.

There was no formal surrender of the city. The Americans simply
extended their patrols until they reached the sand hills marking the outskirts of Veracruz. Outside the municipal buildings and the hotels and on
the street corners American invaders were transformed into sentries, policing the bewildered Mexicans who began emerging from hiding. By afternoon of the third day, the journalists were out looking for stories. One spied
a nervous bluejacket stopping an old man and his son trying to get from
their house to the corner. The American sailor refused to let them pass.
Searching the elder man, he found two bottles. Informed by the Mexican
that they contained medicine for his sick daughter, the bluejacket hurled
the bottles to the pavement.[17]

In the seizure of the city Americans suffered seventeen killed and
sixty-three wounded. No accurate count of Mexican losses was possible,
though a United States naval doctor, using the number hospitalized as a
guide, estimated the defenders had 126 killed and almost 200 wounded, but
he neglected to count those who received no medical treatment or who were
killed and hastily buried. Some of the bodies of those killed the first day
went unclaimed. In the fetid atmosphere they began to decompose rapidly.
For sanitary reasons, American patrols began loading the corpses on carts
and ferrying them to central locations for rapid interment. Others were
disposed of in more expedient fashion. One unit from the *New Hampshire*
piled its cartload of corpses atop creosoted railroad ties and set them afire.
Ens. Glenn Howell passed the funeral pyre of five Mexicans, detecting the
unmistakable stench of burning flesh. "It was not a pleasant sight," he
remembered. Though forbidden, some of the Americans took photographs
of these public cremations. Others posed with their weapons in the hunter's
position, with their kill lying before them.[18]

9. The Rulers of Veracruz

The seizure of Veracruz precipitated hemispheric and even international editorial comment. A major Guatemalan newspaper referred to the occupation as nothing more than an "international incident," but a Mexican paper, understandably, called the landing an "international crime." Even from the remote perspective of Tokyo, Wilson's decision, which had been officially described by Washington as a reprisal, looked more like the president's determination to punish the Mexican people by taking a portion of their territory.[1] In Argentina, which vied with the United States for leadership in the Pan-American system, one political review ran a cartoon showing a repulsive Uncle Sam demanding of an abused Mexican: " 'Salute my flag like it deserves or I'll take off your hat with a cannon shot!' " The League of Latin American Solidarity, hostile to American penetration of the tropics, declared: "Wilson has conspired with bandits and allied with traitors to foment the internal revolution in Mexico."[2]

The president responded to these denunciations of his action in equally fervent language. Less than a week after Admiral Fletcher's bluejackets had stepped ashore at pier 4 on the Veracruz waterfront, Wilson gave an emotional assessment of his Mexican policy to a *Saturday Evening Post* correspondent. "My ideal is an orderly and righteous government in Mexico," said Wilson, speaking with a face so taut that sinewy cords showed on the nape of his neck, "but my passion is for the submerged eighty-five percent of the people of the Republic, who are now struggling for liberty." With these words he brought a clenched fist down with such force that the blow shook the desk, scattering its contents. Then, his passion exhausted, "he sat back in his chair and half closed his eyes. His fingers laced and interlaced. Then he began to talk, clearly, simply, with a clarity of diction, a sequence of thought and a lucidity of expression that seemed even more remarkable than it really was when compared with the muddied speech of many of our statesmen."[3]

Elsewhere in Mexico the landing precipitated violent outbursts against American residents. In Tampico the military governor, anticipating an invasion by American forces, called for public resistance. On April 21, as Fletcher's troops were going ashore, Admiral Mayo withdrew all his vessels from the Pánuco River in preparation for getting underway to Veracruz, leaving the American residents in Tampico unprotected. The Mexican crowds that formed after the governor's decree vented their rage by throwing stones at the Southern Hotel, at Sanborn's, and at the American consulate. Mayo decided to risk an evacuation and solicited the aid of officers of the *Dresden,* a German cruiser, and a British war vessel. The Americans were thus evacuated from Tampico with the assistance of two European ships. Later the refugees praised the *Dresden*'s captain, who had trained his guns on the Southern Hotel, threatening to fire on the gathering mob if it continued its assault on the Americans huddled inside. But toward their own government the 2,600 Tampico refugees became quickly embittered; they were persuaded to leave hastily, assuming that Mayo would then attack the city. Left virtually destitute by their sudden departure, they were sent by Mayo to Galveston, where they were quarantined while the governor of Texas debated whether to accept them.[4]

In the Mexican capital crowds of angry Mexicans harassed foreigners, not only Americans but German and British residents as well. Mobs broke windows of hotels catering to tourists and attacked the American Club and prominent American-owned businesses. In desperation the American colony organized its own defense force, anticipating evacuation to Veracruz or, ominously, an American drive from the coast to take the capital. The British chargé, Sir Lionel Carden, an old hand in the British diplomatic service in Central America before his arrival in revolutionary Mexico, began evacuating British citizens. Most of the early arrivals from Mexico City into Veracruz were British and German nationals, but Carden made an effort to arrange for safe passage for Americans as well. To disrupt the traffic, a Mexican force tore up the track a few miles outside Veracruz, piled the creosoted crossties in huge stacks, and set them ablaze.[5]

As happened in other American military interventions in the Caribbean, the occupying force operated without precise instruction from Washington. The original goal of seizing the customhouse was quickly modified by the fierce resistance of the Mexicans themselves, so that Admiral Fletcher, using his "good judgment," shifted his objective to securing the city. The regular Mexican garrison, retired at Tejería only a few miles outside Veracruz, obviously posed a threat. Less than three days after the initial fighting, rumors of a counterattack from Maass's six thousand men (the estimate Canada gave to the State Department) were rife throughout the city. So the marine force under John Lejeune (one of four future Marine Corps commandants participating in the Veracruz affair) advanced to the sand hills marking the urban boundaries and beyond to the pumping stations at El Tejar and El Garto, which provided the city's water supply. Later, after the army took over in Veracruz, a guard of 250 marines remained at El Tejar. The Mexicans tried to frighten them away and cut off the water to the city, but the marine commander sent a call for help and soon received a reinforcement of 960 men. After that, the Americans used a biplane—fitted with pontoons for landing in the harbor—to survey Mexican troop movements as far as twenty-five miles inland.[6]

The restoration of authority in Veracruz proceeded in a legally haphazard fashion. Fletcher had orders to work through Mexican city officials so that the United States, to use the State Department's phraseology, might "indicate to the Mexican people ... the policy which this Government desires to pursue at Veracruz."[7] But Fletcher had to find municipal employees willing to serve; they refused to cooperate with the invaders because of fear of reprisal and punishment under the old law prohibiting any Mexican official from assisting an invader. While Canada was jubilantly reporting the resumption of normal urban life (as evidenced in the giving of daily concerts in Veracruz's plazas by military bands from the American ships), Fletcher despaired of maintaining order. On the morning of April 26, he reluctantly declared martial law.[8]

Already the Americans in Veracruz were indicating by their improvised rule how they intended to run things. Following Fletcher's decree they began disarming the civilian population and started cleaning the city. Within a day of his arrival Ensign Foster of the *Utah* became sanitary officer and ad hoc provost marshal. He released the Mexicans imprisoned in the dank cells of the Municipal Palace, organized them into sanitary brigades, and had them clean the places of their confinement. Lacking authorization to convene courts-martial, he dispatched the disheveled Mexicans brought before him by patrols to sanitary detail in the area around the palace or to picking up the bodies of Veracruzanos still lying in the streets. Foster worked "day and night" and by the third day of the occupation was receiving pleas "from all over the city" to get the streetcars running, the lights turned on, etcetera—all in the belief that an ensign in the United States Navy had "unlimited authority and manpower to accomplish all of the near miracles requested." Richard Harding Davis, describing Foster's frenetic pace during the early days of the occupation, called him the "Boy Poo Bah of Vera Cruz," because the ensign was "granting permission to open shops, to move families or to make business trips, to hold marriages and funerals, to go to sea with fishing craft, or to leave for inland destinations."[9]

Had Wilson turned affairs in Mexico over completely to his new commander in Veracruz, Frederick Funston, American troops would have marched on the capital. Funston was probably the army's most flamboyant officer of the prewar generation. He had advanced in the service through an unusual route. Born in Iowa six months after the Civil War ended, he

Searching a Veracruzano for weapons, 1914.   *National Archives*

had grown up in Kansas and attended the state university, where he studied botany. Weighing only one hundred pounds and standing five feet, five inches tall, Funston gained a reputation as a scrappy fighter. He joined the Agriculture Department, participated in the famed Death Valley expedition of 1891, and navigated a canoe fifteen hundred perilous miles down the Yukon River. When the Cuban insurrection broke out in 1895, he volunteered for Gen. Máximo Gómez's artillery brigade, served for eighteen months, but deserted the rebel cause after the revolutionary junta refused him leave to the States to recover from his combat injuries. When war erupted between the United States and Spain he sailed for the Philippines as a volunteer under Maj. Gen. Arthur MacArthur. He distinguished himself in the insurrection that broke out in the Philippines after McKinley proposed annexation of the archipelago and seemed destined for a regular commission, though a general in the regular army declared: "Funston is a boss scout—that's all." Funston made himself useful once more when, in a brilliantly executed ruse, he and six comrades captured the Filipino rebel Emilio Aguinaldo. The brazen act earned him McKinley's praise and his long-sought commission.[10]

Once Veracruz became an occupied city, the administration had to decide which service could better carry out the role of occupier. In Cuba—in the occupations of both 1899–1902 and 1906–1909—the army, reinforced by a brigade of marines, had represented American military authority within the country. Funston had lost out in his ambition to be supreme military commander in Cuba in 1906. Since then he had languished in the ranks (though he had found time to write his memoirs, *Memories of Two Wars,* published in 1910). The tense Mexican situation in early 1914 found him a brigadier general commanding an invasion army poised along the Rio Grande. When the president decided to name him military governor in Veracruz, Secretary of the Navy Daniels asked for retention of Fletcher, arguing that Funston was "Rooseveltian in methods . . . [and may] do something that may precipitate war." Daniels may have had some insight into Funston's ambitions. Less than a week after he became military governor, Funston proposed an expedition of seven thousand soldiers and marines, its supplies loaded on the many railroad flatcars abandoned by the Mexicans and pulled along the tracks by horses and mules. Such a vast undertaking, which some Republican critics of Wilson had been advocating, would have meant the navy's resumption of shore duty in Veracruz. But Funston was convinced his plan was practicable. He feared an attack on Veracruz by Maass's army, during which the city's inhabitants, "smarting over their recent humiliation," would rise up against the American occupiers. "Merely give the order," he wrote confidently to the adjutant general, "and leave the rest to us."[11]

Within a week of the landing Veracruz was returning to normal. "Things are really pretty quiet around here now," wrote Fred Delano to his mother; "a shot is the exception and then only at night. The natives are pretty well cowed in some respects, [but] are beginning to realize that we are not making war on them personally."[12]

Funston's military government of mostly army personnel took over from the navy on May 2. Where possible, the civil offices were staffed by Mexicans or, as they were called in the official reports, "natives." But so many of Veracruz's former municipal bureaucrats refused to serve that Funston had to rely on Army officers to fill civilian posts. By every standard of the efficiency of municipal government, these hastily appointed city bureaucrats gave a good accounting of themselves. The port's new customs collector (who happened to be a naval officer), for example, dutifully counted every peso in his possession (27,020) and set the money aside until it was determined how the funds might properly be used.[13]

The Mexican fear of retaliation once the Americans departed and the understandable reluctance to work for an occupation government increased Funston's burdens. Thus the army major appointed to supervise Veracruz's public educational system could boast of the reopening of four schools but added lugubriously that few of the former teachers could be persuaded to resume their duties. Those who agreed to teach under the military government did so without pay—the inference being that they were not really serving the Yankees if they received no salary. In the public safety division, the number of Mexicans employed was much higher; 50 percent of Veracruz's street patrols were composed of former city policemen.[14] But they operated under severe restrictions; they could arrest only civilians and not military personnel. And they had to comport themselves deferentially in the presence of uniformed Americans. "The 'Spig' policemen have to salute our officers," one marine stationed in Veracruz gloated, "and they cannot arrest an enlisted man for two reasons. First he is [sic] not allowed to and second he is not able to."[15]

Military governments can often exhibit paternalistic or even puritanical temperaments. Wood's regime in Cuba had had such a reputation, and the second Cuban occupation of 1906 had demonstrated a puritanical demeanor, though it was dulled considerably by Magoon's vapidities. Most who observed Funston's proconsuls in Veracruz—even the staunchest critics of American intervention in the Caribbean in this era—were impressed with the labors of the occupation government and, above all, its patent fairness. One who visited the city during these days and went away with a favorable judgment was Jack London. To London, Veracruz was an unkempt mestizo hovel that the Americans were desperately trying to clean up. The occupiers ("white-skinned fighting men who know how to rule as well as fight") brought decency and order to the city. City streets were now "quiet and seemly." The military government had weeded out the "riff-raff" and the "able-bodied loafers." At one inferior court established by the Americans, London observed a "blonde lawgiver," a .45 automatic strapped to his waist, dispensing justice in several cases simultaneously—to an accused thief, an Indian woman charged with public drunkenness, and a brothel owner—before proceeding with a stern warning to a hotel keeper about "unclean premises" and a sermon to another man on the subject of wife beating. The Mexicans hauled before this military solon were raucous and garrulous, but the American lawgiver remained patient and certain in his duty.[16]

In the spirit of municipal reform, American rule emphasized public order and, manifestly, honesty in public office. Graft was endemic in Veracruz, but the Americans strived to put a stop to official malfeasance. Suborning of policemen and judges virtually ended. Stolen goods were now recovered; before the occupation, it was said, one could find stolen property only at the petty bazaars around town. The police could no longer be bribed, and citizens arrested for some violation of ordinance left the courts dumbstruck over not having to pay for their freedom. The provost courts tried criminal cases (there were two murders in the city during the seven-month occupation) and, because it was presumed the decrees of civil courts could be voided after the Americans left, heard civil disputes as well. Virtually every imaginable civil contest made its way into the provost courts; six thousand rent-dispute cases clogged the legal channels created by the American proconsuls.[17]

Occasionally American regulations clashed with local custom. The military government prohibited the "so-called sport" of bullfighting, punishing violators with a thousand-peso fine and six months' imprisonment at hard labor. When July 4 approached, however, the judge advocate consented to a request from a group of enthusiastic promoters who wanted to celebrate the American Independence Day with a bullfight. He agreed, provided the Mexicans employed amateur matadors. Funston placarded the city with signs prohibiting spitting in public places and warnings against dumping garbage in the streets.[18]

The proconsuls pointed to sanitary measures as the hallmark of their rule, and rightly so. Veracruz had a reputation as one of the filthiest of international ports, and the task of sanitizing its streets and public places was made more difficult by the influx of some 15,000 refugees from the revolutionary torment in the countryside and the political discontent in the capital. The number of prostitutes rose to such an alarming number that the occupiers were compelled to institute strict regulations for the operation of bordellos, medical examinations for venereal disease, and, using an old

Mexican law, registration of prostitutes with the police. Finding the houses in the old district dilapidated and unhealthful, Funston created a new district where prostitution was tolerated in Veracruz's suburbs.[19]

Two weeks after Funston became military governor the Department of Public Works, responsible for municipal sanitation, proudly announced "a carefully planned campaign against dirt and rubbish." Teams of inspectors visited each house, warning the occupants about new penalties for unclean premises and improper disposal of garbage. The department began its sanitary campaign with $10,000 in hastily appropriated funds. With this money it launched an enthusiastic effort to rid the city of disease and filth. Restaurants (whose menus theretofore had offered "chicken cooked in its own moist") and public buildings were now required to install flytraps and dispose of garbage in sealed cans. Eventually, such measures were extended to private residences. Veracruz was woefully short of garbage cans, so the director of public health requisitioned 2,500 cans from the United States, which were dispensed to Veracruzanos at two dollars each. The *zopilotes* paid the ultimate compliment to the sanitary campaign; finding nothing to scavenge on the streets or along the wharves, they abandoned the city.

All this was impressive, yet the American occupiers seemed to deny their Mexican subjects personal dignity. Martín Luís Guzmán in his classic account of the revolution, *The Eagle and the Serpent,* remembered the judgment of an aged Veracruzano:

This military occupation is a preview of what may happen on a larger scale. From the material standpoint, the North Americans have made, or pretend to make, certain contributions, certain unimportant external improvements. For instance, they have screened the market place and meat market to do away with the flies. It is not much. But spiritually. . . . To understand what this means spiritually—leaving out the basic factor of the humiliation—all you have to do is observe what happens when one of the officers or soldiers of the invasion dismounts at the door of a store or bar; the bystanders fight for the honor of holding the horse's bridle, and for the tip. When the officer or soldier comes out, he gets on his horse and throws the lackey a coin.[20]

The taking of Veracruz had little immediate effect on Huerta's grip on the Mexican presidency. His popularity, which had steadily declined throughout the preceding year, seemed to escalate noticeably as the American military fastened its hold on the country's second-most-important city. Expecting Huerta's political enemies to praise—or at least to acquiesce in—his bold stroke, Wilson received a blow that was as damaging to his resolve as the news of casualties of April 21. With the exception of Pancho Villa, the revolutionary chieftains condemned the United States. Bryan sent a personal assessment justifying American policy to Carranza, but the first chief of the Constitutionalists was implacable: In reply he denounced Huerta's crimes and then denounced the American government for its invasion of Mexican soil. One of Carranza's aides suggested an appeal to the American people to avoid an "unjust war" against Mexico.[21]

Taken aback by the hemispheric criticism of the landing, Wilson welcomed an opportunity to demonstrate that he was not waging war against the Mexican people. Four days after the first troops went ashore at Veracruz, representatives of Argentina, Brazil, and Chile (the ABC powers) proposed mediation of the dispute. Wilson eagerly accepted; under pressure from the British chargé, Huerta agreed to a peace conference. But Carranza reacted suspiciously; when the mediators asked him to suspend hostilities during the negotiations, he called the request an inconvenience and continued the struggle against Huerta.

The conference began on May 20 at Niagara Falls, Canada, chosen after Huerta insisted on a neutral site. From the beginning session until the final meeting more than a month later, the mediators tried vainly to grapple with a lengthening list of issues, not only the seizure of a Mexican city by American forces but the struggle still going on in Mexico. The United States declared that its action at Veracruz rested ultimately on the rights and duties of states under international law; Huerta's call for an armistice, the State Department announced, was superfluous because no war had been declared. On the nagging subject of Huerta's retirement from politics, which Wilson had undeviatingly pursued since his own inaugural, the conferees had to contend with the almost immovable force of Carranza, who declared that he would neither negotiate peace with the dictator nor permit an election in which Huerta or Huerta's followers participated. On the question of American evacuation of Veracruz, Wilson steadfastly refused to compromise. In the end, as John Lind had predicted in April ("The mediation will drag on for weeks without result"), the conferees adjourned with little to show for their labors. They declared that Mexicans must decide on the issue of a Mexican provisional government, but, once installed, it would be recognized by the United States.[22]

In the final protocol of the Niagara conference, the American delegate added a disclaimer from Bryan that nothing in the document constituted diplomatic recognition of Huerta's government, a parting insult to the Mexican leader Wilson had so implacably opposed. The conference did not end the Veracruz occupation, as the ABC governments had naively presumed they might accomplish, nor did it reconcile Huerta and Carranza. The latter, importuned by Wilson to negotiate with the dictator, refused and awaited Huerta's resignation. That came, finally, on July 15.[23]

When the Niagara Falls conference held its final sessions, Veracruz was baking under the 100-degree days of summer that annually drove the city's

Above: Col. L. W. T. Waller (center) at Vera Cruz with (in front) Lt. Col. W. C. Neville, Col. John Lejeune, Maj. Smedley Butler, Maj. R. C. Berkeley. *National Archives. Below:* Ceremony for formal U.S. flag raising, April 24, 1914, Vera Cruz. *National Archives*

wealthier families into higher country. American rule had settled into dreary routine. The marine brigade, now commanded by a burly imperialist of the banana wars, Littleton Waller Tazewell Waller—each name representing a fine old Virginia family—camped in canvas tents staked out on the hills on the outskirts of town. The marines cursed the sand more than Mexicans or even the temperature, because it got into every crevice of body and clothing. Occasionally a dilapidated lorry, requisitioned locally in the initial days of occupation, "U.S. Marine Corps" crudely painted on its side, puttered along the city's narrow streets. Even Funston's usually frenetic pace slackened in Veracruz's summer torpor, though the military governor periodically shook the political scene with a blast at one of the numerous journalists who had taken to writing critically of American rule. Mostly, as Jack London soon realized, military government in Veracruz had become boring. Fred Delano, who wrote insightful letters about occupation life, retained his faith in American paternalism: "The people of Vera Cruz realize that never before have they been so well governed and are bitterly opposed to our leaving—can't say I blame them."[24]

Veracruz may never have been so "ably governed," but its residents were not "bitterly opposed" to American evacuation. As the summer wore on, Wilson himself felt powerful pressures for withdrawing his troops from Mexican soil. Huerta was gone from power and had departed the country. Carranza ruled now, but he governed by decree, refusing to hold the elections Wilson advocated. Carranza argued that Villa and Zapata, who defied him as they had Huerta, must first be dealt with before Mexicans enjoyed the democratic luxury of voting for new leaders. Until then, the first chief of the Constitutionalist army intended to rule as he had for a year—without American dictation. He desperately needed Veracruz's revenue, and he pressed for American evacuation of the port, but the wily old chieftain also realized that Wilson's reason for holding the city had vanished with Huerta's downfall. On September 16, the day of national independence, Carranza got an oral commitment of American intention to withdraw from Veracruz.[25]

The Americans fought for three days to take Veracruz; they would require two months to evacuate it. One explanation lay in the predictable bureaucratic delays that even a small military operation can entail. Funston could easily give an order and have seven thousand men packed and ready for transport ships in a few days. But he had potentially troublesome matters to be settled. The first was the burgeoning population of refugees, many of them former Huertista officers, who had been streaming into the city ever since the American takeover. Some had arrived virtually destitute; others had brought script that purchased nothing locally. Some were fearful of reprisal and began booking passage on steamers for Cuba, Spain, and the

United States. In mid-October Funston estimated that two thousand had departed since the public learned of the impending evacuation three weeks before.

Funston had a special concern for the Catholic priests who had fled the anticlerical fervor of the revolution and also for the Mexicans who had served the occupation government. Though Carranza was pressed to give assurance there would be no retaliation against public officials who had worked for the Americans at Veracruz, he refused. Funston drew up a list of 297 Mexicans, most of them employees of the military government, who asked for evacuation. The military governor suggested a temporary sojourn in the United States and return to Mexico when animosities against Mexican employees of the military government subsided.[26]

Carranza remained silent on the subject of reprisals, and Wilson, equally adamant, delayed in ordering the evacuation. When the American emissary delivered the conditions for withdrawal—no retaliation against Mexicans who worked for the occupation government, no demands for payment to Mexico from revenue received at Veracruz by American authorities, and creation of tribunals to administer justice to those still charged with crimes during the occupation—Carranza in turn sent the demands to the special convention of revolutionaries meeting at Aguascalientes. The American conditions for withdrawal, he told the delegates, were matters affecting the "sovereignty of Mexico" and could readily be settled by its government, but if imposed by the United States, they "constituted an outrage." Capitulation to the United States insulted national honor.[27]

But the revolutionary delegates, persuaded by the presence of Villa's and Zapata's agents, turned against Carranza and named another general as their leader. Carranza was furious; he called his representatives back to the capital and declared war on his rivals. Once again Mexico was plunged into fratricidal violence. The Constitutionalists, outclassed by the armies of the convention, retreated, forcing Carranza to flee the capital. Assailed by the other revolutionary chieftains, he decided to accept Wilson's requirements for evacuation, though Carranza's capitulation was cleverly framed so as to appear to be a response to petitions by leading Veracruzanos. On November 10 the State Department announced that American troops would leave Veracruz in ten days.[28]

The final order for evacuation required Funston to leave Veracruz with all moneys in the city's coffers, including customs duties and taxes, records and accounts, and an inventory of goods stored in the customs warehouse. Though instructed to avoid "any arrangements with . . . Mexican representatives . . . that could make it seem that you are recognizing the right of Carranza to jurisdiction over the city," Funston had already met informally on November 18 with a correspondent of Isidro Fabela, Carranza's secretary of foreign relations, and confirmed the date of evacuation.[29]

The evacuation was carried out without incident on November 23. Seven thousand American troops marched through the streets down to the piers, went aboard the huge transport vessels that had docked the night before, and by 2:00 P.M. were gone from Mexican soil. Already Constitutionalist troops of Gen. Cándido Aguilar were moving into the city. There were a few random shots in celebration; otherwise, the retreating and the newly occupying armies acted with admirable composure.

Within a short time Veracruz reverted to its pre-occupation habits. Bribery and graft reappeared in public affairs, and the city's residents began tossing their garbage into the streets. The sanitary brigade dissolved when the Americans departed and, in time, the *zopilotes* returned.[30]

The tension in Mexican-American affairs still did not abate, however. Carranza, driven out of Mexico City, took up official residence in Veracruz while Zapata and Villa occupied the capital. As the civil war raged on, Wilson once more grew irritated with his factious neighbors, and in summer 1915, following a lofty presidential declaration that Mexicans should settle on a leader, rumors of another intervention circulated in the American military establishment.[31] Wilson continued to proffer aid to Carranza, and Carranza haughtily refused it. His generals, notably Alvaro Obregón, subjected Villa to defeat after defeat. In October, after a collective statement from the ABC powers and several smaller Latin American governments, the United States recognized Carranza as president of Mexico. Enraged, Villa began his murderous assaults on American lives and soil, which culminated in the bloody raid on Columbus, New Mexico, and the chase of Villa by John J. Pershing's punitive expedition into Mexico.

Memories of the Tampico affair and the Veracruz intervention soon faded in American recollection of the history of the banana wars, but among Mexicans the bitterness generated by the seven-month occupation of the nation's major port ran deep for several generations. The American military, whose marines and bluejackets had dramatically affected the course of Nicaraguan politics only a few years before, had not achieved a similar goal in Mexico. There it was restrained by a determined president who remained almost self-righteously convinced that forceful persuasion was a morally preferable policy to full-scale intervention. Closely supervised by its civilian commander throughout the crisis with Mexico, the military could not carry out its plans for a drive into the interior and the ultimate occupation of the Mexican capital.

This distinction has of course made little difference to Mexicans who persist in excoriating Wilson "the moral statesman" for the "immorality" of his Mexican policy. Condemned by Roosevelt for not being tough enough, Wilson, despite his sometimes blind stupidity in dealing with Mexico, at least understood the lamentable consequences of his secretary of war's recommendation for a drive on the Mexican capital. Mexico was riven by civil conflict and fratricidal war, but Wilson realized that an American invasion would have turned the warring Mexicans against the United States and plunged the two countries into a second Mexican-American war.[32] In Nicaragua, full-scale intervention, urged as much by the civilians as by the military, had apparently worked because, among other things, the United States created a pro-American element, not because it had taught the Nicaraguans to "elect good men." But in Mexico it found no one—certainly not the crusty old Carranza—willing to play the role of lackey. Carranza may not have fulfilled the social goals of the revolution, but he kept the gringos out of Mexico City.

PART III

Civilizing the Tropics

10. Turbulent Hispaniola

In the nineteenth century the island of Hispaniola—containing the two very different countries of Haiti and the Dominican Republic—had played a less compelling role in the American vision of tropical empire than had Cuba. The United States had tried to acquire naval leases at Samaná Bay in the Dominican Republic and at Môle Saint-Nicolas on Haiti's isolated northwest coast. The first dream had perished, presumably, with Ulysses S. Grant's abortive Dominican annexation scheme in 1871. The second was destroyed in the early 1890s by the latent xenophobia in Haiti despite the blandishments of an expansionist administration that had dispatched to Port-au-Prince America's best-known former slave and an admiral of Italian ancestry to negotiate a treaty.

After the victory over Spain, with new responsibilities in the Caribbean, the United States Navy looked anew at Hispaniola's strategic location between its Cuban protectorate and its Puerto Rican colony. In December 1900 the General Board reminded the State Department of Hispaniola's "important and commanding position . . . in war strategy" and warned of the baleful consequences of the "feeble and chaotic condition[s] of the Governments in that Island [that] make it easy for any country to obtain concessions without great expense."[1]

The navy never acquired a base at Samaná, though it maintained an intensive interest in Dominican affairs and continuously patrolled Dominican waters. Roosevelt's famous *modus vivendi* of 1905, which allowed the president of the United States to name the republic's customs collectors and provided for the gradual repayment of the enormous international debt incurred in the nineteenth century, became with modifications the Dominican-American treaty of 1907. In approving the special relationship with the beleaguered Caribbean nation, however, the Senate made clear there was no Dominican "Platt Amendment"; references to American "respect for the territorial integrity" of the republic and commitments to regulate its internal affairs were omitted. With American supervision of Dominican customs collection, it was presumed, the republic would achieve internal political stability. As Roosevelt himself said in a letter to anti-imperialist Andrew Carnegie, the United States had a treaty especially designed to prevent the need of any interference by us or by any foreign nation with the internal affairs of the island, while at the same time securing the honest creditors their debts and to the government of the island an assured income, and giving to the islanders themselves the chance, if only they will take advantage of it, to achieve the internal peace they so sorely need.[2]

And in 1907 Roosevelt's smug assessment seemed to have some validity, for the republic's tortured political system had produced in Ramón Cáceres a leader capable of ruling its numerous factions. Cáceres, affectionately called "Mon" by his admirers, was in the gun-toting tradition of strong-willed Dominican leaders. He had been the main assassin in the squad of alienated young Dominicans who had gunned down Heureaux in 1899, survived the civil wars that followed, and finally in 1906 compelled then-president Carlos Morales, who had negotiated the customs receivership with the Americans, to vacate the presidential office and leave the country. A huge man with a commanding presence, Cáceres, in the words of Sumner Welles in his ponderous history of the republic, "lacked the qualities of statesmanship" but possessed both "vision and rare good sense."[3] (Welles usually measured Dominican leaders according to their "practicality" and Caucasian ancestry.) "Mon" enthusiastically expanded the government's virtually nonexistent public works program, laying out, under the direction of an American engineer, the nation's first highway system and promoting public ownership of its infant utilities.

Such vigorous public activity contrasted sharply with Dominican political tradition of using power to line one's pocket or to dispose of enemies. But Cáceres opened the country to foreign entrepreneurs who accumulated large holdings of sugar estates. He did not vanquish his enemies or cure the republic, as Roosevelt would have said, of its "revolutionary habits." In the end he perished in the same way as Heureaux, by an assassin's bullets, on November 19, 1911, as his carriage rolled along a Santo Domingo street near the American legation.[4]

Under Cáceres the Dominican Republic had been something of a model of limited American tutelage of a tropical society. With his death the country reverted to its old ways, leaving Taft and Knox, busily trying to sell the Senate on new financial treaties for Central America, without a workable example of dollar diplomacy. American observers grew disenchanted with the Dominican experiment. Only the customs collectors and the American minister, both appointed by the American president, preserved traditions of honesty and civic responsibility, wrote Secretary of War Henry Stimson, who visited Santo Domingo in the summer of 1911. As did others, Stimson blamed Hispaniola's unsettled politics on the "pall of negro despotism." "This beautiful island," he confided to his diary, "probably the most fertile of all the West Indies, was weighed down . . . by a far more hopeless population than existed when Columbus discovered it four hundred years ago."[5]

The warring of the republic's political factions continued into 1912, and the country seemed no closer to any semblance of order when Wilson became president in March 1913. In the last months of the Taft administration, the Dominican assembly had chosen a prominent cleric, Archbishop Adolfo A. Nouel, as provisional president after his predecessor, who had exhausted the national treasury trying to suppress a rebellion, was driven from office when Knox threatened to shut off customs revenues if he did not resign. To back up the threat, a special investigating team reinforced by 750 marines had descended on Santo Domingo.[6] But Nouel lasted only a few months and was followed by still another provisional president, whose inauguration preceded by one day the outbreak of rebellion.

In the interior valleys, on the rugged Dominican frontier, and on the north coast, rebellion flourished because Santo Domingo was shut off almost completely from the interior by the lack of roads. Historically, few Dominican leaders had been able to intimidate the country's warring political factions. American customs officials generally saw themselves as the bulwark of orderly society. One, Thomas Morris, who served from 1913 to 1916 at various posts along the Haitian-Dominican border, observed after the resurgence of one rebellion: "There is absolutely no law now other than that of the customs service." Morris favored an American takeover to settle Dominican affairs.[7] On the northeastern coast in Samaná, even less accessible to Santo Domingo's control, American naval officers sometimes mediated between the fractious rival bands. In 1913 Walter Anderson, an ensign on the *Des Moines,* composed a hasty armistice between two rebel generals. Surmising that the document had to be written in lofty phraseology, he began, "In the Year of our Lord 1913, of the Independence of the United States, 142 [*sic*]," followed with the pertinent details, and ceremoniously presented it to the two Dominicans for their signatures. "Believe it or not," he recalled years later, "they respected it. That ended the war."[8]

Such were the ephemeral glories of naval diplomacy. The incident bespoke the method and customs the navy had been following for generations in dealing with random Caribbean fighting. And it reflected also the contempt that American military officers held for Dominicans generally. Landing bluejackets or marines to deal with some unpleasant situation in Hispaniola had been accepted practice in the nineteenth century. One of the earliest landings of marines had occurred at Puerto Plata in 1800. And in the Haitian republic United States warships had landed marines on eight occasions between 1867 and 1900.

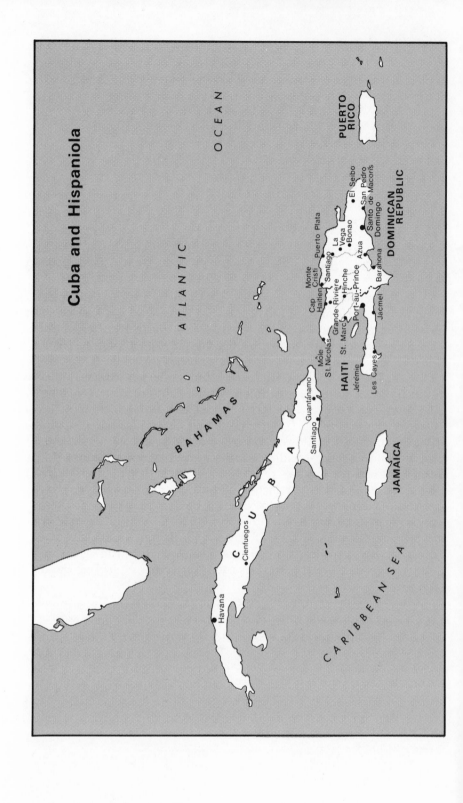

Cuba and Hispaniola

OCEAN

ATLANTIC

PUERTO
RICO

DOMINICAN
REPUBLIC

El Seibo
San Pedro
Santo de Macorís
Domingo

Puerto Plata
La
Vega
Bonao
Santiago   Azua
Monte
Cristi
Cap
Haïtien
Grande
Riviere   Hinche
St. Marc   Port-au-Prince
Barahona
Jacmel

Môle
St. Nicolas
HAITI

Jérémie
Les Cayes

BAHAMAS

Guantánamo

Santiago

C
U
B
A

JAMAICA

Havana

Cienfuegos

CARIBBEAN SEA

Thus the military interventions in Haiti and the Dominican Republic in the Wilson era, often portrayed as drastic departures from American practice, had ample historical precedent. What was different about Wilsonian policy toward Hispaniola was the degree of political interference undertaken by the United States to reform its admittedly backward societies and, that failing, the willingness to use military intervention as a means of bringing about reform. It can be argued that Roosevelt had done much to set the pattern for such interfering behavior in the Dominican Republic's internal affairs with the customs receivership. But Roosevelt had established strict limitations on what he believed the United States should and should not do in the republic, and the 1907 treaty had reaffirmed these restrictions. We would collect the customs, set aside 55 percent for satisfying foreign claimants, and give the politicians of Santo Domingo the remainder. We would protect the customhouses from the perils of insurrection. After that, if their political house was in disorder—and it usually was—it was *their* house.

That was Roosevelt's and Root's approach. Their policy for the republic involved no sweeping American prescriptions for reordering Dominican finances or tinkering with the republic's chronically disturbed political system. Taft and Knox went much further. In 1912, when revolutionary outbreaks disturbed the frontier, the American minister, William Russell, recommended military occupation of the customhouses and indeed a takeover of the country to bring to an end what he considered barbaric practices —forced recruiting into warlord armies, pilfering of public funds, and judicial corruption.[9]

Wilson and Bryan advocated even more stringent requirements for the Dominican political system. The president personally directed Mexican policy, and he gave to Bryan and the State Department considerable latitude in Dominican and Haitian affairs. The Great Commoner was easily the most controversial of Wilson's cabinet appointees. Acting on the impulse that he must cleanse the foreign service, he zealously removed most of the appointees who had secured their posts under the nascent professional standards inaugurated by Hay and appointed wheelhorses and party hacks in their stead. For Latin American posts Bryan's housecleaning resulted in the dismissal of ministers with an average of fifteen years' experience and knowledge of the language of the country to which they were accredited. Most of Bryan's nominees were simply incompetent, though the new minister in the Dominican Republic, James M. Sullivan, a former lawyer and prizefight promoter (who had been recommended by the secretary of state as one of his "deserving Democrats"), was both incompetent and corrupt. Eventually public revelations about the circumstances of his appointment and Wilson's intervention brought Sullivan's removal but not before he had seriously damaged American prestige in the republic.[10]

Even more than Wilson, Bryan had been a critic of Roosevelt's and Taft's Caribbean policies, and he reviled the machinations of predatory capital in the tropics with the same intensity as he had condemned Wall Street. But as secretary of state he readily converted to imperialism, in part because he realized the strategic significance of the Panama Canal, which opened during the second year of the Wilson administration, and also because Bryan became an advocate of what might be called "public dollar diplomacy."[11] Public moneys, not private capital, would underwrite American enterprise in the tropics.

When Bryan discovered that the harassed Dominican president, José Bordas Valdéz, who had taken office in April 1913, intended to use a loan from the National City Bank of New York (which had been secured by his predecessor) to suppress an insurrection, the secretary informed the rebels that if they won the war the United States would neither recognize the new government nor permit it to pay off *its* revolutionary obligations by increasing the public debt. Nor would the new regime receive its allotted share of customs receipts.

The insurrection of course continued. Bordas declared war on one of the republic's most powerful figures, Gen. Desiderio Arias, an outspoken critic of American meddling in Dominican affairs. Apparently Bordas had acted on the advice of Sullivan, but even after Sullivan was recalled American pressure was maintained. In incremental steps Bryan penetrated the inner structure of Dominican politics, beginning with a recommendation for an American-appointed financial auditor in the Dominican government to the highly controversial scheme, the "Wilson Plan," which called for American supervision of the selection of a new president and a reordering of Dominican finances. Bordas tried to retain power beyond the date for his retirement, provoking Arias into another fight. During this conflict the *Machias,* patrolling off the republic's north coast, fired on Bordas's troops at Puerto Plata. Bordas was eventually overthrown in August 1914. In December, following an intensive political campaign in which American demands for Dominican political and economic reforms were a major issue, Juan Isidro Jiménez, leader of the Jimenista faction, became president.[12]

Dominican politics was a complex subject to Bryan, probably because he little appreciated Dominican history and the role played by its political strong men—Santana, Báez, and Heureaux—and the bitter political divisions of the early twentieth century. The Wilson Plan was merely a formula for supervising Dominican finances and selection of its president; the republic's problems dictated a restructuring of society, and such an awesome task, it was later argued, required, and ultimately brought about, military intervention.

Bryan was equally uninformed about neighboring Haiti, though by late 1914, when the State Department began pressing upon the Haitian govern-

ment measures it was urging on Dominican leaders, the secretary of state
had received a long discourse on Haitian history and culture from an
American official in the Banque nationale. At the end of what must have
been a fascinating lecture, Bryan remarked: "Dear me, think of it. Niggers
speaking French." That was perhaps more blatantly racist than the observation of old Alvey Adee, the longtime assistant secretary of state, who had
described Haiti as a "public nuisance."[13]

Haiti had received less official attention after the frustrating efforts in
the 1890s to get a naval lease at Môle Saint-Nicolas on the north coast. The
navy maintained its interest in the Môle, however, with stern statements
that the United States could not tolerate the cession of a base in Haiti to
any foreign power. In the early years of the twentieth century, when fears
of German designs on Caribbean territory ran strong in American military
circles, Haiti seemed especially vulnerable to foreign influence. In 1897 two
German ships threatened to shell Port-au-Prince because of allegedly arbitrary treatment of a German national by the Haitian government. Under
pressure from the American minister, the Haitian president gave in to
Berlin's ultimatum. Afterward Germans began migrating to Haiti in significant numbers, marrying into the French-speaking Haitian elite and creating
a vigorous German business community in the capital.

In the McKinley years the American minister in Port-au-Prince had
advanced a proposal for a financial protectorate (along the lines of the later
Dominican model), but Secretary of State John Sherman rejected the plan
as tantamount to creating a "colonial dependency." Haitians, he might have
added, were suspicious of foreign designs, an understandable apprehension
given the legacy of the rebellion against French rule and the fears of reprisal
against the world's first black republic.

American naval officers on patrol in Haitian waters after the turn of the
century, when the country was plunged into civil war and political intrigue,
made observations that would have validated old Adee's denigratory comment about Haiti as a "public nuisance." In 1902, when a revolt in the
North (where Haitian revolutions ordinarily began) threatened the tiny
foreign community in Cap Haïtien, the most important town on the north
coast, the commander of the *Machias,* Henry McCrae, was on the verge of
landing troops when the shooting died down. Later, McCrae issued a
provocative warning to a rebel gunboat threatening Cap Haïtien: "I am
charged with the protection of British, French, German, Italian, Spanish,
Russian, and Cuban interests. You are also informed that I am directed to
prevent the bombardment of this city without due notice [and] to prevent
any interference with commerce." The legitimate government's agents received no greater consideration: McCrae brusquely informed a Haitian
admiral that any attempt to search an American ship entering Cap Haïtien
"would be considered an act of piracy and treated as such." Even Adee was

taken aback by such forceful language and sent a gentle rebuke to the secretary of the navy. But the view of a chronically unstable society that would have to be "shaped up" by the "civilized Powers" remained a fairly common assessment of Haiti among American naval officers for another decade, when the civilians would adopt a similar outlook. As one sailor succinctly put it in 1908, another year of Haitian troubles: The Haitians cannot "maintain a stable government by their own endeavor. . . . The one question is how long the civilized nations of the world will permit such conditions to exist."[14]

After 1908, when the dictator Nord Alexis was driven into exile in Jamaica, political unrest combined with recurring financial crises in the government made Haiti even more vulnerable to outside influence. In 1910 the Taft administration became embroiled in a financial power struggle involving French, German, and American banking interests for control of the Banque nationale, which controlled the flow of funds to the Haitian government. Two American concerns, Speyer and Company and National City Bank, had tried the previous year to expand their operations in the Banque, but a European consortium masterminded by German investors had stopped them. When the Europeans began their reorganization of the Banque, Taft and Knox, in the spirit of dollar diplomacy, insisted on inclusion of American bankers in the scheme. Fear of German designs in Haiti was a powerful incentive to State Department pressures on behalf of the American banks. The reorganization left the Banque with its headquarters in Paris but with three Americans serving as directors. Since the Haitian government depended on the Banque for loans, its influence in Haitian politics was considerable.

But Haiti's financial crisis seemed only to intensify political agitation. Following Nord Alexis's overthrow in 1908, Haitian presidents entered and left office in unsettlingly brief intervals, usually as the result of a revolution. Haitian executives were expected to serve seven years; from December 1908 to December 1915 there were seven presidents. Most were turned out by *caco* armies hired by Haitian political aspirants (who it was suspected were financed by German residents expecting 100 percent return on their investments). The *cacos* were semiprofessional soldiers living in the mountainous interior who survived mostly by robbing Haitian peasants, but in times of political discord their leaders sold their services to revolutionary causes. It was an old tradition followed by scores of *caco* chieftains in the nineteenth century. In 1911 Gen. Cincinnatus Le Conte drove out Auguste Simon, who had deposed Nord Alexis three years before, in a revolution organized with *caco* bands in the North. Le Conte managed to survive for nine months (during which time he accumulated vast amounts of explosives for future use against his enemies) when he was blown up in the National Palace. His successor, Tancrede Auguste, died eight months after taking power, in a less noisy fashion, by poison.

During revolutionary disturbances in October 1914, two American warships carrying eight hundred marines appeared off Port-au-Prince and cowed Haitian discontents into accepting the current government of Joseph Theodore. In December Bryan grew alarmed that reserve funds in the Banque nationale were being siphoned off to finance another revolution. A squad of eight marines armed with nightsticks and pistols removed $500,000 in gold from the bank and carried it through practically deserted Port-au-Prince streets to the *Machias* for shipment to New York. The bank itself had requested the transfer to ensure the bullion's safety, but the action left in the minds of Haitian leaders the impression that Banque funds were out of their reach.[15]

By mid-1915 the State Department had come around fully to the view that Haiti desperately needed the same kind of reforms—a customs receivership, claims settlement, protection of foreign lives and property, and firm assurances against European (i.e., German) encroachment—that it was already pressing upon the Dominican Republic. In fact the Wilson Plan for the Dominican Republic was retitled and sent to Port-au-Prince to Arthur Bailly-Blanchard, the first white to serve as American minister to Haiti. *Le Matin,* Port-au-Prince's most prestigious newspaper, had already characterized these pressures as simply another variation of dollar diplomacy, "a policy that would demand the use of Marines."[16] Though Bryan was on the way out because of his disagreement with the president's German policy, his successor Robert Lansing was, if anything, even more eager than Bryan to implement Haitian reforms. His motives were never clear, however. In 1918 he told an admiral that fear of German involvement prompted the occupation of Haiti, but Lansing had earlier argued against American intervention in Mexico because such action would play into German hands. His views of Haitian capability were unambiguous: "The experience of Liberia and Haiti show[s] that the African race are devoid of any capacity for political organization and [have no] genius for government."[17]

American naval activity in Haitian waters had picked up considerably since early 1915 when the commander of the Crusier Squadron, Rear Adm. William Banks Caperton, a sixty-year-old veteran cast in the mold of nineteenth-century officers, had been dispatched on the *Washington* to Caribbean waters. In late January his flagship had anchored off Cap Haïtien, Haiti's important northern port, just in time for the admiral to assess the strength of revolutionary activity in the region. It was here that Caperton met Gen. Vilbrun Guillaume Sam, the next Haitian president, "a very gorgeous black gentleman arrayed like a head bellhop at the Waldorf." They conversed pleasantly, Guillaume Sam promising to preserve order, to restrain his troops from robbing the villages, and in general to conduct "humane warfare."[18]

Caperton sailed for Port-au-Prince and a conference with Bailly-Blanchard. The American minister, cataloging the declining economic fortunes of the government, believed American intervention was imminent and wanted to coordinate activities. The navy had already drawn up plans for seizing Santo Domingo and Port-au-Prince. The Dominican capital, the plan anticipated, could be seized and held with a force of about one thousand bluejackets and marines from the *Washington* and its sister vessels, *Prairie, Hancock,* and *Castine;* Port-au-Prince, virtually unfortified, could probably be taken with an even smaller force. But as Guillaume Sam's armies pushed southward, Caperton grew more apprehensive and radioed for additional ships. On February 25, having cut off the capital from the rest of the country, Guillaume Sam triumphantly entered Port-au-Prince. In a few weeks a special American mission arrived to foil rumored plans of French financial scheming, including a bizarre tale (because France and Germany were at war in Europe) that Roger Farnham (vice-president of the Banque nationale) passed on to the credulous Bryan to the effect that the French and Germans were actually cooperating in Haiti.[19]

Caperton sailed for Veracruz. But on July 1 he returned to Haitian waters, brought from Mexico by an urgent navy message telling of disorders in Cap Haïtien and the landing of French marines from the cruiser *Descartes.* Haiti was going through another of its bloody cycles. French activity in the Caribbean did not arouse State Department suspicions nearly so much as German maneuverings. After all, Haiti had once been French domain, and its elite spoke French, sent their children to French academies, and, mistakenly, looked to France as protector of the black race. In any event, the United States could no longer allow French troops to police the Caribbean, and Caperton's orders now were to thank the French commander politely and assume responsibility for maintaining order. The disturbances in Cap Haïtien were the work of Dr. Rosalvo Bobo, who had raised a *caco* army and planned to use it in overthrowing Guillaume Sam. Bobo was fiery and articulate, a graduate of the University of Paris and formerly Haitian minister to the Dominican Republic, a delicate assignment for any Haitian diplomat. Bobo was also a critic of American influence in Haiti; Guillaume Sam, he declared, was betraying the country by arranging with American commissioners for a customs receivership.

Guillaume Sam was in fact negotiating with the Americans, but he had not yet turned Haiti into a financial protectorate of the United States. He was busily harassing his political enemies, the social elite of Port-au-Prince, using funds seized from the Banque nationale to raise an army and drive Bobo's *cacos* across the border into the Dominican Republic. July 1915 witnessed a reign of terror in the capital. Martial law was proclaimed, and anyone suspected of opposition to the regime was imprisoned. Some of the president's enemies took refuge in the city's foreign legations. A few managed to plot a coup and invaded the presidential grounds, sending Guillaume Sam, wounded in the affray, into hiding in the French legation. The disturbance signaled the onset of a massacre of 167 of the president's opponents in the national prison, two of them former Haitian executives.

News of the grisly executions—by strangulation, hacking, and in one case gouging out of the eyes—spread throughout the city. The commandant of the prison, who had supervised the executions and then taken refuge in the Dominican legation, was taken out by a mob and slaughtered, his corpse left on the street for a day before being soaked with oil and burned. The *Washington,* meanwhile, was steaming at full speed for Port-au-Prince. Caperton could be expected to quell the rioting as he had done at Cap Haïtien, though as yet he lacked specific orders to do so. At the sight of the approaching American cruiser, a large group of young Haitian men, relatives and friends of those slain in prison, believing that Guillaume Sam would find sanctuary under a foreign flag, rushed the French legation. They found the wounded Haitian president cowering in a bathroom and dragged him outside. The American chargé, brought to the scene by the din, described the gruesome spectacle:

I could see that something or somebody was on the ground in the center of the crowd, just before the gates, . . . when a man disentangled himself from the crowd and rushed howling by me, with a severed hand from which the blood was dripping[,] the thumb of which he had stuck in his mouth. . . . Behind him came men with the feet, the other hand, the head, and other parts of the body displayed on poles, each one followed by a mob of screaming men and women. The portion of the body that remained was dragged through the streets by the crowd.[20]

Representatives of the foreign community, terrified by the events of late July, crowded on the *Washington,* beseeching Caperton to act. The city lacked any organized authority, he was informed. Presuming the worst, he concluded that the mobs might randomly turn on foreign nationals, reenacting the horrible events of the last days of the Haitian revolution for independence, when the Haitians ran the French out of the country and massacred the whites who remained, a story embellished with such racial hatreds and fears that it made Haiti a pariah among "civilized" societies. The killings and executions confirmed in the minds of foreign residents that Haitians were cruel, even beastly, a character trait borne out by the violent overthrow of successive Haitian leaders, and that the disorder had now reached a state of mindless savagery. But, as a distinguished Haitian his-

Rear-Admiral William Banks Caperton, USN, aboard USS *Washington*.
Defense Audiovisuals

torian later wrote, the "mob" had been composed of Port-au-Prince's better classes and had been very selective in its victims. No one in the French legation except Guillaume Sam had been harmed; his pursuers had paid scant attention to the French minister who had provided sanctuary for the former president. The American flag had not been insulted, nor had any American citizen suffered at the hands of the mob.[21]

But in such an atmosphere Caperton was in no mood for detached analysis. The *Washington*'s battalion of shipboard marines and bluejackets landed at Bizoton, the dilapidated Haitian naval station about a mile from the center of the city, on July 28, the day Guillaume Sam died. The admiral's French-speaking aide, Capt. Edward L. Beach, had gone ashore earlier to inform the Revolutionary Committee of Safety, hastily created to preserve order after Guillaume Sam's death, of the admiral's intentions. Under protection of the *Washington*'s guns, the battalion marched into the city at dusk and began searching buildings and confiscating weapons. The committee had decided not to resist, so there was no disturbance save for a few scattered shots. Beach had told the Haitians that any threat against the Americans would mean severe retaliation. About twenty-five Haitian soldiers barricaded themselves in an army post in midtown, wrapping the national flag around the lock on the gates, and set up an ancient gun inside. They were ignored for several days before a fifteen-year-old marine carefully removed the flag, picked the lock, and opened the gate. The soldiers fired a shell into the street and then quietly surrendered.[22]

In the beginning of an occupation that would last nineteen years, Caperton declared that the intervention would be of short duration. At the same time he was busily sending fragmented reports of his actions, reassuring his superiors that Port-au-Prince was under control but requesting additional ships and more marines. Ashore, his aide negotiated a makeshift arrangement with the city's Revolutionary Committee, granting it responsibility for policing the city if in turn it recognized Caperton's jurisdiction. The suspicious Haitian press was informed that the American military presence did not threaten Haitian sovereignty.

Caperton was not being deceptive about his plans; he had not yet received any detailed order about his future course, only a brief message authorizing his landing of troops (which had of course arrived after he had already done so). He had intervened in Haiti to restore order during the bloody disturbances of late July; in another time, in another place, he might have withdrawn his forces quickly, but his government had manifested its disapproval of Haiti's turbulent political cycles of the last seven years, and it had already advanced a specific remedy for Haiti and the Dominican Republic. Neither country had yet consented to take the medicine the American government was prescribing, but that was not Caperton's concern. The turbulence of the past few days not only had precipitated American action, he could argue, but warranted the measures he was now taking.

On July 30, only two days after the landing, the Chamber of Deputies importuned Caperton to hold an election. He put the assemblymen off with objections concerning the uncertain political situation and the presence of *caco* armies to the north and disorganized bands of *cacos* in the capital. "The election of a chief magistrate while the populace was so worried and anxious," Caperton wrote, "would be productive of further trouble." For the Chamber, however, such conditions were normal; its function when there was no executive was to choose one, usually the candidate with the greatest show of *caco* strength.[23] And the man who seemed now to have the backing of the *cacos* was Dr. Rosalvo Bobo, critic of American meddling in Haitian affairs.

Extracting a pledge of support from the Revolutionary Committee, Caperton dispatched a special commision of Haitian notables north to Cap Haïtien to negotiate the surrender and the return to Port-au-Prince of a government garrison of 760 men. The commission prevailed on Bobo to call in his *caco* allies. Bobo agreed to return to the capital, but the *cacos* refused. Caperton remained apprehensive, however; almost daily he had minor squabbles with the Revolutionary Committee, aggravated by its announcement supporting Bobo for the presidency. His orders from Washington, though congratulatory, lacked specificity. Instructed to withhold power from the Haitian elite in the capital as long as the *cacos* exerted any influence, Caperton felt compelled to secure his position by disarming the population (an act that had the reluctant approval of the Revolutionary Committee but irritated the city's French and German nationals) and disbanding the *cacos* brought into the capital by the former president.

For this task, help soon arrived on August 4 with Col. Eli Cole's Second Marine Regiment. This contingent, composed of scattered companies from navy yards, was the advance force in Haiti of the First Marine Brigade, under Col. Littleton W. T. Waller, headquartered at Philadelphia. The First Marines' regiments included experienced infantrymen, many of whom had served in Veracruz the previous year. When Cole's marines arrived, Caperton sent them immediately to seize the barracks and police stations. The leathernecks began disarming the Haitian soldiers straggling about town in a manner similar to the Veracruz operation, though in Port-au-Prince there was no sniping on the invading American force. After Caperton's declaration ordering the *cacos* out of the city, the marines began arresting those who remained. When Bobo and the other Haitian dignitaries arrived from Cap Haïtien, American military forces controlled Port-au-Prince.

All the prospective presidential candidates were generally familiar with the American proposals for Haitian reforms that had been advanced in 1914. But one, Philippe Sudre Dartiguenave, was more attractive to Caperton than the others, for Dartiguenave, in an interview with Beach, had disclaimed any desire for power and, more importantly, favorably commented on the prospects of a more harmonious relationship between Haiti and the United States. By the time Bobo arrived from Cap Haïtien, Caperton and Beach had decided on Dartiguenave as the best candidate for American interests and so informed Secretary of State Lansing. Bobo had a popular following (he had been enthusiastically received in Cap Haïtien) and might cause trouble, so the admiral decided to settle matters before the Haitian politicians entered the city.

Wearing a frock coat and high hat, Bobo boarded the flagship of the U.S. Cruiser Squadron bearing a suitcase with "Dr. Rosalvo Bobo, Chief of Executive Power" printed on the sides and followed by a retinue of four dignitaries. One of the awaiting American officers, greeting Bobo with "Howdy-do, Doctor," ushered him into the cabin for a dressing-down by Beach. Despite his professions of patriotism, Bobo was humiliated. He could not be a candidate for the presidency because the American government forbade it. Even more, Bobo was told he must sign two orders prepared by Beach, one to his *caco* generals telling them to surrender their arms and a second to Cap Haïtien's Committee of Public Safety acknowledging the first order. Only then did Bobo meet Caperton. The admiral was gracious but still wary. He watched through his telescope as Bobo went ashore to greet his followers. But there was no spontaneous outburst against the Americans on Bobo's arrival. The red-haired mulatto who had been so outspoken against American interference in Haitian affairs abruptly began courting American support.[24]

Not until August 10 did Caperton receive more detailed instructions about his government's intentions in Haiti. The United States, the message read, would not recognize a Haitian president who could not end the country's disorder. Each candidate for the presidency must be willing to accept American control of Haitian customs and "such financial control over the affairs of the Republic of Haiti as the United States may deem necessary for an efficient administration."[25] Two days later, under the strict supervision of Eli Cole's marines, the assembly balloted for a new executive. Outside, the marines disarmed onlookers, but Caperton, after an appeal by numerous assemblymen, permitted those voting to carry their weapons, "with the understanding," he wrote humorously, "that they would be free to shoot themselves while in session, but not others."

Dartiguenave won an overwhelming victory. "The Haitians themselves, without outside influence," observed Caperton, "had made him their president."[26] Back in Washington the events of late July and early August in Haiti and the navy's role in them had made Secretary of the Navy Daniels something of a celebrity among his cabinet colleagues. The secretary of the interior, the jocose Franklin Lane, announced Daniels's appearance at one meeting with the salutation, "Josephus the First, King of Haiti." In keeping with the mood of joviality, another inquired: "Will the candidate you and Lansing picked out manage to squeeze in?"[27]

11. The Pacification of Hispaniola: 1

The American rulers now responsible for Haiti's destiny knew little about the country or its people. Their first impression of the capital was much like their initial reaction to Veracruz: a beautiful vista from the sea but indescribably filthy when at last one descended from the ship at the pier. Port-au-Prince offered the visitor far fewer distinguished edifices than Veracruz. Its most striking features were the towering cathedral and the verdant mountains looming beyond, which shielded the city from the interior. In 1915 it had a population estimated roughly at 60,000 to 100,000 souls, and the observer in August 1915 would have been convinced that every one of them was crowded into the squalid marketplace, chattering incessantly or haggling over chickens or baskets or sandals. Faustin Wirkus, a disembarking marine, described the city as "Fairyland . . . turned into a pigsty." Moving to a higher elevation, one encountered the finer residences of the Haitian elite, the mulattoes and foreign nationals who lived in gabled Victorian structures surrounded by lush growths of flowers and blossoming trees. Here stood the American legation, an impressive two-story mansion with its lovely garden, where the American minister, Bailly-Blanchard, had received Rear Admiral Caperton to discuss the recurrent stories of Haitian turmoil that had led so inexorably to American military intervention on July 28, 1915.[1]

Haiti now had a new president, a mulatto, a man, to use Wilson's words, "we can trust to handle and put an end to revolution." Caperton, the de facto ruler of Haiti in August 1915, put the matter more accurately: "[The] United States has now actually accomplished a military intervention in [the] affairs of another nation." A newcomer to the Haitian scene, the admiral learned quickly the Haitian hostility to the outsider. There had been little overt resistance to the occupation because the opposition had had so little time to organize. Caperton had already taken over the customhouse at the capital, witholding its precious funds from even Dartiguenave until the Haitian-American treaty was approved. Seizing the customhouses in the other seaports required more force than the one armored cruiser, two gunboats, and fifteen hundred marines at his command in mid-August; he supplicated the navy for another marine regiment, the marine artillery battalion, and three more gunboats. Alert to Haitian wariness over American intentions, Caperton warned: "These contemplated operations [should] be kept . . . secret and undertaken only when force is available and custom service organized and ready. This secrecy extremely important now pending treaty negotiations."[2]

Even Lansing sensed that the pressure the American government was employing to get a Haitian-American treaty made a mockery of Haitian sovereignty. He told Wilson: "I confess that this method of negotiation, with our marines policing the Haytian capital, is high-handed. It does not meet my sense of a nation's sovereign rights and is more or less an exercise of force and an invasion of Haitian independence." But, he added almost gratuitously, "from a practical standpoint . . . it is the only thing to do." The president concurred in words indicating he was not in the least troubled about Haiti's subservience to American wishes.[3]

The measures that the Americans were presenting for Haitian "approval" were touted as vital to the republic's internal peace and future prosperity. The customs receivership, the proposed treaty's most important provision, commenced without Haitian consent on August 21, when American functionaries began taking over the customhouses. A closely related feature of customs collection was the proposed office of financial advisor, also nominated by the United States president, who would exercise considerable influence over the Haitian budget. In other areas of public service the Americans intended to create a Haitian gendarmerie (to police the countryside), launch an ambitious sanitary and medical campaign (as they had done in Cuba, Panama, and Veracruz), and improve Haitian agriculture and commerce.[4]

Haitians rarely accepted willingly even the most well-intentioned advice from outsiders. At the first meeting of his new cabinet, in a room crowded with dignitaries including the ubiquitous Beach, Dartiguenave spoke in such a halting voice about his program that he was immediately shouted down by his fiery foreign minister, Páuleus Sannon, who demanded to know at whose invitation Caperton's troops had invaded the country. Within a month Sannon was gone, replaced by the wily Louis Borno, who in the 1920s would replace Dartiguenave as America's client president of Haiti. And to reinforce American determination, Caperton declared martial law (on September 2) and censored the increasingly strident anti-American Haitian press. When the desperate Dartiguenave pressed him for money he was told that "funds would be immediately available upon ratification of the treaty."[5]

Dartiguenave knuckled under on September 16. (A marine legend has it that a grimly determined Smedley Butler carried the treaty through Port-au-Prince streets to the president's residence. Butler's reputation for personal harassment had preceded him, so Dartiguenave hid in the bathroom. Momentarily put off, Butler lost his patience and burst in on a startled Dartiguenave, dressed in top hat and pin stripes, seated on an elegant porcelain commode reading an issue of *Petit Parisien.* The unruffled Butler shoved the treaty and a pen to the Haitian president for his signature.)

But the assembly, composed of elitist mulattoes with a long tradition of bickering over spoils, still had to approve the treaty. The lower house capitulated almost immediately, but the Haitian Senate, its members alert to the ominous activities of *cacos* in the yet unsubdued North, held out until November 11, acquiescing only after Caperton informed them that he intended to maintain the American military presence in Haiti with or without a treaty as legal foundation. Bailly-Blanchard, as determined as Caperton to launch the protectorate, hastily composed (in soft-lead pencil) an interim agreement that included the provisions the American Senate eventually approved.[6]

The pressures exerted on Dartiguenave and the suspicious Haitian Senate to approve the Haitian-American treaty of 1915 have been characterized by Caperton's biographer, David Healy, as the diplomacy of conciliation. Caperton's authority rested, ultimately, on the military force at his disposal; he dealt with the Haitian leaders firmly but with a velvet glove, in the best tradition of nineteenth-century naval diplomacy.[7] But the American admiral had a force even more effective than the tireless Captain Beach to bring about Haitian acquiescence in the American presence.

From the onset of the occupation the marine units in Haiti, which Caperton felt compelled by circumstances to augment continuously, had played a small role in the diplomatic bargaining with the Haitians. Using Beach as intermediary, Caperton negotiated—with Bobo, Dartiguenave, the revolutionary committees, and other disaffected Haitian leaders—assigning the business of occupying Port-au-Prince to shipboard marines and regiments of the First Marine Brigade. Caperton's officers talked and debated with the Haitians; Eli Cole's marines disarmed them. For the first time in the banana wars, bluejackets played an inconsequential role in the seizure of a Caribbean city.

The arrival of the First Marine Brigade brought a new marine commander in Haiti, Col. Littleton Waller Tazewell Waller. If Caperton typified the Anglo-Saxon naval aristocrat turned diplomatic negotiator, Waller was the twentieth-century American military imperialist. His repu-

Mounted marines, Dominican Republic, 1916. *National Archives*

Marine officer inspecting Haitian gendarmes. *National Archives*

tation as ferocious pursuer of revolutionaries and bandits went all the way back to the campaign against Filipino insurrectionists in 1902, when he had been court-martialed (and acquitted) on charges of murdering Filipino guides who he believed had betrayed him. He had served as marine commander in the second Cuban occupation and at Veracruz in 1914, but in those interventions the army had run the military governments and Waller had exercised a less grandiose role as occupier in the tropics. His dealings with Haitians of all classes offered a marked contrast to those of Caperton. The admiral may have held quaint Anglo-Saxon prejudices about persons of color, but he ordinarily held them in check, even in his private correspondence. He never considered the Haitian mulatto elite as equals, but at least he treated them as such.

Waller had the assigned task of negotiating with the Haitian chieftains, cajoling and bribing them into surrendering their arms and *caco* followers —all of which meant he had to haggle with Haitians in accord with Josephus Daniels's instruction to American officers "to regard themselves as friendly brothers of the Haitians, sent there to help these neighbor people." But Waller was not back in Virginia exhibiting a gentlemanly philanthropy to a Richmond bootblack. Treating Haitians as brothers grated on his sensibilities. Dartiguenave, he wrote, was a "crook," not a surprising epithet, considering Waller's view that "there is not an honest man in the whole of Haiti." In a letter to John Lejeune he poured out his bitterness and private humiliation at conducting business with Haitian mulattoes: "They are real nigger and no mistake—there are some very fine looking, well educated polished men here but they are real nigs beneath the surface. What the people of Norfolk and Portsmouth would say if they saw me bowing and scraping to these coons—I do not know—all the same I do not wish to be outdone in formal politeness." That he was not to be "outdone in formal politeness" he demonstrated by lecturing Butler, his close friend and chief enforcer of the occupation in the North, on the need for tact in dealing with Haitians![8]

Waller became increasingly pessimistic about the Haitian situation, something not altogether explained by his racial convictions. Dartiguenave might very well have accommodated to the American presence by mid-September, but Waller suspected some of the president's cabinet were conspiring with German merchants in the capital to sustain *caco* opposition in the North and around Gonaïves, an important coastal city at the upper end of the huge bay marking Haiti's western boundary. Caperton had dispatched a marine force in early August to secure Cap Haïtien. Other marine companies, ferried by ships of the cruiser squadron, protected Les Cayes, Jérémie, Port de Paix, Jacmel, and Saint Marc.

At first Caperton's plan called for disarming the *cacos* by offering a bribe of ten gourdes (about two dollars in U.S. currency) to soldiers and one hundred gourdes to officers, but this tactic produced only one significant surrender of arms (512 at Saint Marc). The bribe was increased to fifteen gourdes, but the raise only negligibly affected the number of surrenders. More apparently the offer whetted the Haitian appetite for an even larger sum. Working through Dartiguenave, the American naval commander tried negotiating with Haitian intermediaries (Charles Zamor, a northern political chieftain; and Charles Le Conte, the minister of war), who wrangled a deal with *caco* leaders to disarm for sixty thousand gourdes. Waller and Cole hurried to Cap Haïtien to bolster the negotiations and met 136 *caco* chiefs (whom Waller privately referred to as "murderous chicken thieves"), but the agreement fell through.

Defying the *cacos*, Waller took a train through their domain from Cap Haïtien to Grande Rivière du Nord. He returned to the capital and wrote bitterly to Lejeune: "I believe we may as well make up our minds either to get out of this country or to take steps to crush the *cacos.*"[9]

What the Haitian peasant desperately wanted, Waller argued, was peace and protection, a condition that could be achieved only with a forceful American presence. By late September he was busily sketching out on his crude map all the places that required more marines: Jacmel in the South; Gonaïves, where a local general had been suborned but was demanding more money and committing "outrages" in order to get it; Ouanaminthé in the interior, only a few miles from the Dominican border town of Dajabón. Officers who hesitated in this vigorous campaign, like Eli Cole, the cautious marine commander in Cap Haïtien, would be replaced by less timid warriors like Smedley Butler. Old Gimlet Eye had been dispatched to Gonaïves to chasten Pierre Rameau, a *caco* chieftain who had shut off the town's water supply and urged the inhabitants to throw out the Americans. The marines caught up with Rameau and his men at Poteaux, where Butler dragged Rameau from his horse and beat him. Butler's tactics well suited Waller's plans. "Hesitation at this time with these people," Waller wrote, "means bloodshed. Positive firmness means they will give up."[10]

Even the hesitant Cole, spurred by Waller's impatient directives, became more aggressive in harassing *cacos,* pushing out from his Cap Haïtien base into the area around Quartier Morin and forcing the chieftains to resume negotiations. Waller's tough policies were generally sweetened with promises of payments for surrendered arms, guarantees of amnesty from Dartiguenave, and opportunities to serve the republic by joining the gendarmerie. The marine proconsul went further, promising employment in the Haitian government and medical treatment in Cap Haïtien hospital.

But Waller's most effective enforcer of the new policy of "positive firmness" was Butler. By mid-October 1915 the last defiant *cacos* had been pushed into a broad swath of territory stretching from Grande Rivière,

Major-General Smedley D. Butler, USMC. *Defense Audiovisuals*

south of Cap Haïtien, to Ouanaminthé. The terrain was among the most forbidding in the tropics, and few white men had traversed it since the eighteenth century. Butler was not the kind to be discouraged; this was not Nicaragua in 1912, and there was no railroad to commandeer and push through enemy territory. So Old Gimlet Eye began patrolling the region with marine companies, trying to lure the *cacos* into a fight.

On October 24, near Fort Rivière, the Americans were ambushed by about four hundred *cacos* while trying to negotiate a deep gorge. The attack confirmed *caco* strength in the area and prompted Waller to commence offensive operations. With command posts at Le Trou and Grande Rivière, the marines began an aggressive pursuit of the *cacos* of the Departement du Nord. The *cacos* attacked Le Trou; failing to drive the Americans out, their assault nonetheless belied the myth that Haitians could neither organize nor fight a traditional military engagement, a racist canard that persisted in American minds. In the first two weeks of November, the marines drove the *cacos* completely out of the region around Le Trou. On the fifth, Butler took Fort Capois but did not slow the fifteen-mile-a-day advances of his weary marine units. By midmonth the remaining *cacos* had taken refuge in Fort Rivière, an ancient masonry structure south of Grande Rivière. On November 17 Butler attacked. With one company blocking an escape, he took three marine companies and converged on a breach in the west wall that served as entrance into the fort. Under a withering fire of Benet-Merciers, they stormed through the opening, led by two marines who daringly plunged ahead, miraculously surviving *caco* fire. The Haitians fought with rifles and sticks and even hurled stones at the invaders but were routed after ten furious minutes of combat. The fifty or so dead Haitians —the number was inexplicably increased two years later when Assistant Secretary of the Navy Franklin Roosevelt visited Haiti on an official inspection—were tossed into a trench in the center of the fort. Two days later, under Butler's satisfied supervision, the marines brought in dynamite on pack mules and reduced the fort to rubble.[11]

The year ended with Caperton ruling Haiti from his cabin on the *Washington* and Waller policing the countryside with his marines. The *cacos,* who had disrupted Haitian politics for generations, coming down from their mountain lairs every six months or so to vandalize towns and overturn governments, had been crushed in Butler's sweep in the North— at least for the time being. But the Haitian aristocracy, the one hundred families who suffered ignominiously as the Americans cut off their livelihood, was not yet finished. Among them was Antoine Pierre-Paul, who had once referred to President Dartiguenave as "that fat pig from Anse-à-Veau." In the dead of a January evening Pierre-Paul and his cohorts attacked the National Palace and the Bureau de la Place (which the marines were using as provost marshal's office) in a wild shooting spree. The "Pierre-Paul revolt" was financed by Antoine Simon, a wealthy mulatto from Les Cayes, who intended to humiliate the Americans, bring down Dartiguenave, and name Sannon, whom the president had removed in September for his impertinent outbursts against American interference, as chief of executive power. Marines handily crushed the uprising, which amounted to little more than wild shooting, and Waller demonstrated magnanimity in victory, granting Pierre-Paul amnesty with the contemptuous remark that the Haitian was "politically dead." In late May 1916 there was another clash when some of Pierre-Paul's followers bribed their way out of jail and began firing buildings and shooting up Port-au-Prince before they were driven off and then captured when Haitian peasants betrayed their whereabouts. On the march back to the capital the rebels tried to escape and were cut down by the marines' Springfield rifles.

In a few weeks Pierre-Paul was happily drinking champagne with President Dartiguenave.[12]

By this time Caperton had moved his command to Santo Domingo, where the American military had recently instigated a full-scale intervention and was laying the basis for a military government.

Ever since the election of Juan Isidro Jiménez in late 1914, American officials had grown increasingly exasperated with Dominican leaders. The State Department had closely supervised the Dominican presidential election, which had been conducted under the Wilson Plan with the understanding that afterwards the new executive would undertake thoroughgoing reforms. These were, essentially, the same as those the United States was forcefully introducing into neighboring Haiti: close supervision of public finance and creation of a more professional national army.

Old and sickly, Jiménez was inclined to go along with American financial supervision of Dominican affairs, but the National Assembly opposed him. With the Dominican Republic—unlike the pre-1915 relationship with Haiti—the United States had a contractual understanding (Roosevelt's 1907 customs receivership treaty). Article 3 of the treaty forbade the republic from increasing the public debt, though it had been commonly understood by Dominicans that "public debts" in the meaning of the 1907 treaty did not encompass the ever-growing internal obligations of Dominican governments. But Bryan and especially Lansing systematically expanded the meaning of article 3 (and other provisions of the treaty) to permit much greater involvement in Dominican internal affairs than Roosevelt and Root had ever envisaged. As Frank Polk (of the State Department's Latin American division) put it: The United States must amend the treaty to permit carrying out its reform plan for the republic or "should interpret the [treaty] so as to give us the right to [do] the things necessary."[13]

Intimidated by the new American minister, W.W. Russell, even more aggressive than his predecessor in pressing American reform schemes on the Dominican government, Jiménez confronted in 1916 renewed bickering and then outright opposition from the republic's other major political faction, the Horacistas, led by Horacio Vásquez, and the mercurial and outspokenly anti-American Gen. Desiderio Arias, minister of war. When Jiménez finally turned on Arias, the Dominican lower house impeached the president. In retaliation Jiménez fired Arias from the cabinet, but Arias had control of the army, and troops loyal to him seized the capital. Though Jiménez received fitful support from elements in the interior, he could not regain the city.

Nor could he bring himself to ally with Admiral Caperton's naval forces lying menacingly off Santo Domingo and crush the assembly. In the tense atmosphere of early May, with Arias's soldiers patrolling the city, Jiménez and his loyal cabinet members took refuge in Fort Gerónimo, which had been built in colonial days by the Spaniards. There he received an offer of American military assistance from Russell, who had already called for 300 marines from the *Castine* to guard the American legation and was ready to ask for more, and from Capt. Frederick ("Dopey") Wise, a fiery-tempered marine veteran commanding about 150 men from the *Prairie*. A nervous Jiménez tentatively agreed to accept American intervention (with loyal troops fighting alongside the Americans) if Arias refused to leave the capital. Wise found Arias at Fort Ozama. The Dominican general was defiant. Told that "this damned business of having revolutions . . . had to cease" and that "he must get out and let the President come back into the capital," Arias smiled and replied sarcastically: "Has the United States sent people down here to teach us how to behave?" It was not often that the volatile Dopey Wise was intimidated, but he knew that Arias had at that moment a much larger force ashore than the Americans. Back at Fort Gerónimo, Jiménez listened to Wise's account of the meeting with Arias, then abruptly withdrew his offer of alliance with the Americans. "I cannot keep my word with you," he told them; "I can never consent to attacking my own people." Berated by Wise, the crestfallen Dominican president offered to resign the following day. "You'll do no such damned thing," Wise shot back, "you'll sign it [resignation] right now." On May 7, facing impeachment by the assembly, a capital thronged with disloyal soldiers, and the ominous threat of American intervention, the fifth Dominican president since the death of Cáceres in 1911 stepped down.[14]

Caperton did not arrive in Santo Domingo until May 12. Four U.S. warships (and a French vessel, the *Marseillaise,* dispatched to evacuate French nationals) now hovered off the Dominican capital. The admiral made his way to the American legation, a prominent structure that had received several hits in the sporadic fighting of the past few weeks. He found the American minister in an agitated mood. In his negotiations with Dominicans, Russell ordinarily displayed a noticeable arrogance, but in assessing the present situation he seemed "particularly anxious," wanting Caperton to move quickly in demanding the "surrender and disarmament of the rebel forces."

But Caperton remembered all too well what had happened in Port-au-Prince the previous July. He must land more troops before dealing with Arias. The rebel general (whom State Department memorandums characterized as a "troublemaker") had only about 250 regular soldiers to the government's 800, but Jiménez's troops had no weapons. Most had withdrawn into an area around Fort Gerónimo. Arias had equipped his regulars with the finest rifles, five Gatling guns, numerous artillery pieces, and, to embolden their confidence, the minister of war had disseminated arms to most of Santo Domingo's males, including teenage boys who swaggered about town brandishing weapons. In a showdown with 130 bluejackets and 150 marines, Caperton estimated, Arias's followers might put up a fight. So the admiral, in a move as much political as military, called for reinforcements from nearby American ships. By daybreak of May 13, having been in the Dominican capital for only twenty-four hours, Caperton had doubled his strength ashore to 600 bluejackets and marines.

Armed with an ultimatum countersigned by Russell, Caperton went to see Arias. The rebels must surrender to American troops; if Arias refused, Caperton told him, then he would occupy the capital and "forcibly disarm the rebels." The presence of American troops in the city was already beginning to undermine Arias's strength, for many of the rebels began deserting. That night, with about three hundred followers, the Dominican general stole out of Santo Domingo and headed for the interior. Arias did not realize that the Americans intended to remain in the republic and in time would come after him.[15]

The next few days in the Dominican capital proved as hectic for Caperton as his initial experience in Port-au-Prince the previous summer. He had arrived on the Dominican scene as a harassed Dominican president resisted internal threats and external pressures from an American government bent on reforming the country. Caperton had run the most defiantly anti-American politicians out of town, just as he had snuffed out Rosalvo Bobo's bid to become Haitian president. But in the Dominican assembly, as in its Haitian counterpart, prevailing sentiment ran strongly against American interference, and the legislators looked to Arias as their choice for president.

Caperton now determined to augment his forces ashore in order to control the city. At 6:00 A.M. on May 15 he landed four companies of marines who had just arrived from Haiti and Guantánamo, Cuba, and a small contingent of bluejackets. In less than two hours the American invaders had scaled the old walls and were in the city. Dominicans awoke to read proclamations of occupation stating the Americans were taking over their capital to ensure "peace and order" during the revolutionary strife. The order prohibited the carrying of firearms, a cherished Dominican custom; in Haiti peasants rarely carried firearms, but in the Dominican Republic a male's rite of manhood generally meant the time when he began toting a pistol, a tradition appropriately summed up in an old saying of Dominican women, "Two revolutions ago, my son took a gun and went into politics." The occupation of the capital went off without firing a shot, though Santo Domingo's press was bitterly critical, and some editions appeared with mourning borders around the masthead.[16]

In the days following the occupation, Caperton's activities bespoke those of a man carefully charting some new venture of American foreign policy in the internal affairs of a small Caribbean state. He began shuttling more troops from Port-au-Prince to Santo Domingo in preparation for a major invasion of the north coast at Monte Cristi and Puerto Plata. Arias had moved into the remote Dominican interior and was once again raising the flag of defiance and revolt, using his base at Santiago to defy the American invaders. Logistically, to pursue the defiant Dominican by crossing the mountains north of the capital made little sense, but forces disembarking at Puerto Plata and Monte Cristi, Caperton reckoned, could successfully strike at Arias from the north.

Meanwhile, Caperton held off the importunate Dominican assembly with statements that the situation was too unstable to permit it to elect another president. On May 19 he moved the remaining members of Jiménez's cabinet, who had fled with the deposed president to Fort Gerónimo, back to their offices. Then he scurried to the legation library, "wondering what the future policy was."[17]

And, as he and Beach had done in Port-au-Prince, the admiral began looking for a suitable candidate, someone who could work "harmoniously" with the United States. With Russell serving as translator, Caperton interviewed Federico Henríquez y Carvajal, president of the Dominican supreme court. They suspected Henríquez was an "Arias man" because he was so popular among the pro-Arias faction of the assembly. Sensing he now had to thwart Henríquez's candidacy, Caperton sent another urgent "request" to the Dominican assemblymen asking for further delay in choosing an executive.

But the Senate defied him and began balloting. Anti-American agitation picked up among Santo Domingo's residents. Leading political figures and professionals formed *juntas patrióticas* in the major towns of the republic. Their intention was the creation of a national front that would persuade the Americans to retire to their ships. As a first step, they resolved on getting Arias's acquiescence in dissolving the assembly, whose frenetic politicking had caused so much of the trouble and precipitated the American intervention. Representatives from Santo Domingo's junta visited Caperton, who politely informed them that his mission was peace and the preservation of order, which he intended to maintain until the "revolution" ended. The juntas had no army to enforce their collective will, but Caperton did, and he now resolved to use it against the "troublemaker" Arias.[18]

The domain of Gen. Desiderio Arias was the Cibao, the heartland of the Dominican interior. Some of the earliest cities in the New World had been founded here by the Spanish conquerors—Moca, La Vega, and Santiago de los Caballeros, the republic's second-largest city. The Cibao was the breadbasket of the republic, but until the Americans built a road across the mountains north of the capital, its links with the capital had been tenuous. Dominicans traveling into the interior ordinarily took one of the Clyde Line steamers and sailed around the eastern coast of Hispaniola to Puerto Plata or Monte Cristi. Even Puerto Plata, the main Atlantic port, only twenty-five miles from Santiago, was shielded from the interior by the northern cordillera running from Monte Cristi in the northwest almost the breadth of the island to the Samaná peninsula in the northeast. From Puerto Plata an old railroad ran into the interior toward Santiago, but the rebels had torn up large sections of track.

On June 1 the gunboat Sacramento landed 130 marines and a company of bluejackets at Puerto Plata. The city had about five hundred Arias irregulars. Before the landing the Sacramento had taken on seventeen Americans huddled on the dock in defiance of the local governor's ban on evacuation. At the time the Sacramento's captain had delivered a warning to the governor that the fort guarding the harbor, which was infested with rebels, must be surrendered or it would be fired on. The governor, an Arias man, had refused. The American captain put the first shot over the structure, trying to scare the rebels, then ordered a ten-minute fusillade that reduced the fort to rubble. Approaching the sandy beach, the landing craft ferrying bluejackets and marines began receiving intermittent rifle fire. (One shot struck marine captain H.J. Hirshinger in the temple; he died on the beach, the first American marine to die in hostilities in the Dominican campaign.) But the Americans swiftly quelled the rebel fire with machine guns and the Sacramento's guns.[19]

At the same time, to the west, the Panther was seizing Monte Cristi. The ease with which the town was occupied may have owed something to the indefatigable Dopey Wise, who had arrived on the northwest coast to reconnoiter several days before the landing. Discussing plans with the American consul, Wise obtained the names of the local Arias chieftain,

Miguelito, and the German consul, Lempke, who was married to a Dominican and ran a store on the side. Miguelito, located at the town hall recently vacated by the governor, was a swarthy man with a prominently displayed pistol strapped to his waist. Wise was customarily arrogant: "We intend to run you out of town." Miguelito snapped back, "You won't have the easy time you had over in Haiti."

For the second time Dopey had been faced down in a verbal confrontation with a Dominican. He retired to the *Panther* to assess the plans for seizing Monte Cristi, which called for shelling the two forts guarding it. The prominent red-tiled roof of the German's house, lying beyond the forts, would be used to sight the guns. It suddenly dawned on Wise that the consul of Wilhelm II would not want his house blown up by American shells, so Dopey went back into town to tell Lempke what the Americans intended. The German responded that there would be no trouble from Miguelito. The *Panther's* landing party took Monte Cristi without incident, and Wise concluded that Lempke "must have packed a bigger punch than Miguelito."

For the first time in its history, Monte Cristi was occupied by American Marines, and the inhabitants resented it. Miguelito had abandoned Monte Cristi to the Americans, but his small force camped outside, firing into the town at night and then cutting off the food supply to its residents. Wise took a detachment and a Benet-Mercier machine gun from the *Panther* and went after Miguelito, bent on luring the Dominican into a showdown. A few miles from town, about 150 yelling rebels led by Miguelito on a roan mule swooped down from the surrounding hills. Apparently, Wise surmised, the Dominican rebels at Monte Cristi had never seen a machine gun. Wise looked on calmly through his field glasses as the Benet-Mercier opened up against the screaming Dominicans. As they dropped "all up and down the line," he remembered, "I could see sheer amazement on their faces." When it was over the marines counted thirty-nine Dominican dead; the rest had scurried down the trail to Santiago, ninety miles away, but Wise did not have enough men to go after them.[20]

The opposition encountered in the North reinforced American assessments of Arias's strength in the interior. Caperton, ever the diplomat, had by now given up on coaxing the Dominican rebel into surrendering. Wanting to rid the country of the American occupiers, several wealthy Dominicans had pooled resources and offered 20,000 pesos to Arias to leave the country, but Archbishop Nouel had informed Caperton of Arias's refusal. On June 19 Caperton announced his intention to occupy Santiago, Moca, and La Vega. The United States was not carrying out territorial conquest of the Dominican Republic, the proclamation stated, but suppressing revolutionists who "prevented reforms."[21]

To carry out his plan, Caperton had a veteran of the Nicaraguan campaign of 1912, Col. Joseph H. ("Uncle Joe") Pendleton. He had just arrived in Dominican waters after a frantic trip from San Diego with the Fourth Regiment, nucleus of the Marine West Coast Expeditionary Force. As in Nicaragua, he distinguished between rebels and peaceful citizens and in his avuncular manner reminded his officers of the political nature of their campaign. "We are not in enemy's country," he told them, "though many of the inhabitants may be inimical to us."[22] They were not invading the Dominican Republic; they were pacifying the rebels who threatened its internal peace.

The operation seemed simple enough: Pendleton's Fourth Regiment would advance from Monte Cristi through the valley carved out by the Yaque del Norte River between the *cordillera central* and the coastal chain. Another smaller force of two companies and the available ship marines from the *Rhode Island* and *New Jersey* would move inland from Puerto Plata as far as possible on the railroad, then march on to Navarette, a small village about twelve miles west of Santiago where the road from Monte Cristi and the railroad from Puerto Plata converged. Here the two columns would rendezvous for the final assault on Santiago. Pendleton's troops would have a much greater distance to cover. Halfway to Santiago, the Fourth would be cut off from its supply base at Monte Cristi and would become, to use Uncle Joe's terminology, "a flying column."

The Fourth's advance on Santiago was one of the illustrious campaigns of the "old Corps." Pendleton's force had a motorized transport unit composed of a "Holt tractor, five Studebaker wagon trailers, two White motor trucks, two Quads, and twelve Ford touring cars," under the command of Dopey Wise. The autos came from the local Ford agency in Monte Cristi, purchased by the regimental paymaster and resulting in an enormous profit, Wise estimated, for the Dominican salesman. But the most reliable conveyance on the rutted trail to Santiago turned out to be the "San Dominican Cart," a two-wheeled, springless apparatus pulled by three mules.[23]

The first day they marched fifteen miles without seeing a rebel. But at Las Trencheras, a ridge where in 1864 a band of Dominicans had held off a Spanish force, the rebels made a stand. This was another Coyotepe, Pendleton thought, remembering the 1912 Nicaraguan battle where his artillery had pounded a hill infested with Zeledón's rebels before he launched an attack. Dragging artillery through inhospitable terrain was paying off once again. The three-inch landing guns pulverized the trenches where the rebels were dug in, as the marines, using the thick brush for cover, inched up the ridge. When the Dominicans popped up, the Americans picked them off. The others ran off down the road, destroying every bridge behind them.

Pendleton's Fourth was traversing a trail through a cactus and brush countryside; unimaginably hot and dusty, it could turn quickly into a quagmire in the torrential rains, bogging down trial-weary men, mules, and the mud-spattered Fords purchased only a few days before in Monte Cristi. On June 28 the rebels, apparently believing that the marine machine guns (which the Dominicans called "sprinklers") would not function at night, attacked in darkness but were beaten off. At Guayacanas (on July 3) the Dominicans made another stand. In this encounter, Pendleton's artillery was of little use because the gunners could not adequately position their weapons. But the machine gun crews hauled their Benet-Merciers to within two hundred yards of rebel lines and opened up with a deadly fire.

The next day the Fourth made Navarette and met the column from Puerto Plata. The two companies from Puerto Plata had ridden as far as possible in boxcars pulled by a dilapidated locomotive, pushing a flatcar carrying a three-inch artillery piece. At Lajas they had had to get off and walk, repairing track and bridges along the way. Here the marines got another commanding officer, Maj. Hiram Bearss, nicknamed "Hike 'em Hiram" because he habitually force-marched his men during the day and amused them at night with wild stories about his exploits. At Alta Mira, where the track passed through a three-hundred-yard tunnel, the Dominicans tried to block the advance, but Bearss and sixty men had plunged through the tunnel, "Hike 'em Hiram" leading the charge while furiously pumping a handcart. The rebels ran off toward Santiago.

As the columns approached Santiago a delegation of citizens came out to meet them to explain that Arias planned to leave the city. The Dominicans asked Pendleton to slow his advance to allow Arias time to depart. Pendleton agreed and occupied Santiago without firing a shot on July 6. The governor of the province implored the citizens to "give [the American occupiers] the frank and loyal treatment of good Christians."[24]

12. The Pacification of Hispaniola: 2

Pendleton's campaign in the North virtually destroyed the rebel military threat in the Cibao, but the unopposed occupation of Santiago by marines in early July 1916 did not shatter the anti-American coalition in the Dominican assembly. Russell and Caperton refused to permit Federico Henríquez y Carvajal to become president because of his pro-Arias leanings and his opposition to American plans for the republic. When he suddenly withdrew his candidacy, the assembly abruptly turned to his brother, Francisco, who had been living in Cuba and had avoided the recent political turmoil in the republic, as provisional president.

Francisco Henríquez, described by one American official as "a scholar and writer but . . . honest," seemed more disposed than his brother to go along with American wishes for a financial advisor and a scheme for reorganizing the nation's armed forces, but he refused to act officially until his government received American recognition and the flow of Santo Domingo's share of the customs receipts, which Russell had cut off, resumed. The American minister, as always suspicious of Arias's continuing intrigue, doubted the Dominican leader's sincerity. His State Department superiors, wary of German meddling in Hispaniola (Arias had already earned the "pro-German" label in Washington), remained intransigent.[1] As Russell negotiated in the capital, American forces in the countryside continued disarming Dominican troops, giving each soldier a token payment and sending him home. Even the foundering of the American cruiser *Memphis* in a sudden storm off Santo Domingo in August, during which Dominicans heroically helped save many of the crew (forty American seamen perished), failed to generate much enthusiasm for the republic in the State Department.[2]

In the fall, the continuing denial of funds to the government aggravated the economic crisis and heightened tensions between marines and Dominicans. On October 24 a marine patrol trying to arrest Ramón Batista, implicated in a raid on the customhouse at La Romana the previous summer, got into a shooting spree with nearby Dominicans, leaving two Americans dead. The following day a similar incident claimed the lives of three Dominicans.[3]

Unable to get a Dominican government to do its bidding, the State Department now vacillated. Once again the United States was faced with the use of force to get its way. The choice seemed to be either to withdraw its forces or to declare martial law. On October 31 a delegation from the State Department met with two naval officers and discussed the alternatives. Given American priorities in the republic, they agreed, withdrawal of American troops was unacceptable. The United States had intervened militarily and controlled the capital, Santiago, and several ports on the north coast. The most expedient way of "legalizing" American actions lay in the establishment of a military government.

Thus, in an almost casual discussion held a thousand miles from Santo Domingo, the legitimate government of the Dominican Republic was overthrown. Secretary of State Lansing sent the recommendation to the president on November 22, noting there existed no alternative to his recommendation. Wilson made a minor change in the proclamation and endorsed it "with the deepest reluctance." One week later, the new commander of the Cruiser Squadron, Capt. Harry S. Knapp, proclaimed the military government of the Dominican Republic with himself as military governor.[4]

Knapp's proclamation stated that the occupation was "undertaken with no immediate or ulterior object of destroying the sovereignty of the Republic of Santo Domingo"—Americans persisted in referring to the entire country as Santo Domingo—but went on to order all revenues paid to the military government. Nothing was said about high-ranking Dominican officeholders until December 4, when Knapp announced that the Departments of Interior and of War and Marine would be staffed by marine officers. The remaining members of Henríquez's cabinet refused to serve in an occupation government, and the deposed president shortly left the country for exile in Cuba. Though the politically astute secretary of the navy wanted to retain as many Dominicans as possible even in an American military government—a view considered by Knapp and his colleagues to be inexpedient and perhaps as ludicrous as Daniels's much-publicized ban on wine for the naval officers' shipboard mess—the new proconsuls in the republic were glad they had a free rein and none of the headaches of their comrades working with a client Haitian government in Port-au-Prince. The lower echelons of the bureaucracy, of course, remained staffed by Dominicans. When the question of a reconvened assembly and its bickering Dominican politicians came up, Knapp resolved the problem by suspending the assembly.[5]

Since the republic was by American standards plagued by uncommon violence, the American proconsuls began their rule by disarming the

Dominican army. Then they began disarming the citizenry. From a population of 750,000 (compared with Haiti's one and a half million), the Americans confiscated more than 50,000 firearms, 200,000 rounds of ammunition, and 14,000 knives. Virtually every male sixteen or older, it seemed, carried some kind of weapon—the official classifications were "rifle, revolver, saber, and dagger"—and the provost courts levied stiff fines on offenders (twenty-five dollars or more, an exorbitant sum in a society where per capita income rose no higher than a few hundred dollars a year) and jail sentences of three to six months. As always, there developed a sociological explanation for the ubiquity of guns: "the arbitrary methods whereby political activities were carried on, frequently culminating in armed revolutions, and the lawlessness practiced by a perceptive portion of the population."[6]

Outside the capital, in the remote Cibao valley and in the eastern provinces, Dominican rebel bands waged a disorganized campaign of harassment against American rule. The intervention did not precipitate banditry in the republic, but the American occupation abruptly transformed the reputation of bandits into that of patriots. Arias had disbanded his army after leaving Santiago in advance of Pendleton's march on the city, but elsewhere various bands wrought havoc on outlying towns and marine patrols. Some were politically opposed to the intervention and had taken up arms against it; others, plainly, were *gavilleros* (highwaymen) or impoverished peasants who had turned to crime out of economic desperation. Still others were agricultural laborers who rented land but earned no money from it and became, as one marine officer described them, farmers by day and bandits by night. There were probably no more than a thousand Dominicans who took up arms against the occupation, operating mostly in small groups of five to ten, but they persevered, eluding marines, who never gained the confidence of local people who knew their whereabouts.[7]

In eastern Seibo and Macoris provinces, where the central cordillera tapered off into coastal hills, banditry was widespread and marine retaliation increasingly severe. The main villages of Seibo were Hato Mayor and Seibo, an impoverished town where in 1808 a ragtag band had defeated an invading force seeking to impose Napoleonic rule over the Spanish colony. The people of Seibo had always been suspicious of outsiders—even those from Santo Domingo—their hatreds sharpened by the number of plantations with absentee landlords who preferred life in the elegant coastal city of San Pedro de Macorís, which boasted electricity and an opera house. In "El Seybo," as the province was sometimes called, people never dreamed of such amenities.

The most notorious rebel of Seibo was a daring Dominican bandit with the nom de guerre of Vicentico Evangelista. For months after the intervention he harassed the local governor of Macorís, a Dominican working for the military government, who finally scurried back to the capital "like a yellow dog," wrote a contemptuous American officer. Evangelista boasted he would kill every American in the republic and began by brutally executing two American civilians, engineers from an American-owned plantation, who were lashed to trees, savagely hacked with machetes, and then left dangling for ravenous wild boars.

In March 1917 Evangelista attacked a marine patrol at Cerrito but was driven off. The marines decided to lure him into a trap. They hired a rival gang to harass Vicentico's band and suborned another Dominican who was a confidant of the rebel leader. A meeting was arranged between Evangelista and a marine sergeant for the surrender of the band and, according to Dominican accounts, for a 10,000-peso payoff for Vicentico. Evangelista complied; most of his men were disarmed and released, and Evangelista himself was arrested with a guarantee of safety but was "shot while trying to escape," in circumstances Dominicans have always thought suspicious. In time he would be enshrined in Dominican national mythology as a patriot fighting the Yankee invaders.[8]

After Evangelista's death banditry in the east subsided but was not completely eliminated. Dominicans of Seibo distrusted American professions of amnesty when word of Vicentico's death circulated. In Hato Mayor relations between Dominicans and the marine occupiers were inflamed; it was here that the notorious Charles Merkel, promoted to captain from the ranks because of the shortage of officers in Hispaniola during the war, earned his reputation as the "Tiger of Seibo." In his regular patrols of the province, Merkel's Dominican guide later testified, the marine captain habitually arrested ordinary country people—men, women, and even children —for allegedly withholding information about bandits. Once, after a march of prisoners back to town, Merkel ordered each captive tied by one leg to stakes driven in the earth around a notched tree, the other leg strapped to the tree itself, with the foot jammed into the notch. Merkel was carrying out the *reconcentrado* policies of Col. George Thorpe, the marine commander in Hato Mayor, which called for the rounding up of the people in the countryside. In one of these drives, the guide said, Merkel ordered two small villages burned, tortured a Dominican prisoner with a knife, pouring salt and orange juice onto the wounds, and completed the interrogation by cutting off the prisoner's ears.

In September 1918, after numerous charges of these and other acts of cruelty, Merkel was arrested. Awaiting court-martial, he blew out his brains with a pistol that the official record states he had secreted on his person. The unofficial version holds that two marine officers visited his cell and left him the weapon and one cartridge.[9]

These atrocities occurred in 1917 and 1918, when the United States was involved in the far more consequential struggle for European civilization across the Atlantic and abler officers in Hispaniola were transferring to combat units in France. Those who stayed behind grew increasingly resentful of occupation duty; their frustration and bitterness over policing "spigs," as they often called Dominicans, made them less sympathetic toward their subjects or their plight. Haitians could be listless and indifferent, but Dominicans resented the intervention and especially the marine occupiers. While Knapp in Santo Domingo spoke glowingly about financial rectitude and the building of the north-south highway, his marine proconsuls in the eastern district camped in grimy little towns, ate canned sardines, rice, fried eggs, and greasy plantains three times a day, and endured Dominican resentment. "We really had to watch the natives," one officer recalled; "they were not very friendly."[10]

Thorpe, who later wrote of the grand accomplishments of the occupation, "used to tell [the new marine arrivals] . . . that they were serving their country just as valuably as were their fortunate comrades across the seas, and the war would last enough to give every man a chance against the Hun in Europe as against the Hun in Santo Domingo." (Much of the banditry in the republic was, after the American declaration of war in April 1917, attributed to German provocation.) He wrote Pendleton: "Whoever is running this revolution is a wise man; he certainly is getting a lot out of the niggers. . . . It shows the handwork of the German." But he was not dissuaded from his mission in the tropics: "If I do a good job of clearing these . . . provinces of insurgents and kill a lot . . . it ought to demonstrate I'd be a good German-killer."[11]

Thorpe apparently genuinely liked chasing bandits. But his comrades found life in Seibo monotonous and the bandit patrols dangerous. Small groups of marines would venture out into the hills of Seibo or Macorís province and sometimes be lost for two or three weeks. Seibo had no usable roads until mid-1918, and so there was no easy way of supplying the scouting marines with trucks.

In 1919 the district command received six Jenny biplanes. The marines developed a crude landing strip in a clearing near Consuelo, about twelve miles from San Pedro, and the biplanes began flying over mountainous Seibo province, scouting for bandits. Occasionally, when a suspicious aviator spotted a Dominican carrying a rifle scurrying below, he tossed a "homemade" explosive from the plane and "bombed" the target. To protect themselves from return fire, the aviators sat on cast-iron stove lids.[12]

For five years an intermittent war between marines and *gavilleros* raged in Seibo. When it became clear by 1921 that the United States intended to dismantle the military government sooner than expected, the marines launched a vigorous campaign to wipe out banditry in the East. Units in Seibo now had radios for signaling and biplanes to spot suspicious activity from the air. Sweeping over huge areas, the planes would signal to marines patrolling in gradually constricting circles on the ground. Every male Dominican encountered in the sweep was arrested, taken to a floodlit detention center, and identified by witnesses hiding behind canvas screens. Some six hundred were captured in these sweeps, but the method so outraged Dominican politicians that the marine commander abruptly dropped it.[13]

One organization created to eradicate banditry and the often violent political activity in the republic was the Dominican national guard. In 1917 Knapp ordered the creation of a new army, the Guardia Nacional Dominicana, which would replace the old republican guard and give the country a desperately needed, modern, national police force. Commanded by "Americans of good character" and modeled loosely on the Pennsylvania State Mounted Police, the guard began with a budget of $500,000 and Knapp's zealous efforts to effect a revolution in the Dominican military. Recruits were drawn from the lower social classes—the guard, in fact, was looked upon as a social equalizer—and then dispatched to the far corners of the republic in order to acquire a sense of national identity.[14]

Problems of staffing the guard with suitable officers inevitably slowed its growth, but by 1921, when Haina Military Academy was established, the guard was using Dominicans as officers. Haina's most famous graduate was an impoverished but ambitious young man from San Cristóbal, Rafael Leonidas Trujillo Molina, who had earned a place in the guard after writing an unctuous letter of application to the commandant in 1918. Trujillo was only one of many Dominicans graduated from Haina in 1921 and 1922, in an era when the Americans had suppressed much of the banditry in the eastern district. (The last uprising, in 1921, had been led by Evangelista's heir apparent, Ramón Natera.) His participation in the campaign was negligible, but after Trujillo became president in 1930 and the orgy of adulation set in, his minions quickly began rewriting Dominican history to show that "El Benefactor" had played a glorious role in pacifying the nation during the occupation.

After Trujillo earned a reputation for cruelty, his critics often alleged he had learned his bestial torture techniques from Charles Merkel, though Trujillo's name never surfaced in the official investigation. One marine officer who remembered Trujillo from occupation days thought him a "bad character" who pocketed the food allowance for the men under his command. In 1920 he was court-martialed on charges of holding a man for ransom and for rape of the seventeen-year-old daughter of the man he kidnapped. He was acquitted on both counts. The guard was experiencing trouble getting recruits and did not want the reputation of its officers sullied. The trial in no way impeded Trujillo's career, though inexplicably the record remained buried in Marine Corps archives until after Trujillo's death in 1961 and the onset of "de-Trujilloization."[15]

Col. L. W. T. Waller (USMC) discussing treaty with Haitians, Camp Haiti, October 1915. *National Archives*

When Harry Knapp proclaimed a military government in Santo Domingo in later November 1916, the first phase of the Haitian occupation had already run its course. Admiral Caperton and Captain Beach, who would write of the "refinement and culture that marks the Haitian highest class" and who developed a genuine understanding of the Haitian situation, had departed. With them went the political finesse schooled into old-line naval officers. Though Knapp, as the ranking American officer in Hispaniola, was technically the supreme military figure in Haiti as well as the Dominican Republic, his duties as military governor in Santo Domingo preoccupied his time. Port-au-Prince was by late 1916 the domain of marines—Waller, Butler, and Cole. Their attitude toward Haitian governance was summed up by Cole: "I see nothing to be done but to let them demonstrate to their capacity," he wrote Knapp, "if such they have, or . . . let them hang themselves so that a military government becomes necessary."[16] The proconsuls of Haiti envied the untrammeled opportunities of their comrades in the Dominican Republic.

Haiti's real ruler was Waller. His official duty presumed a close working relationship with the Haitian president and his ministers, all of whom, Waller believed, were grafters. The marine commander, wrote one of Dartiguenave's ministers, seemed devoid of "politesse, courtesy, or respect." Dartiguenave was polished and cultivated but woefully ignorant of Americans and their ways. He trusted the occupiers to restore peace and aid him in the rebuilding of his country but in a manner inoffensive to Haitian sensibilities. Waller treated this dignified mulatto, steeped in the political philosophy of the Third French Republic and an eloquent orator in his own right, as if he were a subordinate. Once, after a contretemps over Dartiguenave's sending of a written complaint of American harassment to Washington, Waller rebuked him: "You are president because we Americans are in Haiti. If you continue to denounce me, I'll have my government recall its troops for twenty-four hours and by the time we pass by . . . Gonâve [Island], you'll be chased out of the Presidential Palace." Waller had already expressed his conviction about how to deal with Dartiguenave in a letter to his friend Butler: "As far as I am able, this country should be run as a piece of machinery, with no preference being shown any negro owing to a supposed superiority due to the infusement of white blood in his veins."[17]

When the question of a new Haitian constitution came up, Waller showed what he had meant by "running Haiti." In late 1916 a Haitian draft of a proposed constitution arrived in Washington. The State Department, eager to reform Haitian politics and modernize the country, wanted another constitution because the existing one had "unprogressive" features—among them, clauses forbidding the alienation of Haitian territory to foreigners. Within the bureaucracies of both State and Navy, junior officials labored over the document and by mid-1917 had produced a revised copy. (This, apparently, was what Franklin D. Roosevelt, assistant secretary of the navy, had in mind when he indiscreetly boasted in the campaign of 1920 that he had written the Haitian constitution.)

But the Haitian assembly, reconvening in late spring of 1917, fought the American revisions. The American version excised clauses forbidding alien ownership of Haitian land and, mindful of what had happened in Cuba, called for ratification of the laws of American occupation. Waller and Cole blamed Dartiguenave for secretly encouraging the assembly to resist while professing his faith in American guidance. Confronted by the American proconsuls, he tried to provoke them into dissolving the assembly and of course assuming the blame. But Cole made it clear that if the marines threw out the bickering assemblymen they might also kick out the president with them. In their threat the American occupiers had the tentative support of Secretary of the Navy Daniels, who had wired instructions to achieve American goals without using force but at the same time gave Cole "full discretionary power." In the end Dartiguenave acquiesced.

Butler, who liked Dartiguenave personally but thought him an "old rogue," was given the task of handling the president. Storming into the National Palace, Butler compelled Dartiguenave and his ministers to sign the decree dissolving the assembly. Their signatures, he wrote later, were written so small as to be barely legible. When it was over, they agreed that only Butler, as head of the gendarmerie, could deliver the document, fearing that any other bearer of such tidings would be shot by irate deputies.

Arriving in the assembly, Butler was roundly jeered and denounced as a "foreign devil" by an impassioned speaker. In the confrontation, the Haitian gendarmes he had brought with him—who were accustomed to witnessing such scenes—began loading their rifles, and the assemblymen scurried for cover. But Old Gimlet Eye calmly ordered them to unload and rang for order with a dinner bell. The decree was read and the assembly dissolved, as Butler wrote, under "genuinely Marine Corps methods." Dartiguenave and his Council of State now reigned with Waller and Butler overseeing every move.

In June 1918 Haitians voted in a plebiscite on the new constitution and approved it, by a vote of 98,225 to 768. Butler's gendarmes hosted local barbecues and then supervised the balloting of Haiti's illiterate peasants, most of whom had little inkling of what they were voting for—some thought they were choosing a new president; one swore his vote was for a new pope. The American occupation had now been made legal.[18]

The proconsuls of Haiti may have been contemptuous of the country's mulatto elite and convinced that Dartiguenave and his crowd were polished spoilsmen, but the Americans developed a grudging respect for the Haitian peasant, the "ninety-nine percent who did not wear shoes," as Butler described them. The rural population had long suffered from malnutrition, disease, and neglect. American observers presumed that the mulattoes who ruled the country simply did not care about the illiterate Haitian who lived out his life on the land and spoke a Creole patois alien to the French-speaking elite of the capital. (Edward Beach was one of the rare American observers who sensed a latent sympathy for the Haitian masses in the ruling oligarchy, though his grounds for such an observation lay in the old Haitian aristocratic custom of carrying a handful of coins to dispense to the impoverished.)

But had pre-1915 Haitian governments been impelled to redeem the countryside, they would have found it difficult to do so. Haitian peasants lived outside the moneyed economy in remote valleys or mountainous villages. They farmed with crudely fashioned implements and often survived by bartering. Butler later told the Senate committee investigating the occupation about one old Haitian woman who left her crude hut with several bunches of bananas to barter. She returned from her sojourn a week or so later with her exchange—several bunches of bananas. In her travels she made no profit (and in fact had suffered a loss) but picked up a great deal of gossip.

Public services, even in Port-au-Prince or Cap Haïtien, were woefully inadequate even by Caribbean standards. In the capital the waterworks had fallen into such disrepair that it pumped only a few hours a day. Refuse littered about the dusty streets rotted and stank; Port-au-Prince, unlike Veracruz, had no sanitary brigade of vultures. The only adequate schools were those run by the church. Public educational facilities occasionally could be found in the villages, but these rarely held classes, and the teachers were mostly political appointees. An American investigation of the system revealed instances where the state continued to send pay to teachers dead for ten years.[19]

As in the Dominican Republic, the occupiers created the gendarmerie not only as a professional army but as a public service institution. The intent was the eradication of provincial and even familial loyalties and the instilling of national pride in every gendarme. In the Dominican Republic this had been achieved by shunting the guardsmen around the country. In Haiti it was accomplished by giving the recruits a pair of marine-issue shoes, a Krag-Jorgenson rifle to replace the antiquated French-made weapons used by the disbanded army, a sufficient diet (2,500 calories per day was Butler's goal), and medical care undreamed of by any Haitian peasant.

Within a year of the authorization for the gendarmerie, Butler had built a force of 2,500 recruits and more than a hundred officers, the latter, of course, marine officers or hastily promoted noncoms. Sons of the mulatto elite were loath to enlist, and skeptics doubted the professionalism of the recruits or their willingness to serve the American occupier. But in virtually every crisis the Haitian gendarmes proved unswervingly loyal. Faustin Wirkus, who commanded a unit at Perodin in 1919–20 (and later became the "white king of Gonâve") wrote of the Haitians: "They treated us younger officers . . . as though we were younger brothers who for some strange reason of inheritance had absolute authority over them. It didn't matter where we told them to go—they went. If we told them to follow—they ran ahead of us, to protect us."[20]

Thus the Haitian gendarmes were acculturated to the forceful manner of marine occupier, but sometimes, in subtle ways, it was the foreign invader whose political and social views altered during Haitian duty. One marine officer, William Upshur—who like Waller came from an old Virginia family —arrived in Port-au-Prince in the fall of 1915 with settled convictions about the Haitian "problem." "Haiti . . . is easy enough to pacify," he wrote his father, "the trouble is keeping it pacified after we leave." The Haitians were little more than savages, he thought, but they could be taught to behave. Taking as a model the viciously racist tune, "Damn the Filipino," which had enjoined Americans sent to suppress the Filipino insurrection to "civilize 'em with a Krag," Upshur and his musically inclined fellow marines composed a Haitian variation:

In the land of sloth and vice
Where they never heard of ice,
Where the donkeys and the women work all day,
Where the land is full of ants,
And the men don't wear their pants,
It is there the soldier sings his evening lay.

Damn, damn, damn the Haitian cacos
Button-scarred, voodoo-dancing drones,
Underneath the broiling sun,
Let them have the Benet-gun
And return us to our beloved homes.

Yet, on leaving Haiti in early 1917, Upshur mused: "It is strange I should feel a very real regret at leaving this beautiful island and its black people."[21]

Butler zealously used the gendarmerie to build schools, sweep the streets, clean the wretched prisons, and string telegraph lines. But the use of gendarmes and ordinary Haitians in his ambitious road-building operation precipitated a spirited controversy and ultimately an official investigation and scandal.

In the eighteenth century the French had carved out an impressive network of roads throughout their Haitian colony, but by the early twentieth century these had long since become rutted trails or had been swallowed by overgrowth. Port-au-Prince had only a few paved streets and, according to Butler's estimate, there were only about three miles of usable road outside the capital. In the north the trails outside Cap Haïtien were impassable in the rainy season except for horses or donkeys, Eli Cole wrote, but mud rose to the bellies of horses and there were instances, it was sworn, where donkeys had slipped into cavernous mudholes and drowned.

By March 1918, when Old Gimlet Eye departed Haiti, he had supervised the repair and building of almost five hundred miles of road. The link between Cap Haïtien and Ouanaminthé on the Dominican border was reopened, but Butler's most impressive achievement was completion of the Port-au-Prince–Cap Haïtien highway, winding for 180 miles up the coast and through swamps. Butler proudly traversed it by auto in twelve hours in December 1917. The cost per mile, he boasted to a correspondent, was only $1,500, but he added: "It is not well to describe in a letter the methods used by us to build this road."[22]

The "methods" involved the resurrection of an 1864 law permitting the corvée, whereby the state could require the services of citizens in the repair or building of roads in each locale. Since Butler had a limited budget for the gendarmerie and not enough gendarmes for the herculean task of providing Haiti with a road system, he readily exploited the corvée. By late 1917 he had some five thousand Haitians laboring on the roads. At first the corvée was popular among the Haitian peasants, though Butler probably exaggerated later when he portrayed the project as analogous to a country barn raising on the prairie. Technically, the service of the citizen was optional. Cards with the names of those obligated to render service were given to gendarme officials; they in turn notified the Haitian peasant that on a certain day he was to report to work on the roads or pay a tax. Since ordinary Haitians had no money, they had to serve. They were not paid but were provided with lodging and meals and in the evenings "amused" with dances. Butler proudly recalled: "I took the President and members of his cabinet at least once a week to call on the corvée parties and to make speeches to . . . impress upon them that they were doing this for their own country and not for the white men."[23]

Inevitably the system led to abuse. Haitian gendarmes charged with enforcing the corvée would exempt some for a bribe and routinely impress others into service. There were instances where a peasant had served his time working on the road only to be reimpressed by a callous gendarme who tore up his release card. Significantly, the worse offenses occurred after Butler had departed; whatever his flaws, Old Gimlet Eye observed a stern code when dealing with ordinary Haitians. Among the Haitians themselves the corvée's growing unpopularity revived suppressed fears about the reintroduction of slavery. As a missionary to Haiti in these years testified:

The occupation . . . intentionally or ignorantly put a new and altogether erroneous meaning to it [the corvée] by actually turning it into an instrument for oppressing and torturing the Haitian people, and exciting their passions, and apparently some times for no other purpose than to provide them [the gendarmes] with the excuse to beat, if not shoot them down.

Yet such stinging indictments were always juxtaposed with observations about the callousness of human life in Haiti. As one marine recalled years after his Haitian duty: "Their idea of brutality was entirely different from ours. They had no conception of kindness or helping people. . . . They treated their people the same way they treated their animals."[24]

But by fall 1918 the corvée had become so controversial that Butler's successor abolished it. Unfortunately, his action was not in time to stave off another *caco* revolt.

The putative leader of the second *caco* uprising was a six-foot intriguer and political ally of the deposed Rosalvo Bobo, Charlemagne Péralte. In 1918 Péralte had been sentenced to five years' labor for conspiring to steal a payroll in Hinche. Assigned to the menial (and humiliating) task of sweeping the streets in Cap Haïtien, he suborned his guard and the two of them ran off into the mountains. By early 1919 he had organized a formidable *caco* following in the North in preparation, it seemed, for a traditional *caco* strike against the capital to drive out his enemy Dartiguenave and the president's American allies. The corvée, though officially abolished, was still being continued in some remote districts, providing Péralte and his followers with an additional reason for driving the whites out of the country.

The *cacos* hit randomly in outlying areas in fall 1918, but it was not until the following spring that the new marine commander in Haiti, Col. John Russell, realized that Péralte had mobilized as many as five thousand *cacos* in a rebellion. From April to October the marines and their gendarmes had 131 encounters with *cacos;* once they even managed to penetrate Péralte's camp, but the wary *caco* chieftain escaped. Always eluding his pursuers, Péralte grew more defiant; he proclaimed a holy war against the "white infidel" who was reintroducing slavery and raping Haitian women. In October, with about three hundred *cacos,* he brazenly attacked the capital, but alerted marines and gendarmes drove his army back into the hills.[25]

Russell now resolved to capture Péralte. The plan involved bribing another Haitian *caco,* Jean-Baptiste Conze, who hated Americans but hated Péraite even more. Conze would publicly condemn the occupation, gain Péralte's confidence, and then reveal his whereabouts to the Americans. Péralte would be lured into a battle near Grande Rivière. The battle began as planned on October 31, but at the last moment, apparently, Péralte elected to stay behind in his mountain retreat. His American pursuers— Herman Hanneken, a marine noncom with the rank of captain in the gendarmerie and William Button, a marine corporal—went after the *caco* leader.

Dressed in *caco* clothes, they blackened their faces with cork and, with Hanneken's fluency in Creole, were able to make their way past guards into Péralte's camp. Below them a fierce battle raged. They spotted the *caco* leader standing near a campfire just as a suspicious sentry shouted an alarm. Hanneken ran furiously toward Péralte, firing his .45 at the imposing figure, while Button opened up on the scurrying camp followers with a Browning automatic, shooting wildly. Péralte fell dead. Hanneken, who had hit the ground, realized after a few moments of furious firing that the *cacos* had scattered, and yelled for a ceasefire. He crawled in the darkness (the fire had been quickly extinguished when the shooting began) and felt Péralte's body. The dead Haitian leader was wearing Hanneken's pearl-handled Smith & Wesson revolver, which apparently Conze had conveyed to him without Hanneken's knowledge. Angered, and fearful that Péralte might be feigning death, Hanneken fired two more shots into the Haitian's heart.

Hanneken then began a search of Péralte's body for incriminating papers. At daybreak, with gendarmes scouring the camp, Hanneken strapped the body to a door so that four gendarmes could carry it down the mountain. The corpse was brought into Grande Rivière, leaned against a wall with Péralte's standard alongside, and photographed. The photograph was disseminated to prove that the *caco* chieftain was really dead. Despite the evidence of an autopsy verifying that Péralte had died of a bullet wound, Haitians persisted in believing the whites had crucified the *caco* leader on a door.

For his part in the conspiracy, Conze received a reward of $9,600. Hanneken submitted an itemized statement for reimbursement in the amount of $832 for expenses and received a medal for his labors, a deed Woodrow Wilson called "one of the most singularly important acts of heroism in my time."[26]

The death of Charlemagne Péralte quieted the *cacos* of the North. But Péralte had an ally of equal determination, Benoit Batraville, who roused the *cacos* of central Haiti in late 1919 and 1920 in a rebellion the marines and gendarmes ruthlessly suppressed.

In this last campaign against the *cacos*, the marines flew seven HS-2 seaplanes and six Jenny biplanes, which took off from a grassy strip outside the capital. Each Jenny was capable of being converted into a crude dive bomber when a twenty-five-pound bomb in a mailbag was strapped between the wheels and the bomb released by the tug on a small rope held between the pilot's legs. One marine aviator, Edward Ostermann, who won one Medal of Honor in the seizure of Veracruz and another serving under Butler in the 1915 *caco* campaign, dive-bombed a *caco* camp.

A more effective war against the *cacos* was waged by small units of marine-gendarme patrols, some of them commanded by young officers destined for greater fame—Louis McCarty Little, the last marine commander in Haiti, and the legendary Lewis ("Chesty") Puller, who acquired in the second *caco* campaign invaluable knowledge about survival in tropical war. On January 15, 1920, Batraville, in a daring bid, attacked Port-au-Prince with three hundred *cacos* and suffered 50 percent casualties. In the aftermath of this battle, marines and gendarmes began systematic search-and-destroy patrols against the remaining pockets of *cacos*. On one of these forays Little's unit came across the decapitated corpse of Sgt. Lawrence Muth, whose patrol had been ambushed earlier. The body had been split open, the heart removed and, according to confessions obtained later, eaten by his killers. The final push against Batraville's scattered *cacos* witnessed some of the most brutal fighting—some, doubtless, provoked by the cannibalization of Muth's body—in the history of the banana wars. On May 18 a patrol killed Batraville himself and took Muth's pistol from the dead Haitian.[27]

Two thousand Haitians, it was estimated, died in the second *caco*

Charlemagne Péralte. *National Archives*

campaign; twelve thousand more surrendered their arms. Even before the fighting ended, rumors of torture and mistreatment of prisoners taken in the rebellion spread in the press and were reiterated in public condemnations of the pacification of Haiti by the Union patriotique, a Haitian lobby against the American occupation, and the National Association for the Advancement of Colored People (NAACP). Unintentionally the commandant of the corps, George Barnett, fueled the controversy when, after reading a court-martial report of a marine officer accused of shooting a prisoner, he wrote an indignant letter to Russell in Port-au-Prince about "indiscriminate killings" of Haitians. Russell of course denied the accusation, as others had denied the wildest stories now circulating about Haiti, among them that the marines favored white southerners as officers in Haiti because they knew how to "handle niggers." The charges of Haitian atrocities continued, fanned by investigatory articles in *The Nation* on the occupations of both Haiti and the Dominican Republic. The Wilsonian record in Hispaniola became an issue in the 1920 campaign when Warren Harding, responding to Franklin Roosevelt's boast of authorship of the 1918 Haitian constitution, declared that as president he would not impose democracy on "our West Indian neighbors" with bayonets.[28]

In 1920 an embarrassed Josephus Daniels, genuinely concerned about the unfavorable publicity over the way navy and marine officers were running Hispaniola, ordered an investigation of charges of brutality by a special tribunal chaired by Rear Adm. Henry Mayo. The Mayo court grappled manfully with the accusations but concluded that it could not reasonably decide what, generally, constituted a campaign of atrocity in war. Herman Hanneken, the court observed, had been decorated by the president of the United States and condemned as a brute in the liberal press for killing Charlemagne Péralte. As for other incidents, the court noted almost twenty instances of specific acts of unjustifiable violence against Haitians by American military personnel; in each case, the court declared, the perpetrator was punished. Public accusations of systematic torture and brutality in the *caco* campaign, the Mayo tribunal concluded, were "ill considered, regrettable, and thoroughly unwarranted."[29]

But the Mayo court—and the 1921–22 senatorial investigators of the Haitian and Dominican occupations—could explain the severity of the second *caco* campaign only in terms or values understandable to American listeners. One marine, sent to Haiti during the 1919 uprising, remembered the Mayo inquiry and an earlier tribunal, also authorized by Daniels, that investigated a case in which a Haitian troublemaker had been sentenced to death for, among other things, cannibalism. The secretary of the navy, shocked at the accusation, could not accept the punishment and disapproved the verdict saying "such things are unthinkable." Daniels "was just a . . . boob," the marine officer recalled, reflecting on his Haitian experience. "They were thinkable."[30]

His sardonic comment, uttered many years later, perhaps unintentionally reflected the lingering bitterness in the corps over its experience in Hispaniola. Dispatched to the island by a president already frustrated over hemispheric criticism of his Mexican policy, it had had in Haiti and the Dominican Republic an unprecedented opportunity to run things, as Butler liked to say, "according to Marine Corps methods." The army had little interest in the governance of the two countries, and the navy, technically in charge of both occupations, maintained its presence largely in the form of the naval command of the Cruiser Squadron and the increasingly detached scrutiny of Secretary of the Navy Daniels. For the first time in the banana wars and America's penetration of the Caribbean, the marines were their country's imperial proconsuls. Their efforts to alter Haitian and Dominican politics, economics, and even cultural values were predictably thorough; their accomplishments in the rebuilding of what were considered shattered economies were occasionally impressive, if sometimes achieved by questionable and even brutal methods. But in the final accounting, when Haitians and Dominicans and their American critics delivered a verdict on these occupations, it was the style of marine rule, not its accomplishments, that was remembered.[31]

PART IV

The Last Banana War

13. Interregnum, 1921-1925

Despite Warren G. Harding's pointed condemnation of "bayonet rule" in the West Indies, the election of 1920 was neither a repudiation of America's imperial experiment nor a mandate for Caribbean empire.

In 1904–1905, the American press had divided sharply over the wisdom of Roosevelt's ventures into Dominican finance and the enunciation of the Roosevelt Corollary, the legal underpinning for America's Caribbean forays in later years. But the military interventions of 1915–16, when Hispaniola's troubled politics seemed to justify a forceful solution, had broad editorial support. The press accepted the idea of mission in the tropics, often expressing the justification in the strongest racial convictions and stressing in particular the need to end the political anarchy in Haiti and the Dominican Republic. Wallace Irwin's 1904 satirical appeal was by 1915 a call to action:

> Urged by motives nowise harmful
> Beneficial if you will—
> Uncle Samuel's got an armful
> Of republics infantile.
> Uncle hates their constant riot
> But he has the knowledge grim
> That he's got to keep 'em quiet,
> For they all depend on him.
> So he sings in accents gritty
> This enthusiastic ditty:
> "Don't be scared, you're free from harm.
> I can't talk your lingo
> But I'll do my best—by jingo,
> Stop that fightin', San Domingo!"[1]

Various newspapers and periodicals had been incautious advocates of Caribbean intervention in 1915. By 1919, however, many had come to oppose the Haitian and Dominican occupations. During the war these imperial experiments had been largely ignored by the larger dailies ordinarily attentive to Latin American concerns. The *New York Times,* for example, contained only a few references to Hispaniola in 1917 and 1918. Expressing American participation in the Great War as a duty to preserve European civilization, Wilson was soon reminded after the armistice that the lofty goal of self-determination, a cardinal principle of his peace program, contrasted with American prescriptions for Hispaniola. He was reminded again at the Versailles peace conference of the embarrassing violation of Caribbean sovereignty when he received a long memorandum on the subject from the exiled Dominican ex-president, Henríquez y Carvajal, whom Captain Knapp had booted out of Santo Domingo in 1916, and a more plaintive appeal along the same lines from Haitian president Dartiguenave. Wilson tentatively moved to reduce marine strength in Haiti but was dissuaded from doing so by the outbreak of the second *caco* campaign. In 1919 and 1920, the military rule over the island, shielded from public scrutiny during the war, underwent candid investigation by hostile observers. The revelations of atrocities and the Republican attacks on Wilsonian policies in the Caribbean aroused the indignation of the press, which demanded, after the Republican landslide, an impartial investigation of the Haitian and Dominican occupations.[2]

The Senate Select Committee on Haiti and Santo Domingo of 1921–22 produced two thick volumes of testimony from marine and naval officers who had carried out the occupations; publicists such as Horace Knowles, a persistent critic of the Dominican intervention, and James Weldon Johnson, the black literary figure who brought the NAACP into the Haitian inquiry; and Dominican and Haitian protest organizations, the most vocal being the Union patriotique. On the committee itself the most influential figure was Medill McCormick, the chairman, who had endorsed the Dominican intervention of 1916 but by 1921 had grown weary of America's imperial experiment. McCormick wanted reform in, not withdrawal from, Hispaniola. He and two other committee members had even visited Port-au-Prince and Santo Domingo. Under the disapproving gaze of American military officers they had listened to a litany of criticism of the occupations, mostly from politicians but occasionally from an ordinary Haitian or Dominican bearing the physical imprint of American rule. If not an unqualified endorsement of American management of Hispaniola, the final report was not a repudiation of the occupation. After hearing occasionally damning testimony, the committee perfunctorily summarized the material accomplishments in the Dominican Republic and advocated continuation —with an implicit plea for reform—of American rule in Haiti.[3]

Wilson had been planning to evacuate the Dominican Republic as early as 1919, when Bainbridge Colby, his third secretary of state, embarked on a campaign to improve relations with the Latin American republics, an effort culminating in Colby's goodwill tour of the Southern Hemisphere. Military withdrawal from the Dominican Republic, Colby argued, would do much to offset rising Latin American criticism of American imperialism. But it was equally apparent that the administration could not move quickly enough to get credit for ending the occupation. "Concerning Santo Domingo," the president told William Gibbs McAdoo, his son-in-law and former secretary of the treasury, a few weeks after the Harding landslide, "I have done what I think is possible and best in the circumstances. I don't care a damn what the Republicans do. I have been part of this record from the first, and there is nothing in it to be ashamed of at any point."[4]

Neither were his proconsuls in Santo Domingo ashamed of the American record. They seemed convinced that United States forces should remain. Having balanced the Dominican budget (at least for several years), reformed the educational system, begun a medical crusade against venereal disease, and launched an ambitious road construction project, the military rulers of the republic, forgotten during the war, were now reaping the accumulated grievances of an occupied society. The Dominican opposition, mute since the early days of American intervention, reacted to the rising criticism of the intervention in the American press with its own denunciation of military rule.

In late 1919 the military governor, Thomas Snowden, a rigid disciplinarian who, unlike Harry Knapp, never consulted Dominicans about anything, issued a sweeping censorship order prohibiting publication of material advocating "bolshevism" or exciting "public unrest, disorder, or revolution." When the distinguished editor Horacio Blanco Fombona published on the front page of *Letras* a photo of a Dominican allegedly beaten by American soldiers, a squad of marines invaded his office and closed the review. Blanco Fombona went to jail, as did the poet Fabio Fiallo, director of *Noticias,* for writing "inflammatory" editorials that were "virtually a call to arms" against the military government. In May 1921 Fiallo published in *La Tribuna,* a Managua, Nicaragua, daily, a poem, "The Anguish of Santo Domingo," which the commander of the Special Service Squadron angrily labeled "vile." A quatrain went:

> With folded arms, with mouth gagged,
>   Without a press to denounce their laws of terror;
> What atrocious infamies, what vile torments, in
>   Four long years of wicked intervention.

The poem so enraged marines of the legation guard in Managua that an invading squad ransacked *La Tribuna*'s office.[5]

In December 1920 Snowden dutifully issued a proclamation announcing the intended withdrawal of American forces but wrote in his quarterly report that the "sudden change of policy . . . struck the military government at a most unfortunate period." At the time he was cracking down on "agitators" who wanted to embarrass the United States and pleading for assistance in getting a $10 million public works loan. Business would benefit by these moneys, Snowden added, but Dominican entrepreneurs were fearful of retaliation from the "old politicians" returning to power after American withdrawal. Admiral Knapp, his predecessor, was more explicit about the need to retain control over the republic, telling Daniels that the "only hope of those negroes is wise white guidance . . . ; it would be fatal to turn the gov[ernment] over to the negroes, as fatal or worse than [it was] to turn the South over to the negroes after the [Civil] war."[6]

Snowden left Santo Domingo a few months later. Testifying before the General Board of the Navy, he poured out his anger at the Dominican "politicians" who were demanding that the United States pull out. "The mass of the people, say nine-tenths of them," he averred, "want the United States to remain indefinitely." The military government acquired a new governor, another naval admiral, Samuel S. Robison, who shortly found himself negotiating with a consultative committee of prominent Dominicans. A loan of 1922, bitterly resented by the committee because it would financially burden the republic for years, made possible the last grand accomplishment of the occupation—the northern road into the Cibao. The loan, declared the *Listín Diario,* the country's most prominent paper, "fastens the noose around our necks for twenty years." Another paper argued that the highway owed as much to the initiative of Ramón Cáceres, the powerful president from 1906 to 1911, as to the American occupiers.[7]

In the last months of the occupation the American military played a subordinate role in the relations between the United States and the Dominicans preparing to take over. When opponents of the military government balked at complying with Snowden's (and Robison's) proclamations, which required approval of the acts of the occupation, Sumner Welles, who played a central role in the formulation of interwar policy toward Latin America, negotiated with them. In the interior the marine occupiers began pulling back to central points—Puerto Plata, Santiago, and the capital—leaving the policing of the countryside to the Dominican national guard. The provisional government assumed power in October 1922, as the last marine commander in the republic implored his troops to accommodate Dominican sensibilities: "Our conduct here is our country's conduct." Two years later, the old political chieftain and newly elected president, Horacio Vásquez, offered to commission marine officers in the national guard. All refused, saying the stipulations for service were too political. In September 1924 the last marines departed Dominican soil.[8]

Reluctantly abandoning the Dominican Republic to the gaggle of politicians they had run out of power in 1916, the occupiers of Hispaniola reorganized their administration of Haiti. In 1922 Senator McCormick declared that Haiti could not be set adrift but that the occupation needed reform. Haiti got a high commissioner, John Russell, the Georgia-bred marine who had followed Waller and Butler in 1918. Russell was an old-line officer but possessed ample social grace to mollify the more outspoken Haitian nationalists. The nomination for the post almost went to Smedley Butler, whom Secretary of State Charles Evans Hughes apparently preferred, but a young State Department officer, Dana Munro, aware of Old Gimlet Eye's bad reputation among the Haitian elite, dissuaded Hughes. Under Russell, the occupation carried out its rule through the five treaty services—customs, finance, police, public works, and health.

In 1922, when Dartiguenave defied American wishes in negotiating a public loan delivering Haiti's debt to New York banks, he was shunted aside in favor of a cabinet minister, Louis Borno, an outspoken advocate of American paternalism and intellectual devotee of Benito Mussolini's fascist experiment in Italy. Borno willingly complied with American strictures, accepting Russell's pronouncements that the Haitian masses were unfit for self-rule.

For the marine occupiers of Haiti the twenties were good years, especially if one were assigned to Port-au-Prince. "The routine down there was quite relaxed," recalled Carson Roberts, a marine officer. In the early days of the occupation the marines, forced to leave their wives in the states, had mingled socially with Haitian women. Now, with the *cacos* beaten and the policing of the country in the hands of a gendarmerie, Haiti was considered safe, and officers' spouses arrived in Port-au-Prince. In the capital they could have servants and all the social amenities customarily enjoyed by the elite. In the interior, of course, life for a marine wife could be more demanding. Lester Dessez remembered one "petite and feminine" marine spouse who always went about with two .45s strapped to a tiny waist.[9]

Those officers who went into the gendarmerie had to endure the privations of living in isolated coastal or interior towns and were shut off from the social life of the capital and its marine-organized Polo Club. But Haiti was a highly sought assignment for a struggling young officer in the States because it was possible to live on gendarmerie pay and save one's regular Marine Corps pay. Merwin Silverthorne, who arrived in 1923, wrangled an appointment to the gendarmerie from Borno and was sent to Les Cayes, on the southern coast, about 125 miles from Port-au-Prince. The road to the capital washed out regularly, so the station was independent duty for most of the year. "When I took it over," he recalled, "the former commander had lost his mind, had killed a native, and had been relieved under guard." On the way back to prison in the States, he crawled out the porthole of the ship and was drowned. Living in Les Cayes, Silverthorne had a "sort of shaky authority" over the dozens of communes in the interior, sitting in communal meetings, approving budgets, overseeing a crude justice, and supervising some five hundred state employees, among them priests and nuns. He patrolled by auto and horseback, inspecting the rural police stations and lodging in private homes.

Back in Les Cayes he served as his own secretary, filling out monthly reports and filing them "because the filing system was beyond the intellect of the average gendarme." In the mornings he ran the office and in the afternoon drilled squads of illiterate gendarmes. With his wife and two children he lived in a French-style house with no glass windows and shuttered doors. The family made its own furniture from old crates. Malaria still plagued the southern Haitian coast, so at night they slept under nets. Before leaving Les Cayes he supervised the construction of a barracks and a small prison.

In Les Cayes and later as police and fire chief in Port-au-Prince Silverthorne halfheartedly tried to suppress voodoo but soon realized the hopelessness of the task. A myth persisted among Americans for years that the marines stamped out voodoo in Haiti. The problem, Silverthorne recalled, lay in the fact that Haitians "from the president on down" believed in voodoo. Anyone arrested for practicing the ritual received a fine of ten gourdes (about two dollars) or less and was released. Arrests were always made by gendarmes "stumbling onto" a ceremony; white men never witnessed anything but a staged ritual. "I could hear the drums on the weekends," Silverthorne said, "but . . . never could get to them."

Like other marines serving in Haiti during these years, Silverthorne developed a grudging respect for the peasant and a noticeable disdain for the elite. Ordinary Haitians referred to the marine as "papa Blanc." "I liked the Haitians," Silverthorne said; "the people are happy go lucky." As for the mulattoes, "the educated man [was] the schemer" who got his education in France and returned to Haiti to "live off the product of his less fortunate people." The average Haitian, tutored by American philanthropy and inspired by the work ethic, would, the occupiers contended, improve his lot. That proved an unrealized dream.[10]

Americans retained their initial distrust of the elite, denigrating the mulattoes for their anti-democratic politics and European ways. Already American social standards penetrated polite society. Segregation flourished, but Russell would occasionally step over the color line to mingle with the upper-crust Haitian. The marines had their American Club, off limits to Haitians including Borno, but the Port-au-Prince elite had *its* Club Bellevue which, following a gaffe by a gauche American, remained closed to anyone in uniform. Upper-class Haitians suppressed their resentment of American racist slights, the most publicized of which occurred when the marine-trained gendarmerie band once saluted President Borno with a rousing rendition of "Bye, Bye, Blackbird."

The generation of mulattoes maturing in the occupation rejected the Frenchified social philosophies of their parents and the practical exhortations of self-help and material progress preached by the Americans. They discovered a new cultural salvation in their African past, their negritude, which held that the races *were* different.

The goals of the occupation—agricultural diversification, technical education, financial rectitude, public health, and a nonpolitical army—were laudatory endeavors touching the lives of thousands of ordinary Haitians. But the elite saw in them a threat. The sons of the aristocracy rejected the technical education parceled out by the Americans; and the much-publicized efforts to introduce a "competitive spirit" among employees in the customs service met with widespread indifference. "For the most part," the Marine Corps history of the occupation dourly notes, "Haitians failed to respond enthusiastically to either training or rewards."[11]

The Wilsonians made Mexico and Hispaniola the crucible of American empire; their Republican successors took their imperial stand on the isthmus of Central America.

Retreating from Hispaniola after Harding's victory and the Senate inquiry, American power in isthmian affairs sharply escalated in the early 1920s. In 1921 the appearance of a warship with four hundred marines compelled Panama, which had mobilized its army, to accept the arbitral decision of an American Supreme Court justice in the republic's long-standing territorial dispute with Costa Rica. Panama was more a colonial appendage in 1924 than it had been in 1904. When the distinguished Panamanian diplomat Ricardo Alfaro (who a decade later would declare that Theodore Roosevelt had treated Panama with respect) protested American economic policies in the Canal Zone, Secretary of State Hughes bluntly reminded him that the United States conducted affairs in the zone "as if it were sovereign," irrespective of Panamanian claims.[12]

In the early 1920s the United States reentered the century-old debate over Central American federation. After World War I interest in a Central American union revived, inspired by the political triumph of a unionist party in Guatemala in 1920 and a formal request from El Salvador for a conference to reconsider the 1907 treaties. When the conference finally met in San José, Costa Rica, the delegates immediately ganged up on the Nicaraguan representative because of his country's subservience to American policy, and he stalked out. Costa Rica's assembly rejected the federalist scheme, but Honduras, El Salvador, and Guatemala plunged ahead, meet-

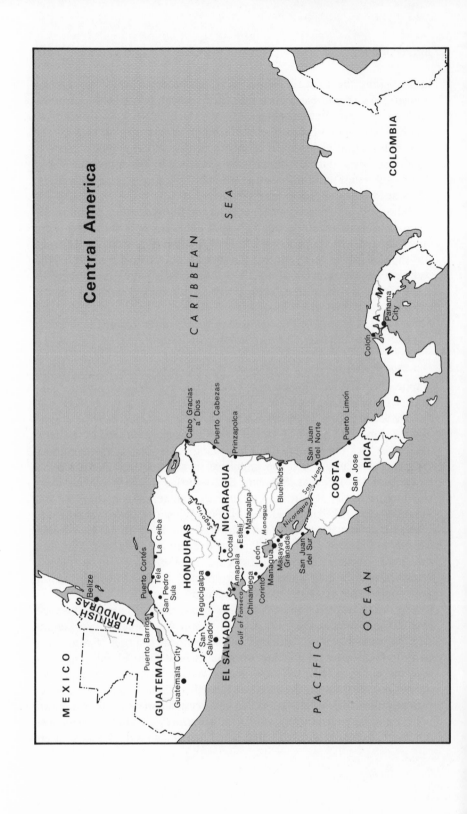

ing in Tegucigalpa in mid-1921. A special delegation from the new union descended on Washington but was coldly received by a State Department thoroughly disillusioned with Central America's frustrating record in federalism and irritated by the union's challenge to American sway over the isthmus. Rejected in Washington, the unionists suffered another blow to their cause when a coup in Guatemala City toppled the prounion party.

Some months later a brief war scare among Nicaragua, El Salvador, and Honduras sent their respective presidents scurrying aboard the U.S.S. *Tacoma* to settle the squabble. Under the reassuring supervision of naval officers, they sent a peace proposal to Washington. The outcome was the Central American Conference of 1922–23, held in Washington under the tutelage of Sumner Welles. Theodore Roosevelt's and Elihu Root's 1907 prescription for isthmian peace was updated and strengthened. In the treaties of 1923 the Central Americans made no effort to revive the union. Instead, they created a new isthmian court to hold inquiries into disputes among the five states, leaving unmentioned the unhappy demise of the Central American Court of Justice, ignominiously brought down in a quarrel over America's canal policy in Nicaragua.

The 1923 treaties dealt with the Central American states as if they were an extended family of perpetually bickering cousins and in-laws who could not survive without stringent ground rules. If a political aspirant shot his way into power, his government would not receive diplomatic recognition from the other Central American governments or from the United States, which meant that he could not borrow money from American bankers. With Welles's reluctant blessing, the delegates added an inflexible provision: Even if elections sanctioned a revolutionary government, none of its high-ranking members (or close relatives) in power six months before or after the election could become president.[13]

The first test of the 1923 treaties came in Honduras. Since the turn of the century Honduras had been a perpetual victim of the isthmus's often bitter interstate feuding. It shares a boundary with three Central American states—Guatemala, El Salvador, and Nicaragua—and in the Zelaya era numerous battles had been fought on Honduran soil. Because revolutionary elements plotting against neighboring governments occasionally used Honduras as a staging area, the treaties of 1907 had declared the republic neutral territory.

The civil war of 1924 was essentially a struggle between Liberals and Conservatives vying for patronage and the support of the fruit companies operating on the north coast—Standard, organized by a Sicilian family out of New Orleans, the Vaccaro brothers; United, founded in 1899 by the brilliant entrepreneur Minor Keith; and Cuyamel, headed by the legendary Samuel ("Sam the Banana Man") Zemurray, who merged Cuyamel with United in 1929. Tegucigalpa, a drowsy place protected by towering mountain peaks, was virtually shut off from the north coast and its busy ports and bustling banana plantations. The banana companies imported huge quantities of supplies for their bastard-gauge railways and ugly company towns with their yellow frame houses and monotonous plantation stores. Practically everything the companies needed came in duty-free at Tela, Puerto Cortés, or La Ceiba.

The banana magnates learned very early how to play the game of Honduran politics. They paid off local chieftains, loaned money to desperate governments, bribed presidents, and generally tried to keep the warring Hondurans away from the north coast. Fighting in the port towns could be costly, as the Vaccaro brothers found out in 1911 when a rebel force under Lee Christmas, the legendary filibuster, and former Honduran president Manuel Bonilla (who had allegedly plotted their invasion in a New Orleans brothel as U.S. federal agents staked out the building) shot up La Ceiba and routed government troops from the town. Another problem was the presence of so many exiles who worked on the plantations, many run out of Nicaragua by the American-backed government. When the Honduran government ran low on money or soldiers, it generally got both by squeezing the banana companies.[14]

The rebellion began over a spirited contest for the presidency in fall 1923. Among the candidates, the most popular—and most feared—was a moon-faced general with a walrus moustache, Tiburcio Carías Andino. Carías had an army of zealots along the Nicaraguan frontier who talked of putting him in the presidency by force of arms if he were cheated out of an honest election. Solicited for its opinion, the State Department solemnly asked for a "fair" election, an absurdity to anyone familiar with Honduran politics. As the campaign wore on, President Rafael López Gutiérrez grew more agitated over Carías's support, but he found reassurance in the advice of the American minister, Franklin S. Morales, ex-bartender of the Hotel Pratt in Tegucigalpa with powerful connections to New Jersey's political machine, who told López to rule firmly. The president responded by cracking down on Carías's exuberant supporters. Carías claimed victory in the election, but he won only a plurality, and the decision was thrown into the National Assembly. When the assembly failed to raise a quorum López declared martial law and began arresting Carías's organizers.[15]

Genuinely embarrassed by its minister's gaucheries, the State Department withdrew recognition from López's government but could hardly extend it to Carías, who raised the flag of revolt. The north coast was already under patrol by the Special Service Squadron, commanded by Rear Adm. John H. Dayton. The Special Service Squadron had been created after the war to assume the duties theretofore performed by the Cruiser Squadron —to patrol the American empire in the Caribbean and the Pacific coastline of Central America, showing the flag and supplying forceful support to the efforts of American diplomats to keep the peace. Its flagship, the *Rochester,* was, like the vessels of the Cruiser Squadron, a tired castoff from the fleet with the appropriate nickname, the "Rambling *Rochester.*" Dayton, like other naval officers in such stations, could use his own judgment in landing troops to protect "American lives and interests."

Both López and Carías began pressing the banana companies for loans and other favors. United stood to gain most by a Carías victory, but all three pestered the State Department for a signal as to American intentions to recognize Carías's government if his side won the civil war—vital information if the companies intended to "loan" money to the cause. The response was a mild rebuke to the banana companies for meddling in local politics and a restatement of the intention of the United States to protect American interests.[16]

By late February Dayton had the *Milwaukee* at Amapala, on the Pacific coast, and the *Denver,* to which he moved his command, at La Ceiba. He was no sooner in La Ceiba than a battle (remembered by locals as the "Ceiba horror") erupted between a large army of Blues (rebels) and Reds (government troops) on February 28. In the engagement the Blues slowly got the better of the contest, and Dayton decided to land a detachment of marines and bluejackets. The Americans set up headquarters in a Vaccaro brothers warehouse and, following another naval tradition in the tropics, declared the area a neutral zone. Within La Ceiba, however, the battle raged, each side taking turns burning and looting the town, sending some three thousand Ceibeños into the protective custody of Dayton's bluejackets and marines. The American consulate received so many hits that the consul himself fled to sanctuary on a banana plantation.

Trouble followed at other ports on the north coast—at Tela and Puerto Cortés—and there was more fighting when a government force commandeered a United steamer in Tela and sailed for La Ceiba on March 8. The next two days witnessed another round of burning and looting, during which the marines took in more refugees and sent others into the interior on Standard's rail line.[17]

Carías won the war on the north coast, and his army pushed on to the capital, but he was denied the final victory. In April Sumner Welles arrived in Honduras after a hectic trip from Santo Domingo. Hughes had given the peripatetic diplomat virtually complete authority to settle the Honduran squabble. Welles arranged a conference of leaders from the various factions aboard the *Milwaukee* at Amapala. As Tegucigalpa was subjected to shelling and its businesses compelled to make forced loans to Carías's cause, Welles negotiated an agreement among the Honduran factions, cleverly keeping Carías's representatives away from the ship's radio and thus denying them vital information about Carías's impending military triumph.

Welles's solution was not a radical one: a provisional presidency followed by an "honest" election. Anticipating victory by Carías in the general election, the provisional president stacked his cabinet with Carías followers. His Liberal enemies charged fraud and raised the flag of revolt. Once more fighting erupted on the north coast, and the banana companies resumed payments into Carías's coffers. Welles castigated the banana entrepreneurs for much of the trouble; Morales was removed and was followed by an American minister who applied strong pressure against the companies and shut off the flow of loans to Carías. The government crushed the Liberal revolt, but Carías was so embittered by this experience that he dropped out of the presidential race. Instead, an ally, Miguel Paz Barahona, a permissible candidate under the 1923 accords, became president of the republic.[18]

The Honduran violence, costly as it was to the republic, did not alarm either the State Department or the Navy Department nearly so much as the Nicaraguan conflict of 1909–10 or the sanguinary war that would break out there in late 1926. Not only was the American strategic and economic stake less important in Honduras than in Nicaragua—especially so if one discounted the banana companies of the north coast, which played a political role in the republic not always consistent with American policy—but Honduras had not yet offered a nationalist leader who could challenge American power. Nicaragua had produced such a figure in Zelaya; in 1927 it would find another.

14. The Second Nicaraguan Civil War, 1925-1927

The installation of Adolfo Díaz as president of Nicaragua in 1912 brought an imposed peace to that republic, symbolized by the presence of one hundred marines "protecting" the American legation in Managua and the subservience of Nicaragua to American direction. Desperately short of funds, Díaz signed a canal convention with the United States—American planners had not given up on building a Nicaraguan canal—providing some $3 million and a guarantee of Nicaraguan independence. In return the United States got an option to construct a second canal across the isthmus, the cession of Great and Little Corn islands where the navy contemplated building a Caribbean base, and still another naval concession on the Pacific side in the Gulf of Fonseca.

This treaty had been hastily negotiated by George Weitzel, the American minister in Managua, in the closing days of Taft's presidency. Assuming command of the State Department, William Jennings Bryan inherited the convention and the related squabble when Nicaragua's neighbors, who had strategic interests in any transisthmian canal, protested Nicaragua's concessions. Costa Rica had claims on the use of the San Juan River, which formed a portion of the route of the proposed waterway, and El Salvador and Honduras objected to the alienation of territory in the Gulf of Fonseca. To speed ratification, Díaz even suggested a proviso similar to the Platt Amendment, by which Cuba had been incorporated into the American empire, but the proposal was quietly dropped when Bryan and Nicaraguan minister to the United States Emiliano Chamorro drew up a new treaty in 1914. (As partial compensation for his cooperativeness, two years later, when Chamorro was a candidate for the presidency, he returned to Nicaragua aboard an American warship and in so doing cowed his opponents into submission.) Concurrently American bankers took over Nicaraguan finances, assuming control of Zelaya's old debts with European syndicates and reorganizing the republic's monetary system. Since 1911 an American appointee had been collecting Nicaraguan customs.

The Senate finally sanctioned the Bryan-Chamorro Treaty in 1916, the approval delayed by persistent attacks from the former secretary of state and now senator Elihu Root, who expressed dismay that the Wilson administration could sign a convention with a government that hardly represented the interests of its people and flagrantly disregarded the rights of its neighbors. In the final debate, the Senate was assured that the interests of Costa Rica, Honduras, and El Salvador were not being violated. Nicaragua's assembly hastily approved the treaty, though Díaz wound up with only about 20 percent of the $3 million, the other 80 percent going to pay off the republic's restless creditors. When Costa Rica, El Salvador, and Honduras laid their protests before the Central American Court of Justice, the court in two decisions upheld them but added ominously that it had no jurisdiction over the United States. Neither the United States nor Nicaragua moved to undo the treaty, and the court, humiliated by the affront, soon disbanded.[1]

Nicaragua antagonized its neighbors by signing the canal convention with the American government, but, unlike the old days under Zelaya, it had at least stopped making war on them. And its often turbulent internal politics, typified by the fratricidal rivalries between Granada's Conservatives and León's Liberals, had become subdued under the stern measures prescribed by the republic's American overseers.

The dominant political figure after 1916 was Emiliano Chamorro. Scion of a proud Conservative family, he was adulated by ordinary Nicaraguans. His father had been mercilessly mistreated by Zelaya, and in vengeance Chamorro had helped the Americans crush the Mena revolt of 1912. In the election of 1920, unable to succeed himself, Chamorro was able at least to shift his aging uncle, Don Diego, into the presidency. The ever-conspiring "General," as the masses always called Emiliano, took up the post of Nicaraguan minister to the United States, effectively controlling his country's destiny from Managua and Washington.

Afterward the republic's politicians returned to their principal concern —the American presence. Liberal publicists periodically condemned the erosion of national sovereignty and the economic subservience of the country to American bankers, but old Don Diego forthrightly responded to such accusations with ringing praises of the republic's orderliness and prosperity. The marines encamped at Campo de Marte, within sight of the National Palace, occasionally grew so weary—"gone tropical" was the expression describing this phenomenon—of the humdrum routine of policing a dusty little city isolated from the real world that they occasionally unleashed their frustrations at the slightest provocation. Clashes between marines and Nicaraguan police, in which three policemen were killed and several more wounded, occurred in 1921 and again in the following year. An angry

Nicaraguan assemblyman introduced a resolution calling for withdrawal of the legation guard; the resolution failed, but the United States had to apologize once more for the violent actions of its marines in Managua and went so far as to pay an indemnity to the families of the victims and to relieve the entire guard with substitutes from the brigade in Haiti. But in 1922 the legation's guardians performed a signal service to President Chamorro. A small band of rebels captured the fortress atop La Loma; historically, whoever took this hill commanded the city. The invaders surrendered meekly when the American minister bluntly warned them that any firing on the capital would be returned by the marines.[2]

Don Diego Chamorro died suddenly on October 19, 1923, as his energetic nephew sailed for the United States to negotiate a $9 million loan from New York bankers. The vice-president, Bartolomé Martínez, as politically ambitious as any Chamorro, immediately succeeded to the executive chair. But Emiliano no sooner returned to bury his uncle than he began conspiring to move into the National Palace. As Nicaraguan representative to the Central American Conference, he had dutifully signed the 1923 treaties with their stringent provisions on presidential succession, but the overseer of the rules—the United States—was now showing signs it no longer wanted to interfere in the internal affairs of the Central American republics. Secretary of State Hughes had so declared in a bracing speech commemorating the centenary of the Monroe Doctrine, and an American political scientist from Princeton University, Dr. Harold Dodds, was busily drawing up an electoral code for Nicaragua which, it was hoped in Washington, would be dutifully followed in the 1924 election.[3]

Almost a year before this election the State Department had officially informed the Nicaraguan government of American intention to withdraw the legation guard as soon as a properly staffed constabulary (modeled on the Dominican guard) could be organized. The Liberals, out of power for a decade, wanted the marines to remain long enough to guarantee a "fair" election, which, it was presumed, Dr. Dodds would closely monitor.

Martínez went along with the delay on removal of the guard and complied with the suggestion for a constabulary, but he was noticeably reluctant to allow Dodds and his assistants to supervise the election because he had every intention of cheating. Dissuaded by a polite demurral from the State Department to his query about his own candidacy, Martínez resolved to keep Emiliano Chamorro from becoming president. He craftily fashioned a symbiotic coalition of anti-Chamorro Conservatives and disaffected Liberals into a union called the Conservative-Republicans, who nominated Carlos Solórzano, an amiable old capitalist with a penchant for spending his own money to get ahead in politics, for president, and Dr. Juan B. Sacasa, a prominent physician and Liberal, as his running mate.

Martínez controlled the election, and Solórzano won a stupendous victory. But in triumph he suppressed an inner fear that the popular Chamorro, who knew the election was fraudulent ("irregular" would have been more apt), would try to annul the results by proclaiming a revolution. The State Department was genuinely befuddled: It questioned the fairness of the election but could hardly encourage Chamorro to undo matters. Sensing the American predicament (Central American politicians had already acquired a sixth sense in divining American quandaries), Solórzano inundated Washington with pledges for reforms—electoral reforms, economic reforms, and military reforms. The enfeebled Nicaraguan government even managed to muster enough resources to purchase the national bank from American creditors, and in June 1925 it hired Maj. Calvin Carter of Elgin, Texas, as head of the proposed constabulary.

On August 3 the marines of Managua boarded a train for Corinto. A jubilant crowd bade them farewell at the railroad station, their departure captured by a newsreel crew intently focusing the camera on the windows of waving leathernecks. As the train chugged off, President Solórzano jumped in front of the camera and began waving an enormous Nicaraguan banner.[4]

"Peace reigned in Nicaragua," wrote Harold Denny in his spirited account of American rule in the republic, "for three weeks, four days, and thirteen hours after the marines departed."[5]

Stung by his defeat, Emiliano Chamorro retired to his plantation to raise corn and plan his revenge in what Calvin Carter later called the "Kentucky feud" in Nicaragua. On August 28, 1925, a band of Conservatives invaded the International Club, disrupting an exquisite dinner party for the capital's most prominent families, President and Mrs. Solórzano, various members of the president's cabinet, and a goodly number of guests from the American colony, including the American minister, Charles C. Eberhardt, and Roscoe R. Hill, Nicaraguan high commissioner. At the height of the merriment, as champagne glasses were hoisted in toasts, a prominent Conservative outfitted in breeches, boots, and spurs, obviously drunk, strode into the grand ballroom firing a pistol. Trailing behind were less gaudily attired young ruffians, some wearing straw hats and all armed. Women fainted and scuffles erupted. A few of the less combative guests scurried for cover underneath the billiard tables in the game room.

The invaders had come to liberate the president from the clutches of his Liberal allies, their leader proclaimed. Fortunately, the Solórzanos had departed early, but the invading mob began arresting prominent guests, including one Liberal who grabbed Minister Eberhardt by the coattails, beseeching protection. Gen. José María Moncada, a future president, was led away with a pistol nuzzled against his head as he cursed his captor. The liberators took their prisoners to La Loma and defied the president to meet their demands. At one point Major Carter urged the harried Solórzano to take a detachment of troops and storm the citadel and even promised to shoot the Conservative dandy who had invaded the International Club, but Solórzano demurred, saying, "He's my brother-in-law." In the end the president dismissed the Liberals in the cabinet, and the party crasher acquired a bribe of $5,000, a house, and a membership card for the International Club.[6]

Solórzano was so agitated that he began pestering Eberhardt to call for an American warship to bolster his resolve. When Chamorro, presumably the instigator of these shenanigans, appeared in Managua, Carter gave him a stern lecture about political agitation. But the marines were gone, and the general believed they would not be returning to Nicaragua. His followers seized La Loma, and Chamorro demanded a coalition cabinet with himself as general of the army. The next move called for a convenient resignation from the assembly, so that Chamorro might join that body. Cleverly he maneuvered a bill of impeachment against Sacasa through a compliant assembly, whose members saw fit to inflict more pain on the vice-president by attaching to it a decree of banishment from the country for two years. In March 1926, after an orchestrated campaign that may rightly be described as psychologically torturous, Chamorro compelled the president to resign, beginning with an offer to make Solórzano minister to the United States and, when he refused, threatening to have the president declared insane. As first designate of the assembly, Chamorro became president— all accomplished in a manner vaguely conforming to Nicaragua's tortuous rules on presidential succession. Two years of conspiracy had apparently paid off handsomely.

Both Solórzano and Sacasa fled the country. Solórzano had resigned under duress, but he *had* resigned. Sacasa had been rudely and, his Liberal followers asserted, unconstitutionally prevented from succeeding the former president. A loyal supporter, Gen. José María Moncada, proclaimed a movement to restore Sacasa to power.

The revolt against Chamorro, like the one that began more than fifteen years before against Zelaya, won its first successes on the isolated eastern coast. A makeshift Liberal force assaulted Bluefields, home of the coastal American colony, and seized $160,000 from the national bank. The fighting prompted the local American naval commander to land a detachment of marines from the *Cleveland*, "to protect American lives and interests," and to declare the city a neutral zone.

American involvement in Nicaragua's internal affairs deepened when Eberhardt suddenly left the country, turning things over to his chargé d'affaires, Lawrence Dennis, a moody figure who in the next decade would become an intellectual devotee of fascism. Dennis plunged into the Nicaraguan political maelstrom, offering advice to the warring factions and bluntly telling Chamorro to resign. The Conservative reaction was, predictably, to unite in calls for solidarity; the Liberals rallied even more strongly behind Sacasa in his claims on the presidency.[7]

Throughout the summer the war of nerves between Dennis and Chamorro continued unabated, the president believing that the Americans would not return—even as their marines policed Bluefields—to enforce the 1923 treaties and that, in time, he would receive American diplomatic recognition. He was more successful in prosecuting the war against his rival Sacasa. At the end of May the Liberals had triumphed along the east coast; they had taken Bluefields, Rama, La Cruz, Puerto Cabezas, and the Bluff, controlling the entrance into Bluefields harbor. Within three months Chamorro's expeditionary force had dispersed them to the Costa Rican border and into the wild Nicaraguan interior. But as Chamorro won victories over Sacasa, Adm. Julian Latimer, commander of the Special Service Squadron, quietly increased his forces ashore, sending more marines into Bluefields and, after late September, regularly disembarking marines from the *Denver* at Corinto.

By the fall of 1926 the Nicaraguan affair had become more than a bitter internal feud precipitated by Chamorro's coup, for Sacasa had made a triumphant visit to Mexico, and evidence of Mexican involvement had shown up in captured weapons and ammunition bearing the stamp of a Mexican munitions firm. The Nicaraguan constabulary had even taken Mexican prisoners who confessed they had been given official leave to join Sacasa's rebellion. Chamorro denounced the meddling in words familiar to Americans who had been chastising the Mexican government for its expropriation of American property. In 1926 Secretary of State Frank Kellogg condemned the "bolshevik menace" next door, and President Calvin Coolidge declared that "Mexico was on trial before the world." But, inexplicably, the common hostility toward the Mexicans of Chamorro and Kellogg did not make the Nicaraguan leader a kindred spirit; he was not absolved of guilt for violating the 1923 treaties.[8]

Searching for an acceptable course in the Nicaraguan maze, J.H. Stabler, a longtime functionary of the Latin American division of the State Department, resurrected a solution often used by American negotiators when dealing with feuding Central Americans—a conference. Sumner Welles had corralled a gaggle of warring Hondurans aboard an American warship in 1924 and thrashed out a compromise. Now, in neighboring Nicaragua, the State Department decided on a reprise of that performance. The site for the conference was the port of Corinto, the neutrality of which could be assured by the menacing presence of Admiral Latimer's light cruisers.

Corinto, wrote an American ensign who saw it some four years later, was a "typical Central American place with mud-flats to the rear and vultures croaking in the trees." Three volcanoes, the middle one belching "thin smoke," loomed in the background.[9] The talks began on October 6 aboard the *Denver*, with Dennis, the thirty-two-year-old chargé, presiding. Naively, Dennis believed he could now play the role he had failed at in his persistent meddling in Nicaraguan affairs: Under his direction the Liberals and Conservatives would thrash out the issues and divide the spoils in the American tradition. Within a few days he realized that the civil war was not a contest between men with differing political philosophies but an intensely fought feud between antagonistic families with irreconcilable ambitions. At one point the Liberal delegates suggested American arbitration of Nicaragua's quarrel, which brought the predictable response that the republic's troubles were an "internal" concern. Eager to be fair, the American government even arranged an interview with Sacasa, who had sought refuge in Guatemala City, but the man on whose behalf the rebellion was waged emphatically denied any collaboration with the Liberal cause.[10]

Chamorro, however, came away from the Corinto conference with another of his labyrinthine political schemes. Lacking American recognition, he knew it was hopeless to continue as president, but before resigning he secured pledges from Conservative assemblymen supporting him in the 1928 election. The agreement was signed in Dennis's presence in the American legation. An interim executive followed, and under Dennis's prodding the assembly on November 11 named Adolfo Díaz president. Díaz immediately got Chamorro out of the country by naming him general minister to Great Britain, France, Spain, and Italy. The State Department's harried Latin American specialists were delighted, having already cabled to Managua their view that while the United States hesitated to interfere in Nicaragua's politics it nonetheless thought Díaz "would be a wise choice" because he was "honest and capable" and possessed "firmness of character."[11]

The relationship between Díaz and American officials in these trying months for American policy in Central America offered an early example of the "tail wagging the dog," a phrase former Secretary of State Dean Rusk has often used to describe a more recent alliance between the United States and another small country mired in civil conflict. Reluctantly drawn more deeply into the Nicaraguan morass, the United States looked to Díaz ("our Nicaraguan") to unify the country and protect American interests. Schooled in the Central American political art of manipulating Washington, Díaz determined on serving a full term, which meant that the Americans not only would have to maintain their military presence in the republic but would have to augment it. The State Department, alert to Díaz's thinking, hesitated in sustaining him beyond diplomatic recognition, but Díaz then raised anew the charges of Mexican meddling in Nicaraguan affairs.

On December 19 Eberhardt, having returned to his Managua post, wrote: "Were Mexico eliminated it is my ... opinion that the Liberals would immediately be brought to treat with Díaz."[12]

As the war revived in the East, Díaz cleverly played on American suspicions of Mexican designs in Nicaragua. Among American residents of the coastal towns fear of a prolonged struggle ran strong and did not subside after Díaz's election and American reaffirmation of faith in him. Two days before Christmas 1926 Admiral Latimer, responding to pleas for increased protection from American interests, landed forces from the *Denver* and *Cleveland* at Puerto Cabezas, known as Bragman's Bluff to Americans, and declared the town neutral, giving Sacasa's troops until 4:00 P.M. to leave. In the capital an additional five hundred marines formed a guard around the National Palace.

On the east coast, landing of American troops in times of revolutionary disturbances was not uncommon and had generally followed the traditional pattern of a vigilant naval squadron protecting American lives and property. But in Managua and on the west coast, the introduction of American forces meant something more ominous—the United States was undertaking a policing role that could not be fulfilled by the government. It had done so in 1912, when Díaz had proved unable to quell Mena's revolt; it was doing so again because the Nicaraguan executive lacked the wherewithal to crush Sacasa's rebellion.[13]

Díaz had said as much on December 31, when several high-ranking Nicaraguan officials held a secret conference with Eberhardt and the American high commissioner at the American legation. Though virtually destitute, the Nicaraguan representatives declared, Díaz's government intended to carry on the struggle for "national honor" even though it meant forced loans, levies, and, possibly, "suspension of the foreign debt." Alarmed, the Americans replied that such a course would be disastrous, but their Nicaraguan counterparts were resolute, saying that if the Americans did not intervene the Mexicans would continue their support of Sacasa. The alternative to surrender was a "fight to the finish."[14] Given the condition of Díaz's government, that was a fight the United States could ill afford to wage by proxy—and Díaz knew it.

The preservation of order without undue interference in the republic's internal affairs, Coolidge declared in a special message to Congress on January 10, 1927, guided American policy in Nicaragua. The United States, he said, had a "special responsibility" in the Caribbean. Two days later Secretary of State Kellogg followed with a reproachful assessment of the Bolshevist menace symbolized by the leftist course of the Mexican government and its unwarranted involvement in Nicaragua.

Main Street of Chinandega after rebel bombardment, 1927.   *Defense Audiovisuals*

Crest of El Chipote.
National Archives

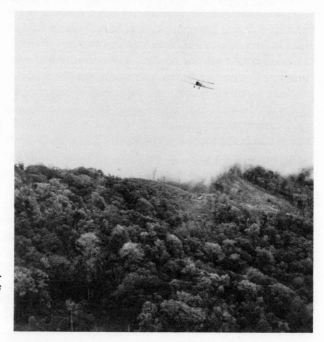

Adolfo Díaz had correctly interpreted the American mood: The United States, frustrated in its efforts to retrench from Caribbean empire, could not repudiate the interventionist doctrines of Roosevelt and Wilson because to do so would mean losing face to Mexico and its inspired leftist course in Central American affairs. The putative reasons for plunging ever deeper into Nicaraguan troubles—preservation of the Monroe Doctrine, protection of the canal route, and security for American lives and interests—sounded platitudinous to such sarcastic critics as William E. Borah, the Senate's most persistent foe of American policy toward Mexico and Nicaragua. Borah called the president's recitation of America's mission in the tropics a "mahogany and oil policy," an unsubtle reference to accusations that the administration was fundamentally more concerned about American business interests in those two countries than with its professed commitments to political stability. Testifying before the House Committee on Foreign Affairs, a student of inter-American affairs questioned the president's use of the Monroe Doctrine to protect Wall Street's investments.[15]

But in the establishment of neutral zones along the east coast, at Bluefields, Prinzapolca, and Puerto Cabezas, the U.S. Navy provided sanctuary to Americans or any other foreign resident wanting to escape the fighting. Admiral Latimer was only vaguely concerned about Wall Street's stake in Nicaragua. His bluejackets and marines protected Americans from the ravages of civil war because it was traditional naval practice in the turbulent Caribbean to do so. The marines at Bluefields, at León, the citadel of Nicaraguan liberalism, and especially those encamped at Campo de Marte in Managua symbolized order in a disorderly society.

Manifestly, the creation of neutral zones favored the government. Sacasa had broad support throughout Nicaragua, but his military strength lay in the isolated East, far from the menace of Díaz's troops. Forbidden to use the coastal towns as bases, Sacasa's armies in that region were driven into the inhospitable Nicaraguan interior. Even so, the war went poorly for Díaz. Sustained by the reassuring presence of American troops in the country's major cities, the president commanded a virtually demoralized army. A Liberal force launched a daring assault on Chinandega, only ten miles from the port of Corinto, resulting in a furious battle for control of the town. In the fighting the town's central area erupted in flames, started, it was later charged, by American mercenaries flying for Díaz's aviation corps. The two aviators had flown over the area, spotted the rebel advance, and flown back to Managua to rouse the government. Joining in the counterattack, they heaved bombs from their planes on clusters of shabbily clad rebels racing about below. Díaz's forces held the town, but the human toll was high, as witnessed by the ghastly sight of feasting vultures among the dead. The battle of Chinandega with all its human and physical destruction was a portent of the suffering to come. On February 12 another Liberal flank —part of a 3,000-man-strong motley army (many of them women and young boys) of General Moncada, Sacasa's ablest officer—which had marched from the Atlantic coast to San Pedro del Norte, routed a government garrison at Muy Muy. Assessing the defeat, Eberhardt wrote gloomily: "It is increasingly evident that without complete intervention there is no likely prospect of an early restoration of order."[16]

But Coolidge and Kellogg, smarting from the attack on American policy by antiinterventionists in the Senate, had in mind another solution to the Nicaraguan puzzle—a dramatic peace mission led by a prominent American who, reinforced by the marine presence in the republic, could impose peace between the warring Nicaraguans. For such a mission the president turned to a distinguished public servant, Henry Stimson, formerly secretary of war and captain of artillery during World War I.

Stimson had picked up a fleeting impression of tropical politics on an official visit to Hispaniola during his tenure as secretary of war in the Taft years, but he knew embarrassingly little about Nicaragua (which he habitually mispronounced "Nicaragewa") or its civil war, though he was to learn quickly and with sufficient depth to write a book on his experience in the country. From the moment this imposing man of sixty stepped from an American warship onto the dock at Corinto, he commanded the attention —and the respect—of Conservative and Liberal alike. His rail trip to Managua offered a sobering education in the nature of civil war; along the way he saw the scars of battle in Chinandega and, in the countryside, scrawny farmers bearing rifles going about their daily chores. A fertile land and rich heritage, he thought, had been despoiled by the ravages of war.[17]

The official announcement sent to the American legation in Managua had made clear that his was not a mission of mediation. There would be no insistence on a mutuality of concession between rebel and government forces; Díaz did not have to relinquish any military advantage in the war. But Stimson would impress upon the besieged Nicaraguan president the need to offer "reasonable generosity" to the rebels (i.e., the expedience of opening up some Liberal posts in the cabinet), with the United States participating in "any permanent arrangement which may be effected for the establishment of peace and order" (an American-trained constabulary). A few days after his abrupt arrival in Managua, in a conversation with Díaz's minister of foreign affairs, Stimson explained "reasonable generosity" in the vernacular of American politics. The solution, he told his Nicaraguan listener, lay in a fair election. Told by the minister that the defeated party in an election resorts to revolution, Stimson replied that the defeated should

192   The Last Banana War

accept their loss "in [a] spirit of sportsmanship." In a jocular mood he told
the minister that Nicaraguans "ought to play more football, baseball, etc."
as a means of learning how to accept political defeats.[18]

Reason and persuasion and a "fair election," then, would prompt the
Liberals to stop fighting and turn in their weapons. But if persuasive tactics
proved inadequate and the rebel armies pressing against the capital from the
interior continued their advance, Stimson had the authority to call on
Logan Feland's two thousand marines to stop them. The United States must
not make the mistake of 1912, he wrote somberly, when it used "naked
military intervention" but made little effort to improve political conditions.
Now the rebels had a "reasonable" choice: They could throw down their
arms and gain a fair election (with the strong likelihood that Sacasa or
another Liberal would triumph), or they could continue the war "with no
chance of recognition" if their cause triumphed militarily.[19]

Stimson met with prominent Liberals of Managua, including a youthful
Anastasio Somoza, founder of the postwar Nicaraguan dynasty, who impressed the American emissary as "very frank" and "likable." But the most
consequential encounter was the meeting with General Moncada, Sacasa's
hard-drinking rebel commander, underneath a blackthorn tree by the
Tipitapa River. Their conversation lasted only thirty minutes, Moncada
insisting that Díaz's continuation in power was immoral, Stimson replying
earnestly that the United States would stick by the president until the next
election—if necessary, by force of arms. The insistent American departed
with Moncada's verbal commitment to call upon his commanders to surrender their arms.

A few days later, Stimson and Moncada exchanged written agreements
at the Hotel Tipitapa. Celebrating at lunch, the American emissary remarked conciliatorily: "From this moment let there be a new era of peace
and true friendship between Nicaraguans and Americans."[20]

15. The Sandino Chase

The Tipitapa accords stopped the rebel advance, and once again in Nicaragua's tortured history a policing force of American marines and bluejackets imposed an uneasy peace. In the towns along the rail line to Managua newly arriving reinforcements from American warships in Corinto harbor peering out dirty car windows must have believed Nicaraguans had been exhausted by the ravages of civil war. In Chinandega, wrote one of Admiral Latimer's bluejackets, "could be seen bodies picked clean by the vultures, and still other bodies with only their abdominal cavities scooped out by the ravaging beaks of turkey buzzards who gorge themselves to a nauseating stupor."[1] Elsewhere there were clashes between American occupying forces and Nicaraguans. In Léon, hostility against patrolling marines among Liberal partisans who felt cheated by American policy and Stimson's commitment to Adolfo Díaz precipitated random violence. And in Chinandega a marine unit stalked a defiant rebel general to his house and into his bedroom and shot him—and his equally combative mistress—dead.

Henry Stimson had pledged General Moncada a fair election, but the distinguished American emissary had first insisted on a general disarmament. Induced by an American promise to pay ten dollars for every surrendered rifle, Nicaraguans began turning over their weapons to specially designated marine units. From mid-May until the first week of June, a vast exchange of arms for money went on, the Conservatives surrendering almost 11,000 rifles and 300 machine guns; the Liberals, 3,100 rifles and 30 machine guns—a discrepancy, observed a marine veteran of the campaign, an astute intelligence officer should have noted. Sacasa vainly urged his supporters to retain their weapons, watched his movement collapse, and quietly left the country.

The disarmament and the lure of profits attracted the more enterprising Nicaraguans to sell their rifles several times over to American purchasers. "We would put [the rifles] in the government warehouse," recalled Robert Hogaboom, detailed by General Feland to one of the three-member disarmament commissions, "and we found that they were being issued out the back . . . as fast as we were storing them in the front." Afterward Hogaboom and his associates began segregating the better weapons for use in the proposed Guardia and dumping the rest in Lake Managua.[2]

The difference in the number of rifles surrendered by Conservatives and Liberals was in large part due to Augusto C. Sandino's denunication of Moncada and the peace of Tipitapa. In late spring 1927 the marine occupiers of Nicaragua knew little of this diminutive Nicaraguan "bandit" who was to preoccupy them for the next five years in a savage jungle war and whose name and cause would soon be invoked throughout the hemisphere in anti-American slogans. (Ten thousand miles across the Pacific in war-torn China a Nationalist military unit took the name "Sandino brigade.") Egocentric but not vainglorious, Sandino projected a becoming modesty beneath his broad-brimmed Stetson—looking, indeed, like an extra in a Tom Mix cowboy film—but he excelled in writing arrogantly boastful letters to his marine pursuers and moving defenses of his cause to the outside world. Of all the "bandits" chased by the banana warriors in the tropics, Sandino alone acquired an enthusiastic audience in the Hispanic world.

The illegitimate child of a landowner's son and a peasant girl, he had grown up in the Zelaya era, when Liberals ran the country and life had been relatively pleasant. The dictator's downfall, which owed much to American harassment, and the coming of the marines in 1912 changed the family's fortunes. In 1920, following a personal feud (Nicaraguans, among Central Americans, had a reputation for personal combativeness), he fled to Honduras, worked for a while on the vast Vaccaro brothers banana plantation near La Ceiba, then in 1923 moved on to Tampico, Mexico, a bustling city dominated by petroleum companies. In revolutionary Mexico, his ablest biographer, Neill Macaulay, has written, Sandino acquired a hurried education in social justice and concern for the victims of American capital in Latin America, feelings that did not abate when Sandino returned to Nicaragua in 1926 with five hundred dollars and a Smith and Wesson revolver.

He began working for an American mining company in Nueva Segovia, a mountainous region that offered sanctuary to his forces in the coming years, but soon took up gunrunning in behalf of Sacasa's cause. Sandino's ties with Sacasa and Moncada were never close, however. He first met the Liberal claimant to the presidency after a pitched battle with Chamorro's army in early November 1926, when Sandino suffered a defeat and moved on to Puerto Cabezas, where Sacasa had established his provisional government. From their first encounter Sandino distrusted Sacasa and Moncada, considering the latter merely an opportunist. When Admiral Latimer's forces occupied the town and began confiscating arms, Sandino's men, with the timely assistance of Puerto Cabeza's prostitutes, sneaked away with thirty rifles and seven thousand cartridges. The Tipitapa accords confirmed Moncada's treachery in Sandino's estimation; when they met later, Moncada had shed his modest uniform for a Palm Beach suit and new shoes.[3] Moncada was now the traitor, but at the time, wrote marine officer Wilburt ("Big Foot") Brown, who later joined the Sandino chase, Sandino had no plan to attack Americans. His rejection of the Tipitapa agreement made him an idol among his men, and he made a glorious entry into Jinotega.[4]

Feland launched a desultory campaign into Nueva Segovia to disperse Sandino's ever-growing band, but the Nicaraguan rebel, now casually referred to by marines as a "mule thief" and "bandit," raided Telpaneca and the San Albino mine, acquiring spoils and more followers. After the San Albino raid he issued a ringing denunciation of American policy and called for the building of a Nicaraguan canal by hemispheric public subscription. A somewhat humorous and mutually insulting exchange began between Sandino and Capt. Gilbert Hatfield, commander of the marine–national guard garrison at Ocotal. In provocative terms Hatfield urged Sandino to surrender, using the example of Emilio Aguinaldo, the Filipino rebel who had successfully defied the United States until his ignominious capture by Frederick Funston. Aguinaldo had "become the greatest of caudillos and splendid friend of the United States." Rejecting the offer a few days later, Sandino threw down the gauntlet: "I want a free country or death."

In the early morning hours of July 16, having infiltrated the village of Ocotal, Sandino attacked the garrison with about sixty regulars and five hundred partisans, including a hundred or so from the town who joined in the assault. Hatfield had only forty marines and a slightly larger force of guardsmen, but the defenders were well protected by the thick masonry walls of the barracks. A furious fire fight raged on through the night and into the next day, relieved only by Sandino's dispatch of a messenger with a flag of truce (accompanied by the mayor, who claimed to be a prisoner) demanding Hatfield's surrender. But the marine captain was as flamboyantly defiant as Sandino, and the battle resumed after the flag bearer departed.

Though the Americans and their Nicaraguan guardsmen suffered only a few casualties to Sandino's hundred or more, the fight for Ocotal was ultimately decided by an air strike of five planes, theretofore employed mostly for observation, armed with machine guns and fragmentation bombs. The squadron had been alerted by two planes flying over Ocotal earlier in the day, which had strafed the Sandinistas before returning to Managua with news of the attack. Under the command of Maj. Ross ("Rusty") Rowell, the squadron took off from a grassy strip, headed out over Lake Managua, and then climbed over the five-thousand-foot mountain chain dividing the western lake region from eastern Nicaragua. Reaching Ocotal by midafternoon, the aviators began strafing and dive-bombing the scattering rebels, killing two hundred of the three hundred Sandino lost

Capt. Gilbert D. Hatfield and Ocotal defenders, 1927. *National Archives*

Sandino's soldiers. *National Archives*

in the battle. At least thirty, it was estimated in an official report on the battle, had perished from the explosion of *one* fragmentation bomb. The timely arrival of the aircraft probably saved the Ocotal garrison, but the dive-bombing technique portended a frighteningly modern quality in the Nicaraguan war.[5]

Sandino and his American adversaries drew differing lessons from the battle of Ocotal. Commenting on the battle a few days later, Sandino maintained that his force had taken control of the town and, even when compelled to retire by American planes, had retreated in triumph. The attack on Ocotal proved beyond doubt that his struggle was for "ideals" and constitutionalism and that he and his followers were not "bandits," as the American marines and Díaz's government declared. Ocotal, Sandino said, showed "we prefer death to slavery." The person ultimately responsible for Nicaragua's agony was Calvin Coolidge, who sustained his "lackey Adolfo Diaz, whom all good Nicaraguans held in contempt." One of his pursuers, Capt. Oliver Floyd, whose seventy-five marines and 150 guardsmen had been sent into Nueva Segovia by General Feland to crush Sandino, put the issue somewhat differently. Reconnoitering in Sandino country between San Fernando and Ocotal, Floyd reported barrios practically deserted save for women and children and "all people encountered . . . unquestionably strong for Sandino." In a somber assessment of his mission, Floyd concluded: "I will have to wage a real blood and thunder campaign and will have casualties every day. I will become involved in a small real war."[6]

Yet, in the evaluation of conditions in Nueva Segovia by marine headquarters in Managua, Sandino was still viewed as only one—albeit the most dangerous—leader of several rebel bands that had not yet been disarmed. The thrust of marine activity, General Feland stated in August, should be "a policy of denial to Sandino of places of assembly and supplies [and] of movement of his contraband in cattle and products and denial of opportunity for his recruiting."[7]

Feland left Nicaragua a few weeks after sending this report, turning his command over to Col. Louis Gulick; in the same month Adm. Julian Latimer, who as commander of the Special Service Squadron supervised American operations in Nicaragua, relinquished his post to Rear Adm. David Sellers. Before departing Managua, Feland once more publicly labeled Sandino a "bandit," though a "dangerous bandit," in keeping with State Department policy of minimizing the Sandino threat. Privately Feland called for more marines to suppress the revolt. A critical press in the United States was already doubting the American government's handling of the Sandino challenge to American policy in Central America. Publicly, Henry Stimson referred to Sandino as just another isthmian bandit, though Coolidge's special emissary to Nicaragua confessed years later in his autobiography that the Nicaraguan rebel was a "skillful guerrilla." But if Sandino were merely a bandit, editorialized the *New York Times* in January 1928, what explained his wide popularity with Nicaraguans?[8]

In his annual message of December 1927 President Coolidge dwelt briefly on the Nicaraguan problem—the Sandino chase had not yet been described as a "jungle war"—noting the threats to American lives and interests but concluding: "the population [has] returned to their peacetime pursuits, with the exception of some small roving bands of outlaws." A few weeks later, in keeping with the president's well-known view about the main function of government, the marine commander reported: "The business situation throughout Nicaragua continues excellent."[9]

Sandino was not yet captured, of course. Since his "defeats" in the summer, he had chosen to avoid direct confrontation with the marines and instead to follow the guerrilla tactic of hit-and-run skirmishes. In late August his band seemed to have been swallowed by the Nicaraguan jungle, prompting Admiral Sellers to predict that the "critical period of pacification has passed and that the country is entering [a] period in which efficient policeing [sic] will be all that is required." But in September and October there were several ambushes of marine patrols by Sandino's men, and information dribbled in that Sandino and most of his force were encamped atop El Chipote, a remote mountain surrounded by virtually impenetrable valleys of ceiba and mahagony trees near the Honduran border—terrain ideally suited for guerrilla war.[10]

Sandino had indeed assembled an army at El Chipote, but it was unlike any the American occupiers had encountered in their wearying campaigns in the tropics. By virtue of his reputation and the changing currents of Latin American attitudes toward U.S. intervention in the Caribbean, the Nicaraguan rebel had become much more than a folk hero among Nicaraguans. He now had followers from every Latin American nation save Peru. Sensing an opportunity to inflict a final defeat on Sandino and rid themselves of this persistent obstacle to American policy in Nicaragua, the marines launched a combined ground-air assault on El Chipote. On November 23, 1927, Rusty Rowell finally pinpointed the location of the mountain on the crude maps marine aviators used to reconnoiter the Nicaraguan wilds. In the days following, the American pilots pounded the mountain and surrounding area with fragmentation bombs. But El Chipote was not Ocotal; the heavily wooded terrain provided protection to Sandino's troops, invisible to their attackers from the skies.

In December the ground offensive got underway with two marine-guard units converging on the village of Quilali. In separate actions, Sandino ambushed both groups, striking first on December 30 just a mile outside Quilali and again on New Year's Day in a skirmish that took the life of Lt. Richard Bruce, who had just written his mother promising to hold

Sandino's head in his hands or perish "like a dog." Bruce's assailants stripped his corpse of pistols, compass, binoculars, and a small American flag, then savagely hacked his body with their machetes.

Taking refuge in Quilali, the harassed marines and guardsmen faced an uncertain fate as Sandino closed in on the village. The Americans turned a grassy street into a two-hundred-yard crude landing strip that allowed supply planes from Managua to land. From January 6 to January 8, Lt. Christian Schilt, operating one of the newly acquired Vought 02U "Corsairs," flew ten missions into the beleaguered village, bringing in 1,400 pounds of medical supplies and evacuating eighteen wounded, three of whom would doubtless have perished had they been taken out overland. For his exploit Schilt won the Medal of Honor.

A second, more devastating bombardment of El Chipote commenced in mid-January 1928. The marines now had newer, more effective Corsairs and Curtiss Falcons to take the place of the lighter de Havilands, and Rusty Rowell's pilots subjected the crude shacks atop El Chipote to unremitting aerial attack. When the scattering Sandinistas ran for cover, the marine aviators dropped fragmentation bombs in their midst with deadly effectiveness. But when the ground assault battalion finally reached the summit of the mountain after three days' march from the base, the marines found only hastily abandoned food supplies.[11]

Sandino is a "small-time Caesar," said marine commandant John Lejeune after an inspection of the Nicaraguan war, who "would rather be a big frog in a little puddle up in Northwest Nicaragua than a respected but otherwise unimportant citizen in Managua." But if Sandino were little more than a fanatic with ideals harassing American troops in a remote corner of Nicaragua, "Why all this fury for [his] annihilation?" queried the *Cleveland Plain Dealer*. Though the policy of confining him to Nueva Segovia made sense, the paper continued, "the dispatch of a considerable American Army and the sacrifice of American lives in a wild goose chase . . . seem to be without rime or reason."[12]

Sandino had by now attracted numerous publicists, among them the journalist Carleton Beals. Much to the displeasure of the marine command, Beals sought out and interviewed the Nicaraguan rebel in his mountain retreat and published a series of articles on Sandino in *The Nation*, noted for its literary antiimperialism and its exposé of the Haitian occupation earlier in the decade. Told frankly that his hit-and-run tactics would mean only the sending of more marines to Nicaragua, Sandino responded:

We are not protesting against the size of the invasion, but against invasion. The United States has meddled in Nicaragua for many years. We cannot merely depend on her promise that she will someday get out. Every intervention is more pronounced. The United State promised to give the Philippines their independence, but American troops still remain in the Philippines; they are still a subject people.

Denying the charge that his army was made up mostly of mercenaries and adventurers from other countries, Sandino boasted: "Our army is . . . composed of workers and peasants who love their country."

In some respects—in the setting and the intensity of the rebel leader —Beals's Nicaraguan foray resembled a later and even more famous interview between an American journalist sympathetic to a cause and a Latin American revolutionary, Herbert Matthews's storied encounter with Fidel Castro in the Sierra Maestra in 1957 Cuba. The Sandinistas fought with American-made rifles and captured marine automatic weapons. An old man showed Beals a homemade bomb fashioned by wrapping rawhide tightly around dynamite, stones, nails, glass, and pieces of steel. But Sandino's claims of victory (eighty of the enemy, the rebel boasted, had perished at Ocotal) were, Beals wrote, "as exaggerated as those of the marines." He did not doubt the urgency in Sandino's denunciation of the American government's using as pretext the need to safeguard American lives and property ("I have never touched a pin belonging to an American," was Sandino's response) when its real purpose lay in sustaining the unsavory regime of Adolfo Díaz and the "economic spoliation" of the country by American banking houses. "We are no more bandits than was [George] Washington," Sandino declared. "If their consciences had not become dulled by their scramble for wealth, Americans would not so easily forget the lesson that, sooner or later, every nation, however weak, achieves freedom, and that every abuse of power hastens the destruction of the one who wields it." This was an eloquent statement, made more compelling by the myth still growing about the name. Sandino would inevitably fall, wrote one Nicaraguan editor, but his image would survive as the "new William Tell."[13]

Morosely assessing the Sandino chase in February 1928, a marine officer attributed the rebel's ability to elude his pursuers to the peculiar difficulties of fighting in inhospitable terrain. Occupying the towns of Nueva Segovia to deny them to Sandino's forces meant fewer marine contingents for patrolling the interior. And there was the added, though often exaggerated, aid Sandino received from the outside. Most of it came from Mexico. The Mexican government's sympathies for Sandino and his cause were widely known, wrote Ambassador Dwight Morrow, who had arrived in Mexico the previous year to resolve the nagging issues in Mexican-American relations, but Mexican authorities were "far too preoccupied with internal problems" to render aid to Sandino. Pro-Sandino committees, which collected funds presumably only for medical supplies, operated not only in Mexico but in the United States. A larger threat to American policy, observed one intelligence report, was the Mexican-based Hands Off Nicaragua Society, a leftist hemispheric organization that drew funds from organizations ranging all the way from the International League against Imperialism to the International League in Behalf of Persecuted Stragglers.[14]

By the early spring of 1928 Beals's prediction to Sandino about inevitable increases in marine strength in Nicaragua had become a reality. Following Lejeune's visit, which returned Logan Feland to command the marine brigade in the republic, 2,000 marines arrived, enlarging the Sandino pursuit force to 3,700 men. Five American cruisers with 1,500 bluejackets patrolled the Nicaraguan coast.

The republic's political system, like an addict whose body had adjusted to daily drug injections, had already begun the quadrennial campaign for the presidency despite the apparent absurdity of trying to elect a chief executive while almost four thousand foreign troops pursued a defiantly anti-American rebel throughout the North. By now the Sandino chase had become an obsession with the interventionists, a cause vital to American *credibility* in the tropics, and in a perverse way Sandino's escapades and the continuing violence served the bickering political parties. As Admiral Sellers observed: "All local disturbances are seized upon by both political parties as militating against our guarantees of free and fair election and agreement to tranquilize the country."[15]

A "fair election"—that had been Stimson's pledge to Moncada and his rebellious Liberals. The followers of Chamorro, removed by the power of American intransigence in 1926, naturally looked on the Stimson accord and the American military presence as an election the Liberals were guaranteed to win. In the fall of 1927, when Nicaragua's politicians began manuevering for the 1928 election, Don Emiliano dutifully went to Washington beseeching American support. At his elegant Long Island home, Colonel Stimson told the general that he was not considered "presidential" anymore. Moncada followed and was enthusiastically received; the former rebel had quickly learned the old Central American art of accommodating the Yankees.

Early in 1928 there arrived a special commission at Corinto, headed by Army Brig. Gen. Frank McCoy, accompanied by a young officer destined for bigger things, Matthew Ridgway, "a master of Spanish grammar," a skill he would soon put to good use. The McCoy commission drew up an electoral code, reminiscent of the one another army officer, Enoch Crowder, had laboriously put together for the Cubans and which they had so cleverly learned to circumvent. Ridgway diligently checked the translation. His work completed, he took Nicaraguan "R and R" by hunting alligators.

Electoral reform posed a greater threat to the Conservatives than to the Liberals, Chamorro quickly recognized. When his minions blocked passage of the enabling legislation in the National Assembly in March, Díaz duti-

fully proclaimed the code by executive decree. Shortly thereafter McCoy
became supervisor of the board of elections and with that post virtual
master of the upcoming election.[16] Driven from Nueva Segovia by the
marine occupation of the province's towns and the frantic clearing of air-
strips for their aerial force, Sandino shifted his campaign into the eastern
lowlands. His war was now directed almost exclusively against the American invaders and their property, and he began a campaign of destruction
of American mines. Having reduced one American mine belonging to
Adolfo Díaz's old employer, the La Luz and Los Angeles Mining Company,
he left an explanation:

Dear Sir: I have the honor to inform you that on this date your mine has been
reduced to ashes, by disposition of this command, to make more tangible our protest
against the warlike invasion that your government has made in our territory, without any more right than that of brute force. . . . The losses which you have sustained
in the aforementioned mine you may collect from the Government of the United
States.[17]

But the attacks in the East and the harsh treatment allegedly meted out
by Sandino's troops to civilians, General Feland wrote in mid-May, meant
that Sandino was now "desperate." When the raids precipitated renewed
violence in Masaya in the West, as Sandino had expected, the disturbance
was quickly dealt with, followed by Feland's reassuring statement: "The
occurrence is of small importance." With Admiral Sellers he undertook a
personal inspection of the eastern theater (which required sailing through
the Panama Canal and up the eastern coast of the isthmus). Returning to
the west coast, Sellers reported confidently: "The military situation has
improved steadily and is now in a very satisfactory condition despite the fact
that Sandino is still at large." Under Díaz's amnesty decree in April, 538
"self-confessed bandits" surrendered—the number rose above a thousand
during the summer—though, inexplicably, only twenty-two turned in any
weapons. But the surrenders meant that "neither Sandino nor his followers
will be able to have any appreciable effect on the outcome of the election."[18]
    For the policing of the election, McCoy had acquired an impressive
staff of twenty-five army, twenty-nine navy, and four marine officers and ten
civilians. There at their behest were 432 marines and bluejackets, one at
each of the polling places scattered throughout the republic. The army had
not played a major role in Caribbean occupation since the days when
Frederick Funston had ruled Veracruz, but McCoy was making the most
of his role. His electoral commission, he believed, would rejuvenate—even
revolutionize—Nicaraguan politics, and his enthusiastic descent on Managua aroused marine resentment. The marines, after all, had been doing the

grubby work of pursuing Sandino, policing the dense forests and boggy wastes of northern and eastern Nicaragua in what was turning out to be, from the perspective in Washington, a futile chase. They (and their navy comrades) were predictably annoyed at Coolidge's abrupt decision to turn to a rival service for inspiration about American policy in Nicaragua and management of the election. McCoy had arrived not only for the purpose of drafting an electoral code and guaranteeing an honest count but also to assess the war and report on marine operations. "People cannot understand why the job [of disarming Sandino] cannot be done," Secretary of State Kellogg had lamely confessed to McCoy before he left for Nicaragua, "and frankly I do not understand myself."[19]

In reviewing the dreary record of fraudulent voting in Latin American politics, American supervision of the 1928 (and 1932) Nicaraguan election stands out as premier example of the honest election. President-elect Herbert Hoover, in his preinaugural goodwill tour of the hemisphere, stopped briefly at Corinto and observed that intervention had inherent limitations. Privately he noted that New York City politics might benefit from application of the American electoral code used in Nicaragua. At polling places the supervisors required each voter to dip two fingers in indelible Mercurochrome. Even President Díaz was photographed complying with the requirement in order to convince wary peasants, who had been told by the Sandinistas that the chemical substance in the bowl was poisonous, to participate.[20]

Yet the conduct of the campaign and the American presence virtually dictated a Liberal victory. The Nicaraguan Liberals, like the Cuban Liberals of 1905, probably deserved to win, but they took no chances. They cleverly spread among McCoy's supervisors stories about Conservative strong-arm tactics in previous elections and even circulated the credible story that the United States favored their cause. General Moncada, the Liberal candidate, ostentatiously traveled with General McCoy on one of his preelection inspections.[21]

The voting went off without much trouble, though one marine officer in charge in Jinotega, where Sandino had threatened to disrupt the election, obtained secret permission to alter the rules to fit the situation. And despite the use of Mercurochrome there was multiple voting. When it was over, Moncada won a stupendous victory. Thus was fulfilled Stimson's pledge at Tipitapa. A few weeks later Admiral Sellers implored Sandino to accept the result and surrender. Leaflets pledging amnesty were dropped from marine planes flying over Sandinista country. Sandino himself sent his old chief an accommodating letter urging their alliance against the Yankee invaders.[22]

Moncada, however, had already made his bargain.

16. The Last Banana War

On a gorgeous Sunday in January 1928—what Leonard Wood would have called the "best sort of Cuban day"—President Calvin Coolidge and former Secretary of State Charles Evans Hughes sailed into Havana harbor. The president had arrived to open the Sixth Pan-American Conference. His illustrious associate had been chosen to head the American delegation in its defense of an anticipated assault on U.S. policy in the hemisphere. At the dock they were greeted by Cuban president Gerardo Machado, a former Santa Clara cattle thief and Cuban Electric tycoon who three years previously had embarked on a businesslike presidency. His most signal achievement as president had been to convince the United States that a Cuban executive could rule firmly and above all protect American interests. Flanked by 200,000 cheering Habaneros along the Malecón, the two presidents, looking like two small-town businessmen headed for a convention, rode triumphantly to the executive palace. The following day Coolidge reminded his Latin American audience: "The rights of each nation carry with them corresponding obligations, defined by laws which we recognize as binding upon all of us."[1]

Ever since James Gillespie Blaine had inaugurated the Pan-American Conference of 1889 in Washington, the American delegation, backed by the awesome power of the United States in hemispheric affairs, had virtually controlled the agenda of these conferences, always managing to keep politically controversial issues like the Roosevelt Corollary from the sharp debates of the plenary sessions. In the period from 1911, when Taft and Knox were espousing dollar diplomacy as the salvation for tropical governments and backing up the policy with gunboat diplomacy, until 1922, the American empire in the Caribbean had reached its zenith. In that decade the conference had not met. But in 1923, when the Fifth Inter-American Conference opened in Chile, the Latin American delegates, inspired by Argentina's aggressive influence in shaping an anti-American coalition in hemispheric affairs, had grown increasingly restive under American domination. Now, as American marines in Nicaragua were hotly pursuing Sandino, Latin American delegations were arriving in Cuba virtually united in their animosity toward America's latest Caribbean foray on behalf of order and protection of American citizens and their property. Intervention—as a concept and as a practice—was on trial.

This challenge to American policy had not been unexpected. Hughes himself had subtly divorced the Roosevelt Corollary, the political bulwark for American interventionist practices, from the Monroe Doctrine in a bracing 1923 centenary address on the subject. At Havana the Latin Americans expected a vigorous defense of TR's famous pronouncement about America's obligation to police the turbulent Caribbean. The local press defiantly published Sandinista manifestos alongside editorials on the conference agenda.

Hughes adopted a strategy of accommodation. In a major address before the Cuban Chamber of Commerce, he lauded the principle of territorial integrity of states. Later, when the Mexican delegate proposed a resolution concerning hemispheric wars—including, presumably, the Nicaraguan conflict—Hughes happily supported it. He deftly helped to defeat an Argentine proposal calling for an absolute ban on intervention, and the Argentine delegate stalked out. In the concluding plenary session, the debate over intervention was renewed, this time punctuated by fervent denunciations of American policy even from the representatives of the captive Dominican Republic and occupied Haiti.

Hughes was stunningly effective in rebuttal. The Monroe Doctrine safeguarded the hemisphere, he told them, and intervention was sometimes the only recourse of a "civilized" state:

What are we to do when government breaks down and American citizens are in danger of their lives? Are we to stand by and see them killed [Some in the audience stated later he had said "butchered in the jungle."] because . . . a government can no longer afford reasonable protection? . . . Now it is the principle of international law that in such a case a government is fully justified in taking action—I would call it interposition of a temporary character—for the purpose of protecting the lives and property of its nationals.

They knew he was talking about Nicaragua. They did not like what he said—given the circumstance of the case he was obviously defending—but they liked the forceful way he had said it, and he sat down amid thunderous applause. In his finely honed legal distinctions, intervention was not aggression.[2]

Within a year, however, the policy Hughes so courageously defended at Havana was disintegrating.

The sometimes subtle shifts in Latin American policy were most noticeably apparent in the altering views held by Henry Stimson, Coolidge's special emissary to Nicaragua in 1927 and, two years later, Kellogg's suc-

206

The Last Banana War

cessor as secretary of state. Stimson was an old-style imperialist cut in the Roosevelt mold. Our duty in the Caribbean, he believed, was to protect American citizens and their property from marauders or revolutionaries when legitimate governments proved unable or unwilling to do so—as Roosevelt said, to prevent harm from those who had "fallen into the revolutionary habit." Such a policy involved the ever-present vigilance of American naval power in the Caribbean and, when necessary, the landing of troops—in other words, limited intervention, which might have to be used recurringly but was something quite different from what the Wilsonians had done in their virtual annexation of Haiti and the Dominican Republic. A corollary to the Rooseveltian maxim of a duty to police the Caribbean was the benign tutelage implicit in TR's laborious efforts to reform Central American politics, a scheme sketched in the 1907 treaties and reconsecrated in the treaties of 1923.

Returning to Washington after concluding the Tipitapa peace, Stimson declared that the central problem plaguing Nicaragua (and all Central America) could be solved by a free election. Supervised by American troops, such an election would in his view assure the choosing of a truly popular leader who in turn would rule with a nonpartisan constabulary to maintain order. An honest ballot removed the primary cause for revolution, and an efficient national guard—unlike the warlord armies of Central America's turbulent past—would effectively deal with banditry and the periodic revolutionary commotions that had historically plagued foreign residents, prompting the navy to dispatch troops ashore to restore order or protect American property.

Taking over the State Department only a few months after the apparently successful marine supervision of the 1928 Nicaraguan elections, Stimson confidently planned for gradual withdrawal of American troops and the training of a constabulary. In early 1929 the United States had almost 5,000 troops in the republic, most of them in the Sandino chase, but in the months following Stimson's assumption of duties at State their number fell dramatically, to 2,500 by July and 1,800 at year's end. At midyear Sandino slipped out of the country and surfaced in Mexico, reinforcing Stimson's early optimistic belief that the struggle against the rebel who had defied his Tipitapa peace settlement was verging on victory.

Stimson's approach to the Nicaraguan dilemma varied from the previous pattern of American policy in the Caribbean. This was more than the limited intervention of landing marines at seacoast towns or prescribing general guidelines for political behavior: The United States had not only landed troops on the foreign-dominated eastern Nicaraguan coast but had dispatched them into the interior. And it had supervised an election with American military personnel. But the Nicaraguan intervention of 1926–27 was patently not of the scope of the Wilsonian takeover of Hispaniola, where American officers had actually administered the government, either directly, as in the Dominican Republic, or through clients, as in Haiti.

There was disadvantage in the first approach because brief interventions severely limited what one could hope to accomplish in the way of lasting reform. But full-scale occupations of the Dominican or Veracruz type wrought equally objectionable results because the mundane functions carried out by the interventionists usually produced not gratitude for enlightened governance but unremitting hatred of the intended beneficiaries. In Nicaragua, as Stimson planned, American policy could avoid the pitfalls of both approaches by adopting the middle course. We would write the electoral laws, supervise the election, train a nonpolitical guard, and leave—all the while permitting the Nicaraguans to govern. In the course of four years he would discover that the middle approach posed unexpected disadvantages, too.[3]

Nineteen twenty-nine brought unanticipated shifts of influence to the civilian managers of empire who had so often in the past lost initiative to their military counterparts. In Haiti, almost forgotten after the 1922 Senate inquiry, serious rioting erupted after a student protest at the agricultural college had spread to public workers in the capital. In Les Cayes a squad of nervous marines fired into an unruly crowd, killing twelve. The American high commissioner, John Russell, tried to restore the shaken prestige of client-president Louis Borno, but the disturbances underscored the widespread unpopularity of the American military presence. The following year a special investigating commission headed by Cameron Forbes, former governor of the Philippines, arrived in Port-au-Prince. Forbes and his associates ignored Russell's restrictions on their activities and mingled freely with Haitians, soliciting their attitudes about the occupation. When Forbes returned he gloomily reported that the American intervention had accomplished much but was not working well anymore.

And in Nicaragua, where the American military held sway over United States policy because of Sandino's defiance of Stimson's peace and Washington's commitment to preserve order, there were tentative reassertions of civilian and a corresponding diminution of military influence. Dana Gardner Munro, a thoughtful scholar of Central American history who had joined the State Department just after World War I, became chief of the Latin American division. In 1922, following the Senate inquiry into the Haitian and Dominican occupations, he had dissuaded Secretary of State Hughes from naming Smedley Butler as Haitian high commissioner. Munro had just completed a term in Managua as legation secretary, and he resisted efforts by the navy in 1929 to "indoctrinate" him on the volatile issue of allowing army officers to "get in" on Nicaraguan operations.

Gen. Sandino and staff en route to Mexico: Rubén Ardilla Gómez (Venezuela), José
Paredes (Mexico), Sandino, Augustín F. Martí (El Salvador), Gregorio Gilbert (Haiti).
National Archives

President
Adolfo Díaz,
January 1929.
National Archives

Ever since the McCoy commission had arrived to oversee the drawing up of a new Nicaraguan electoral code and report on marine activities, the navy and marines resisted intrusion by their rival service. Though the army was never to play a crucial role in Nicaraguan matters—except of course for McCoy's vital work on the electoral code—the presence of army officers, however few, aroused navy and marine resentment. As Admiral Sellers wrote complainingly to the chief of naval operations: "I am very decidely of the opinion that the best results will not be obtained by mixing the army with the navy and marine corps in matters like the present operations."[4]

In early 1930 a former aide to Leonard Wood in Cuba, Matthew Hanna, who had worked with Alexis Frye in revamping the island's educational system, became American minister. The staff of the legation feared at first that Hanna's previous experience would add a severe military tone to the conduct of American policy, but the former army officer, wrote an enthusiastic young chargé d'affaires, Willard Beaulac, was a "diplomat to the core." A few weeks later General Feland, who had tried repeatedly to circumvent the legation in his effort to become Moncada's de facto minister of war, left the country on a new assignment. The marine brigade's new commander, Brig. Gen. Dion Williams, proved less resistant to the legation's revived role in Nicaraguan affairs. Hanna even arranged a reconciliation between Moncada and Chamorro at a legation party, a gala affair of champagne and good cheer at which a nervous Moncada, flanked by submachine-gun-bearing guards, greeted his old adversary.[5]

The military stalemate of 1929 also prompted critics of the intervention to step up their demands for withdrawal of the remaining marine force, allowing the Nicaraguan guard to take over the tedious work of policing the countryside and, under the professional supervision of American officers, the pursuit of Sandino's dwindling army.

Training an effective constabulary, however, was no less frustrating in Nicaragua than it had proved to be in the Dominican Republic or Haiti. For one thing, the republic's political tradition of deeply nurtured factional antagonisms militated against the creation of a truly nonpartisan military. Historically Nicaragua's armies had been the servants of their leaders and often a means for a politically ambitious Liberal or Conservative to gain the presidency or, as in the case of General Mena in 1912, to frustrate or even overthrow an incumbent executive. General Moncada, compelled to surrender his own army after the Tipitapa peace, began putting together another one shortly after his election in late 1928. In his determination to control the reorganized guard he surreptitiously undermined the Tipitapa accords, arguing that Stimson's rules for the constabulary were nullified by his election. Momentarily, Moncada found an unexpected ally in General Feland, who was also resentful of the guard's independent spirit.

Frustrated by American opposition to his tinkering with the national guard, Moncada organized a force of *voluntarios,* staffed by marine officers, who set out for the North in the bandit chase in February 1929. One column, composed of one hundred "volunteers" and forty marines commanded by a Mexican adventurer named Juan Escamilla, left Managua by truck for Estelí and from there hiked to Ocotal. There the expedition learned that another group, which included Lt. Herman Hanneken, still a legend in the corps for his daring assassination of Charlemagne Péralte in 1919, held as prisoner Sandino's chief of staff, Manuel María Girón. After his capture Girón had agreed to help locate Sandino's camp. Under orders Hanneken turned Girón (and another prisoner, a lowly peasant who was caring for one of Sandino's mules) over to Escamilla's volunteers. They were quickly court-martialed and shot, Girón cursing his executioners and dying "with a sneer on his face." Hanneken was a veteran of jungle war and understood its "no-quarter" tradition, but he remained deeply troubled for years about Escamilla's *voluntario* justice. After a spring campaign in the North, during which Escamilla's conduct came under increasing attack by Conservative critics, Moncada reluctantly disbanded the volunteers.[6]

By official American expectations the Guardia nacional operated more as a police agency than a strictly military organization, though it was set up along traditional military lines. There was, moreover, no urgency in Nicaragua, as had clearly existed in the Dominican Republic, to make the guard an instrument for awakening nationalistic pride or breaking down class barriers. But in Sandino country in the North its political role, despite the American insistence of nonpartisanship, was evident. Julian Smith, who commanded six hundred guardsmen headquartered at Jinotega in 1931, declared to his men that their first mission was the "suppression of banditry"; the second, policing the towns and enforcing civil law. He had the power to invoke martial law, arrest bandits or anyone suspected of helping the Sandinistas, impress civilians as guides, commandeer food or animals from property owners, and destroy dwellings that might afford sanctuary to bandits. Yet such severe measures were tempered with additional directives on the need to secure the cooperation, if not the friendly support, of local people. It was presumed that ordinary citizens who helped the Sandinistas were motivated by fear. The guard could not guarantee against bandit reprisal but should spare "no effort . . . to demonstrate the advantages of law and order and to secure their cooperation."[7]

Though the Nicaraguan guard was not a great social experiment, it was in some respects the most competent national police force the banana warriors assembled in their Caribbean interventions. Dominicans remained hostile or intensely political; Haitians had a reputation for indifference; Nicaraguans were born Liberals or Conservatives and doggedly retained family loyalties. But such loyalties, the Americans discovered, were transferable to the familial character of guard units. Nicaraguan recruits could be trained and led, and they exhibited a devotion to American commanders unequaled by any other Caribbean people. They would often take risks in action just to win a coveted "wound chevron."

But the Nicaraguan guardsmen, intensely proud, were extraordinarily sensitive to even casual criticism. They demanded fearlessness in their marine leaders and expected them to be attentive to their well-being. On the ten occasions in the Nicaraguan war that guardsmen mutinied, the precipitating incident was usually retaliation for wounded pride. Of all the banana warriors, marines were the least skilled in dealing with the cultural sensibilities of their Caribbean wards. A guard sergeant, denied a pair of new shoes, was bent on killing the American officer responsible for his deprivation and would doubtless have done so had not another Nicaraguan, devoted to his *jefe,* stood guard over the American. Another marine perfunctorily chewed out a Nicaraguan sentry in the most cherished corps verbal abuse, and the guardsman matter-of-factly shot him as he walked away. Yet relationships between officers and men, between weary "gone-tropical" marines and their Nicaraguan charges, could be close. Robert Hogaboom, who relinquished command of a unit made up of green recruits he had personally trained and subsequently led into action in the north, recalled that the Nicaraguans actually wept when he departed.[8]

Among liberal critics of the intervention the image of American occupier was often that of brutish persecutor of elusive Sandinistas. In actuality marines in the bush lived not much better than their rebel adversaries, and not a few of the marines dispatched to Nicaragua remembered their experience as dreary routine occasionally punctuated by a brief engagement with the enemy. In Managua an officer might live in the Campo de Marte, the famous Nicaraguan army barracks, but out in the smaller stations he could expect modest accommodations. Robert Denig, a marine officer serving in the guard, was billeted at Ocotal, a town of about two thousand where Sandino had launched his first major assault against the invaders. Guard headquarters was an adobe brick structure with big rooms but few of the amenities of home. Water had to be hauled from the river by donkeys, and bathing was done in old gas drums fitted with crude shower heads.[9]

Nicaragua was, Robert Hogaboom recalled, like Vietnam in many respects—an unwinnable war because the Sandinistas could slip across the border into Honduras or escape into the northern wilds. "You had to occupy the centers, you had to identify with the people, you had to make it to their advantage to work with you in that if they worked with you they could operate their coffee places, etc." The intervention in Nicaragua had no television reporters supervising operations, but there was considerable publicity about the Sandino chase in the American press, much of it highly critical. (Carleton Beals was often the target of marine criticism many years afterward for his caustic analyses of this war.) But the marine occupiers of Nicaragua clearly believed their conduct in this war was a marked improvement over the American record in the Dominican Republic or Haiti—a curious assessment when one considers that this Caribbean intervention has retained its reputation as the most savage of the banana wars.[10]

In the last banana war, the marines carried out their rule as enforcers of America's imperial policies by accepting the unalterable laws of jungle war. And the fundamental tenet of jungle warfare was adeptness at bush patrol.

The ideal size for a patrol seemed to be about twenty men equipped with Krag-Jorgenson and Springfield '03 rifles, automatic weapons, and only enough food for subsistence in the bush. Submachine guns were essential because the Sandinistas were masters of ambush, and the "tommies" were excellent for spraying fire and scattering the attacker. The Nicaraguan war was different from the bandit operations in Haiti or the Dominican Republic, where pursuit of rebels was conducted more or less as a traditional military operation and the ambusher could not easily escape across the border. The Haitians had fought with laughably outmoded weapons, but the Sandinistas were as well armed as their adversaries and, after Sandino's initial defeats of 1927, became adept at guerrilla war. Marine commanders in the guard had to adapt to rebel tactics. A patrol could travel twenty to thirty miles in a day, moving single file along trails flanked by dense growth, stopping usually at midafternoon to rest. Since pack mules ordinarily moved slower than men, animals were limited to the minimum necessary for carrying blanket rolls, food, and ammunition. "On many occasions," one marine commanding a guard unit recalled, "we lived off the country, even though the picking was pretty sparse." Everything was sacrificed to speed on the trail, to having men in condition to fight. One had to be able to sense if an upcoming turn in the trail or some particularly dense undergrowth offered a good spot for ambush and get off the trail to reconnoiter, to avoid becoming a "creature of habit."[11]

What could not be carried or scavenged was flown in by the air squadron, a heterogeneous mix of twenty planes—O2Us, which were cast-off navy observation craft; Vought Corsairs; weird-looking Fokker and Ford trimotors; and the "grotesque" but dependable Curtiss Falcons. (Allegedly, the last trimotor Ford built for the military went to Nicaragua.) The planes would come in low over a clearing and drop tightly wrapped bundles of bread, beans, rice, coffee, sugar, corned beef, and ham. Other than the grassy clearing hacked out of the bush near the larger towns, marine aviators had few places to land. To pick up messages, the planes were equipped with dangling hooks underneath the fuselage; when the plane swooped down the hook snagged a mail pouch attached to a line tied to two posts about fourteen feet apart.[12]

In Nicaragua the prototype of the banana warrior carrying on in the flamboyant tradition of Smedley Butler was probably Lewis ("Chesty") Puller, a veteran of Haiti with a flair for jungle warfare and a disarming Virginia drawl. Puller arrived in early 1929, just as E.R. Beadle, the guard's commander, was launching an offensive against Sandino. Puller was eager to join the chase, but Beadle assigned him to a desk job, and Puller proved his worth by zealously exposing fraud in guard transactions with unscrupulous Nicaraguan suppliers. In March, when an American marine in Corinto stupidly rode his horse into a mob and was shot with his own pistol, Puller rushed to the port and restored order. Wading into a crowd of angry dock workers, he took a Thompson submachine gun from his suitcase and sprayed cans floating in the harbor. A few days later, with the situation still tense, he called on one of the ringleaders, storming into the Nicaraguan's office and declaring: "You will be held responsible for any further disorder. With your life."[13]

A year later, after a baptism of fire in a typical Sandinista ambush, Puller and M Company began clearing bandits in the area around Jinotega. With William Lee, a sixteen-year veteran of the corps with a natural instinct for guerrilla war, Puller made M Company into the most feared guard unit in the Sandino chase. Under Puller and Lee, M Company developed discipline, marksmanship and, above all, a thorough respect for the rules of bush warfare. Puller never caught Sandino, but his efficiency—and ruthlessness—in commanding M Company justifiably entitled him to the enviable reputation he acquired in the Nicaraguan campaign.

Sandino did not return from Mexico until mid-May 1930, having made his way in disguise across Honduras accompanied by two marine deserters carrying dismantled submachine guns. From June through the rest of the torrid Nicaraguan summer he conducted a campaign in the region north of Jinotega. The Sandinistas and the guard clashed at Mount Saraguazca, where the rebels successfully eluded marine aviators sent to bomb them and the guard column quickly dispatched to hunt them down; at San Juan de Telpaneca on June 28; at Pasmate near the Honduran border on July 10, where another legendary marine, Evans Carlson, defeated a Sandinista unit with guardsmen fanatically eager to rush the enemy.

Puller took part in the summer campaign, but it was at the battle of Malacate on August 19, 1930, that he earned the sobriquet, "Tiger of the Mountains." M Company had already fought skirmishes at Moncotal and Guapinol in late July when Puller and Lee set out after some "horse thieves" headed for the Honduran border. The chase was slowed by the continual rains, which had turned the trails into muddy bogs, but they caught up with the retreating bandits before reaching the border. Told by an old woman that the rebels were led by a young man, Puller attacked their camp, driving the pursued into the surrounding hills and forcing them to abandon their animals and supplies.[14]

The marines and the guard conducted a hard campaign in 1930, yet for all their determination and even ferocity of pursuit they could not wipe out Sandino's army. The rebels' ability to survive in the bush surprised their marine pursuers. They were as well armed, captured weaponry revealed, as the Americans. Reflecting on his Nicaraguan experience many years later, Julian Smith was still incredulous about the Sandinistas' capacity for survival; the only thing we could have cut off, Smith recalled, was probably salt.[15]

Since early 1929 Henry Stimson had followed an undeviating plan to steadily reduce the number of American troops in Nicaragua. The onset of the depression and its severe effect on governmental expenditures made Congress even less disposed to sustain a large marine force there. This plan Stimson had adhered to for two years as secretary; in early February 1931 he met with high-ranking military officers to inform them that all remaining American marines except for a small training contingent would leave Nicaragua by June 1, even as the Marine Corps commandant testified before a House committee that withdrawal meant problems for the still inadequately trained Nicaraguan guard.

Sandino did not make a reciprocating gesture. In the early spring his armies struck in the northeast, a vast region inhabited by Mosquito Indians, long suspicious of central Nicaraguan governments; immigrants of European stock; and the powerful American entrepreneurs who operated the gold mines, banana plantations, and lumbering companies along the coast. These enterprises had fallen on hard times; some, such as the Vaccaro brothers' Standard Fruit Company and Braggman's Bluff Lumber Company, had sharply reduced their activities, throwing hundreds out of work. Sandino believed that the combination of harsh economic conditions and long-standing grievances against the foreigner would rally more followers to his cause.[16]

Sandino's assault forces under Abraham Rivera and Pedro Blandón (a ruthless rebel leader who ordered the decapitation of a German Moravian missionary accused of being an American spy) were well on their way to Cabo Gracias a Dios and Puerto Cabezas when, on March 31, Managua was devastated by an earthquake. The shock destroyed most of the city, wrecking even the solidly built American legation as Willard Beaulac watched horrified from the legation porch. Samuel Jack, a marine aviator on duty in Nicaragua, was coming in for a landing when the quake occurred: "The whole town just exploded into dust." After the tremors stopped, a fire started, which could be contained only by blasting and creating a firebreak. More than 1,400 Nicaraguans (and four Americans) perished. Though most of the government buildings were leveled, many offices were unoccupied because Nicaragua's high-ranking officials, including the president, had joined other Managuans who had left town in celebration of Holy Week. Anastasio Somoza, then deputy minister of foreign affairs, remained, directing the recovery with energy and authority—in much the same way as another future Caribbean dictator, Rafael Trujillo, had earned praise for his tireless labors to restore order in Santo Domingo during the hurricane that struck the capital of the Dominican Republic in 1930.[17]

Eastern Nicaragua did not feel the shock, and Sandino declared that the quake was God's sign that he was on the rebels' side. Blandón, his lieutenant, struck Logtown, a Braggman's Bluff Lumber Company town about seventy miles by rail from Puerto Cabezas, on April 11. The rebels looted the commissary, fired several buildings (intentionally sparing the workers' quarters), and waylaid a small unit dispatched to protect the town. A larger marine force aided by air patrols from Puerto Cabezas finally subdued the rebels, killing Blandón. But the other Sandinistas closed in on Puerto Cabezas and would have taken the town (just as their comrades to the north were seizing Cabo Gracias a Dios without firing a shot) had not marine reinforcements from the *Asheville* promptly landed. On April 15, as rebels looted Cabo Gracias a Dios, a marine aerial attack dropped fourteen bombs on the town, causing little damage (most of the bombs dropped were "duds," Samuel Jack recalled) but driving the Sandinistas back into the interior.[18]

The March–April 1931 raids on the coast frightened foreign residents, who now clamored for increased protection from the navy squadron patrolling the western Caribbean and stepped-up patrols into the interior. Earlier in the Sandino campaign, Merritt Edson had led a sixty-man patrol up the Coco River from Cabo Gracias a Dios; harassed by bugs, rain, snakes, and the predictable hazards of tropical campaigns, the expedition lost almost all its supplies in the river when its craft capsized. The only engagement with the enemy had lasted three hours and had been indecisive. But the Coco River foray had occurred earlier in the Nicaraguan intervention, when American determination to protect the foreign residents of the coast and crush Sandino's movement had been much stronger. Now, in depression-wracked Washington of 1931, the twin effects of seemingly irreversible decline in revenue and the frustrations of a prolonged pursuit of an elusive enemy prompted Stimson's abrupt announcement of April 18 that the United States could no longer provide "general protection of Americans" in Nicaragua.

Experienced hands in the State Department argued that Stimson's declaration represented no reversal of policy, and a few remembered old Josephus Daniels's chastisement of American investors who had gone to Mexico to "get rich" and expected the American military to protect their property even if it meant war. But even some ordinarily friendly editorialists were taken aback by what seemed to be the abandonment of helpless American citizens in another country to the ravages of war, a change in policy that contrasted sharply with Hughes's ringing defense of "interposition" at Havana and the implicit reassurances of Stimson's 1927 book on American policy in Nicaragua.[19]

Simply interpreted, the statement of April 18 said that American residents in Nicaragua must look to Managua for protection, just as ordinary Nicaraguans did. But the declaration had deeper implications. It signaled that the American military would no longer police the tropics. It meant the United States would find a less forceful way of ensuring political stability in the Caribbean. It marked the end of the banana wars.

Epilogue

In October 1931 Smedley Butler, embittered over his failure to become the commandant of the Marine Corps, watched solemnly as his two-star flag was slowly lowered in a special ceremony at Quantico, Virginia. Two months earlier, Old Gimlet Eye had enraged his fellow Quaker Herbert Hoover by giving what was described as an antiwar speech to a convention of legionnaires:

I spent 33 years . . . being a high-class muscle man for Big Business, for Wall Street and the bankers. In short, I was a racketeer for capitalism. . . . I helped purify Nicaragua for the international banking house of Brown Brothers in 1909–1912. I helped make Mexico and especially Tampico safe for American oil interests in 1916. I brought light to the Dominican Republic for American sugar interests in 1916. I helped make Haiti and Cuba a decent place for the National City [Bank] boys to collect revenue in. I helped in the rape of half a dozen Central American republics for the benefit of Wall Street.[1]

A professional soldier since the turn of the century, Butler was now, at age fifty, caught up in the national debate over the collapse of capitalism and its pernicious influence in American expansion in the Caribbean. He harangued the Bonus Marchers in Washington and in early 1933 told a Brooklyn audience: "I wouldn't want to see a boy of mine march out with a Wall Street collar about his neck." Commenting on his speech, *The Nation,* a persistent critic of American imperialism, declared: "General Butler . . . serves his country better in peace than in war."[2]

Butler's last hurrah was taking place just as the American military expedition to Nicaragua was winding up its affairs. By 1932 the marines had made the guard into an organization that seemed capable of dealing with the Sandinista threat. When Sandinistas tried to embarrass the celebration of the opening of the León-El Sauce railroad by staging an attack on the train a few days before the ceremony, Chesty Puller and his guardsmen drove them off in Wild West Fashion.

Stimson had declared that once the elections of 1932 were held the marines would leave Nicaragua. His original plan for complete withdrawal had been frustrated by the Sandinista attacks in the East in March-April 1931. Once again, as in 1928, American troops and guardsmen supervised a Nicaraguan presidential election; when it was over, Juan B. Sacasa, in whose name the constitutionalist flag of revolt had been raised in 1926, had been chosen president of the republic.

Nicaragua's peace and stability could be preserved, the Americans believed, by the national guard. And the key to understanding the role of the guard in the years following lay in the political ambitions of the man Sacasa named to head it, Anastasio Somoza García. Somoza was, it has often been argued, the personal choice of General Matthews, the retiring American commander of the Guardia nacional. The Americans had been favorably impressed with Somoza since 1927 when the English-speaking Nicaraguan had served as Stimson's interpreter. Somoza had played a vital role in the often delicate political relations between Moncada and the marines. Julian Smith recalled: Somoza "was our liason with Moncada. . . . [He] was always loyal to us. I never knew Somoza to put anything over on the Americans." And when the retiring Americans put into motion their plan for staffing the Guardia command—which anticipated a *nonpartisan* guard but called for appointment on a *bipartisan* basis—Moncada, the outgoing president, had an opportunity to name his protégé Somoza as Guardia commander. The incoming executive, Juan Sacasa, reluctantly approved the choice.[3]

Clearly, Somoza recognized the changing character of American policy in Central America, that direct military intervention was going out of fashion and that in the future the United States would throw its support to strong-willed leaders who could keep the peace and protect American interests. Graves Erskine, a marine officer who became a friend to Somoza, early recognized the Nicaraguan's ambition. Somoza told him: "Erskine, you Americans are a bunch of damn fools. . . . You've got 5,000 Marines down here and you are just not getting ahead, you'll never get Sandino." When Erskine casually inquired how Somoza might succeed, Somoza replied: "It would be very simple. I would declare an armistice, I would invite Sandino in, and we'd have some drinks, a good dinner, and when he went out one of my men would shoot him."[4]

When the marines pulled out, Sandino called off his war, entered Managua amidst cheering Nicaraguans, and publicly embraced Sacasa on the steps of the presidential palace, declaring, "Now we are brothers." The rebels were granted amnesty, and Sandino himself was permitted a personal army of one hundred men. He retired to an agricultural collective but soon grew weary of the sedentary life. Fearful that Somoza was conspiring against Sacasa, Sandino reentered politics. In February 1934 he returned to Managua to talk with the president and the national guard director about the disarmament of the last of his rebel followers. Already Somoza and his fellow officers had begun conspiring; the director of the guard held discussions with the American minister, Arthur Bliss Lane, and came away confident of American moral support, if not direct commitment, in Sandino's removal. Sandino was arrested after leaving a dinner party with the president, taken to a Managua airstrip, and shot—just as Somoza had told Erskine.[5]

Years later, one of the marines who chased Sandino concluded: "He was a patriot who was a nationalist . . . determined to destroy the feudal clerical system which then obtained in Nicaragua. . . . He was a pretty hot number—the Establishment was afraid of him."[6] His murderers were Nicaraguan, not American, but they had been armed and trained by the United States marines, and for years Latin Americans remained convinced that the United States had played a direct role in his death.

But the final act of the banana wars was not the elimination of Augusto Sandino. Haiti, not Nicaragua, had been the test of American empire in the Caribbean, and it was in Haiti that the tradition of military interventions aimed at restoring political order and uplifting backward peoples came to an end.

Ever since the visit of Cameron Forbes and his associates in 1930 the American military in Haiti had been defensive about its long rule. A Haitian activist, Jolibois Fils, continually denounced the occupation, organized street demonstrations, and generally annoyed the American rulers. Once he began a tirade against the occupation in the presence of Haitian gendarmes, and a marine officer, Oliver P. Smith, ordered him to stop, saying, "There's the door." Leaving, Jolibois Fils was defiant: "You say to me, 'There's the door,' and I say to you there's the sea, and that's where we are going to drive you—into the sea."[7] They were not driven into the sea, but after the Forbes report the marine command in Haiti seemed demoralized. The State Department stepped up its program of Haitianization, symbolized among other things by the recruitment of Haitian officers for the Garde.

In 1934 President Franklin Roosevelt arrived in Cap Haïtien aboard the *Houston*. In 1918 the physically fit and dapper assistant secretary of the navy had visited Haiti on an official inspection. Now he was returning to pledge the restoration of Haitian sovereignty in a public gesture that many Haitians still fondly recall. He moved awkwardly down a special ramp onto a barge that carried him to shore, the Haitian onlookers, among them President Sténio Vincent, staring disbelievingly at the labored movements of the president of the United States. Roosevelt and Vincent rode in an auto to the Haitian Club, and there Roosevelt told his audience in his best Harvard French that the marines would soon be leaving. His suit was already soaked from the torrid Haitian heat.[8]

In the last weeks some of the higher-ranking officers, anticipating an incident between departing marines and jeering Haitians, seriously considered leaving the night before the announced departure day. But the chief of staff of the brigade, Alfred Noble, opposed it: "We should go out," he told his fellow officers, "with the band playing and flag flying. We should march down [to the dock], and if they want to throw stones they can throw them. We are not going to sneak out of the country after 20 years!" When the brigade left on August 1, the Haitian Garde staged an appropriate military ceremony, and the marines marched out of Haiti under the gaze of curious but properly behaved Haitians. The retiring Garde commander, Louis McC. Little, dutifully received the military honors of retirement, the ceremony spoiled only by the failure of the Haitians in the fort to fire the guns at the right time.[9]

The departing marines left most of their weapons "on consignment" with the Haitian Garde. Little, a devoted horseman, gave his favorite mount, Blackie, to a Haitian equestrienne. One of his staff officers went to say farewell to George Leger, in whose home the American had once lived. "You will be glad to see us go," the marine said. "Yes," said Leger. "I will be absolutely honest. We know you have helped us in many ways and we appreciate that. But after all, this is our country and we would rather run it ourselves."[10]

The year before, during the tumultuous weeks following the overthrow of the Cuban dictator Gerardo Machado, when idealistic young revolutionaries frightened American diplomats with their socialist rhetoric, Roosevelt surrounded the island with warships. Cubans feared the return of American troops. But instead of pacifying the Cubans with bluejackets and marines, the president relied on his special emissary, Sumner Welles, who skillfully maneuvered among the factious Cubans until he found a former clerk-stenographer in the Cuban army, Fulgencio Batista, who had meteorically risen to higher command after the Sergeants' Revolt and whose peasant cunning taught him that the Americans were desperately searching for a government that would "respect life and private property." Batista became the first surrogate of America's refashioned Caribbean empire, the prototype for a generation of Caribbean strongmen whose line would expire in 1979 with Anastasio Somoza Debayle in the ashes of the Nicaraguan civil war. Yet it was a diplomat, not a soldier, who discovered Batista and shrewdly estimated his worth to American interests in Cuba.

The passing of the banana wars had a curious impact on the putatively typical banana warrior, Smedley Butler, who launched his retirement from the Marine Corps with condemnations of capitalism and spent his last years warning his countrymen against war. But his fellow marines, whose first assignments had been "down there in the tropics," rose in the ranks during the global conflict of the next decade, remembering the banana wars mostly for the instructive lessons in bush warfare and secondarily for the changes they had wrought in Caribbean societies.[11] As they began retiring in the 1950s and 1960s, most recalled their early service in the Caribbean with almost nostalgic fondness. Their recollection of the political and cultural impact of these military interventions in the first third of the twentieth century waned until, inevitably, it became little more than diverse anecdotes about Caribbean personalities and politicians and the obstacles posed by fighting in the bush.[12]

Given the bureaucratic rivalries, not just between the State Department and the military but also among the Navy, Army, and Marine Corps, it was inevitable that the civilians and soldiers developed sometimes differing perspectives on America's tropical empire. Within the Latin American division at State there emerged a coterie of Caribbean specialists who articulated the broad views of Caribbean policy: protection of the Panama Canal, promotion of grand schemes for the financial rehabilitation of individual countries (as in the Dominican and Nicaraguan cases), and the championing of the long-term benefits of peaceful settlement of disputes between small countries and honest elections within them. But the State Department lacked a colonial office to carry out its mission, and until the 1920s, when Sumner Welles and Dana Gardner Munro acquired considerable influence, its agents in the Caribbean were mostly political appointees who generally lacked experience in Caribbean affairs and rarely acquired either the knowledge or the intuitive skills of the colonial emissary.

Thus it was the military the American government ultimately depended on to carry out its policies, though it, too, lacked nineteenth-century colonial experience. So, in ruling America's empire in the tropics, the military often looked to its own traditions and experience: the navy to its historic role as policeman of the sea lanes, protector of foreign lives and property in coastal towns, and uniformed diplomats in remote places; the army to its Indian campaigns in the West and its pacification and governance of the Philippines and Cuba; and the marines to their acquired reputation as fearsome pursuers of bandits, rebels, and "troublemakers," and as tough hombres.

And it was the American soldier, sailor, and marine who ultimately symbolized American rule in the tropics and, in turn, whose words and deeds became the measure by which Caribbean peoples still judge that rule.

Among the countries occupied by American troops during these thirty-six years, the assessment of American empire is uniformly critical, predictably so in socialist Cuba, where Marxist historians have rewritten history to portray the two military occupations of the early twentieth century as examples of capitalist exploitation. But even in harshly ruled Haiti, where social and political conditions are not much changed from the days when Butler and Waller ran the country, the official version of the long American occupation holds that it was a disgraceful era in Haitian life. The dispatch of twenty thousand crack troops to Santo Domingo in 1965 by Lyndon Johnson to prevent a putative communist takeover revived charges that the American government was reverting to a course of military intervention in the Caribbean.

America's great imperial era has passed, but its record is still controversial, and the lessons of that age instructive for our times, when political and social unrest in the Caribbean is growing and diplomatic efforts to quell it are giving way to arguments for direct military solutions. Such a course in modern times would have consequences far more damaging for the United States in the Caribbean than the prosecution of the banana wars. Caribbean countries are not united in military alliance, but they remember their experiences of a half century or more ago and are firmly opposed to the kind of "gunboat diplomacy" and military intervention the banana wars brought.

Of those empires in the Caribbean after the war with Spain, America's has the severest reputation, and the reasons go deeper than the fact that the British, French, and Dutch built their Caribbean empires centuries ago among isolated territories and islands claimed but not colonized by Spain, while the United States, a latecomer in the pursuit of empire, moved in on former Spanish colonies or nominally sovereign states vulnerable to outside pressure. The British left a bloody swath in carving out their empires in Asia and Africa, and the material accomplishments they wrought for their subjects never equaled the American record in the Caribbean. Certainly British racial convictions about the inferiority of the peoples they ruled were no less severe than those held by America's imperial proconsuls. Yet the British reputation as colonial ruler, now that the empire is gone, remains fairly high, even among the empire's former subjects.

America's imperial conquerors disdained the words "empire" and "imperialism." Butler's reference to himself as a "muscle man" for "Big Business" was not only hyperbolic but essentially a mischaracterization of his own career. He had certainly been forceful in dealing with the subjects of American rule, as would a policeman enforcing the values not of Wall Street but of Main Street. Not even in Cuba, where American investment rose dramatically after the war with Spain, and certainly not in Haiti, where on the eve of American occupation the United States had a negligible economic stake, did the military presence represent the House of Morgan as much as it reflected widespread beliefs that the Caribbean was a disorderly (and unclean) place that needed shaping up. To be sure, the imperial proconsuls protected foreign, especially American, property, but they did so out of older nineteenth-century convictions about community well-being as something that rested on a twin respect for law and order and the sanctity of private property.

The obligations of governing they tried to instill in Caribbean political leaders—sometimes in a rough fashion—were basically what most Americans of that age expected from their own local government: decent, democratic societies populated by a healthy, educated citizenry governed by "responsible" leaders. In their efforts to inculcate such views they forgot— or never really learned—that in the Hispanic political heritage the "centralist" tradition in which power flows from the top remained a strong influence in Latin American culture long after the Spanish empire died. In centralist political structure, the political leader is not the "neutral" executor of the laws and wishes of the people; he embodies their beliefs, hopes, and fears and expresses them through his actions. Such governmental appurtenances as national armies, which in the American tradition are looked upon as costly but necessary for national defense, are essential parts of the leader's authority and are not, in the American definition, "apolitical."

The United States failed in its imperial experiment in the banana wars era not altogether because its empire, as have most of the world's empires, rested ultimately on a willingness to use military force to achieve its goals. In fact, the American military reluctantly took up its imperial tropical tasks, and with some exceptions the banana warriors, despite their racial prejudices, were not brutish fiends who delighted in waging war on darker-skinned peoples. Smedley Butler was a flamboyant Pennsylvania Quaker with a puritanical bent; Joseph Pendleton was a Henry George single-taxer; Leonard Wood was a doctor turned soldier; and Fred Funston was a scrappy midwesterner who never lost his boyish adventurousness.

Yet their labors, despite some grudgingly acknowledged accomplishments in health, education and communication, have been harshly judged. They failed not as conquerors—even in the Sandino chase they accommodated well to the demands of bush warfare—but as rulers of conquered places. Striving to teach by example, they found it necessary to denigrate the cultural values of those whom they had come to save. Determined to implant a sense of community in the tropics, they mistakenly assumed that community values could be inculcated with sanitary measures or vocational education or a reformed military where soldiers from humble social origins learned to identify with "nation" instead of prominent politicians or families. Their presence, even when it meant a peaceful society and material advancement, stripped Caribbean peoples of their dignity and constituted an unspoken American judgment of Caribbean inferiority. Little wonder, then, that the occupied were so "ungrateful" for what Americans considered years of benign tutelage. But, then, Americans do not have in their epigrammatic repertory that old Spanish proverb that Mexicans long ago adopted: "The wine is bitter, but it's our wine."

Notes

Introduction

    1. Leonard Wood, Diary, May 1902, Leonard Wood Papers, Library of Congress Manuscript Division, Washington, D.C. (hereafter LC MS Div.).

    2. Quoted in Herman Hagedorn, *Leonard Wood: A Biography,* 2 vols. (New York: Harper, 1931), 1:392; Capt. Frederick Oliver, "Havana Episode," *United States Naval Institute Proceedings,* 78 (Oct. 1952): 1099-1101. The Dominican Gómez was probably the only rebel general who was not estranged by American callousness and indifference toward the Cuban army. In August 1898 he had written Estrada Palma: "Peace will be made but I have not received the least official attention from the Americans. But I am grateful in my heart most profoundly for the aid of the American people in winning our independence. . . . The Americans and I . . . are strangers in this land." Quoted in Enrique Collazo, *Los americanos en Cuba,* 2 vols. (Havana: C. Martínez y Cía., 1905), 2:180-81.

1. Leonard Wood and the White Man's Burden

    1. Graham Cosmas, *An Army for Empire: The United States Army in the Spanish-American War* (Columbia: University of Missouri Press, 1971), pp. 308–9; Edmund Morris, *The Rise of Theodore Roosevelt* (New York: Coward, McCann, 1979), p. 626.

    2. Gerald Linderman, *The Mirror of War: American Society and the Spanish-American War* (Ann Arbor: University of Michigan Press, 1974), pp. 137-45.

    3. Charles Post, *The Little War of Private Post* (Boston: Little, Brown, 1970), pp. 260-61.

    4. Russell Alger, *The Spanish-American War* (New York: Harper and Bros., 1901), p. 426.

    5. Hugh Thomas, *Cuba: The Pursuit of Freedom* (New York: Harper and Row, 1971), pp. 417–35.

    6. Quoted in J.H. Hitchman, *Leonard Wood and Cuban Independence, 1898-1902* (The Hague: Martinus Nijhoff, 1971), p. 6.

    7. Military Government of Cuba, *Civil Report of Major-General John R. Brooke, 1899* (Washington, D.C., 1900), pp. 6-7; idem, *Report of Brigadier-General William Ludlow, July 1, 1899, to May 1, 1900* (Washington, D.C., 1900), pp. 6-9

    8. Hitchman, *Leonard Wood,* pp. 17-18; Brooke to Adj. Gen., Feb. 15, 1900, Wood Papers, LC MS Div.

    9. Hagedorn, *Wood,* 1:260-61.

    10. Quoted in ibid., p. 285. See also Military Government of Cuba, *Civil Report of Brigadier-General Leonard Wood, 1902* (Washington, D.C., 1902), p. 4.

    11. Hitchman, *Leonard Wood,* p. 31; Robert Bullard, "Education in Cuba," *Educational Review* 39 (Apr. 1910):31; Military Government of Cuba, *Civil Report of Brigadier General Leonard Wood, 1901,* 15 vols. (Washington, D.C., 1901), 1:21, 48-49; David Healy,

The United States in Cuba, 1898–1902: Generals, Politicians, and the Search for Policy (Madison: University of Wisconsin Press, 1963), pp. 179-88.

12. Root to Wood, Feb. 9, 1901, Elihu Root Papers, box 168, LC MS Div.

13. Wood to Root, Mar. 23, 1901, Root Papers, box 168, LC MS Div. For a more critical interpretation of American involvement in the war and the character of the occupation that followed, see Philip S. Foner, *The Spanish-Cuban-American War and the Birth of American Imperialism, 1895–1902,* 2 vols. (New York: Monthly Review Press, 1972), vol. 2, esp. pp. 339-465.

2. TR and the Use of Force

1. Adm. George Dewey to Sec. Navy, June 25, 1901, General Board Subject Files, no. 171, "Monroe Doctrine," Naval Historical Division, Operational Archives, Navy Yard, Washington, D.C. (hereafter NHD).

2. Holger Herwig, *Politics of Frustration: The United States in German Naval Planning, 1889–1941* (Boston: Little, Brown, 1976), pp. 101-9.

3. Sec. Navy to Comdr., North Atl. Sta., Oct. 4, 1902, and Comdr., U.S.S. *Marietta,* Dec. 24, 1902, Jan. 24, 1903, Department of the Navy Area Files, 1900–11, Record Group (hereafter RG) 45, National Archives (hereafter NA). See also Henry Pringle, *Theodore Roosevelt: A Biography* (New York: Holt, Rinehart, 1931), pp. 198-203, and Dexter Perkins, *A History of the Monroe Doctrine* (Boston:Little, Brown, 1963), pp. 214-27, who dispute Roosevelt's story of 1916; Howard K. Beale, *Theodore Roosevelt and America's Rise to World Power* (Baltimore: Johns Hopkins University Press, 1956), pp. 395-431, and Seward Livermore, "Theodore Roosevelt, the American Navy, and the Venezuelan Crisis of 1902–03," *American Historical Review* 52 (Apr. 1946):452-71, who contend Roosevelt did threaten Germany.

4. Kenneth Hagan, *American Gunboat Diplomacy and the Old Navy, 1877–1889* (Westport, Conn.: Greenwood Press, 1973), pp. 160-61, 164-65, 178-79; Capt. Harry Ellsworth, *One Hundred Eighty Landings of United States Marines, 1800–1934* (Washington, D.C.: USMC History and Museums Division, 1974; orig. pub. 1934), pp. 46-51; David McCullough, *The Path between the Seas: The Creation of the Panama Canal, 1870–1914* (New York: Simon & Schuster, 1977), pp. 178-79.

5. Ellsworth, *One Hundred Eighty Landings,* pp. 52-56; Comdr., U.S.S. *Machias,* to Sec. Navy, Apr. 19, 22, 1902, and Capt. T.C. McLean to Sec. Navy, Sept. 18, 1902, Navy Area Files, 1900–11, RG 45, NA. The truce ending the Thousand-Day War was signed aboard the U.S.S. *Wisconsin,* Nov. 21, 1902. One Liberal guerrilla, Victoriano Lorenzo, an Indian from Penonomé, refused to accept the treaty; he was later tried by a military tribunal and shot. Panamanians have since incorporated Lorenzo into their pantheon of heroes.

6. Sec. Navy to Comdr., North Atl. Sta., Oct. 4, 1902, Navy Area Files, 1900–11, RG 45, NA; Richard Challener, *Admirals, Generals, and American Foreign Policy, 1898–1914* (Princeton, N.J.: Princeton University Press, 1973), pp. 152-55.

7. William McCain, *The United States and the Republic of Panama* (Durham, N.C.: Duke University Press, 1937), pp. 14-17; the quoted phrase is from Dana Gardner Munro, *Intervention and Dollar Diplomacy in the Caribbean, 1900–1921* (Princeton, N.J.: Princeton University Press, 1964), p. 53.

8. Ellsworth, *One Hundred Eighty Landings,* pp. 134-36; Robert Heinl, Jr., *Soldiers of the Sea: The United States Marines Corps* (Annapolis, Md.: Naval Institute Press, 1962), pp. 147-48; Hubbard (U.S.S. *Nashville*) to Sec. Navy, Nov. 5, 6, 1903, Area Files, 1900–11, RG 45, NA.

9. James Vivian (in "The 'Taking' of the Panama Canal Zone: Myth and Reality," *Diplomatic History* 4 [winter 1980]:95-100), examining Roosevelt's March 23, 1911, speech at Berkeley, concludes the president meant to say, "I took a trip to the Isthmus."

10. Coghlan to Sec. Navy, Nov. 17, 23, 1903, Navy Area Files, 1900–11, RG 45, NA; see also Richard W. Turk, "The U.S. Navy and the Taking of Panama," *Military Affairs* 38 (Oct. 1974):92-96.

11. Quoted in Selden Rodman, *Quisqueya: A History of the Dominican Republic* (Seattle: University of Washington Press, 1964), p. 92.

12. Howard Hill, *Roosevelt and the Caribbean* (Chicago: University of Chicago Press, 1927), pp. 148-68; J. Fred Rippy, "The Initiation of the Customs Receivership in the Dominican Republic," *Hispanic American Historical Review* 17 (Nov. 1937):419-57. In December 1900 the General Board informed the secretary of the navy that "So important is the possession of this Island [Hispaniola], or its military control, that if a foreign country should by a sudden surprise obtain a foothold, at or just before the outbreak of war with this country, it might easily cause what would otherwise be a short campaign to grow into a long and extensive war." General Board Subject Files, no. 87, Dec. 10, 1900, NHD.

13. Sumner Welles, *Naboth's Vineyard: The Dominican Republic, 1844–1924*, 2 vols. (New York: Payson and Clark, 1928), 2:606-7; Comdr., U.S.S. *Atlanta*, to Sec. Navy, Mar. 31, Apr. 14, 21, 1903, Navy Area Files, 1900–11, RG 45, NA; Lt. W.A. Crosley, USN, Memo (1903); Comdr., U.S.S. *Detroit*, to Sec. Navy, Jan. 3, 1904, ibid.

14. Ellsworth, *One Hundred Eighty Landings*, pp. 66-68.

15. Roosevelt to J.B. Bishop, Feb. 23, 1904, in J.B. Bishop, *Theodore Roosevelt and His Time Shown in His Own Letters*, 2 vols. (New York: Scribner's, 1919, 1920), 1:431.

16. Dillingham to Sec. Navy, Jan. 17, 1904, Navy Area Files, 1900–11, RG 45, NA; W.F. Powell to John Hay, Feb. 10, 1904, ibid.; Dillingham to CIC, South Atl. Squad., Feb. 11, 1904, ibid.; Lester D. Langley, *The United States and the Caribbean, 1900–1970* (Athens: University of Georgia Press, pp. 1980), 28-29; Hill, *Roosevelt and the Caribbean*, pp. 160–63. As things turned out, the navy lost in the Dominican arrangement to the army, which was given a role in the management of the customhouses.

17. Charles Sigsbee to Sec. Navy, Jan. 23, 25, 28, Feb. 10, 1905, in Office of Naval Intelligence, "Santo Domingo Correspondence," RG 45, NA.

18. Rear Adm. W.C. Wise to Sec. Navy, Feb. 12, 1904; Navy Area Files, 1900–11, RG 45, NA; Rear Adm. R.B. Bradford to Sec. Navy, Oct. 11, 1905, ibid.; *Listín Diario* (Santo Domingo, D.R.), June 4, 1906.

19. Comdr. W.M. Chambers to Comdr. W.H.H. Southerland, Jan. 18, 1906, Navy Area Files, 1900–11, RG 45, NA.

3. The Second Cuban Intervention, 1906

1. Steinhart to Wood, June 10, 1902, Wood Papers, LC MS Div.

2. On Farquhar, see Charles A. Gauld, *The Last Titan: Percival Farquhar, American Entrepreneur in Latin America* (Stanford, Calif.: Stanford University Press, 1964); and for American penetration of the Cuban economy, see the savagely critical Leland Jenks, *Our Cuban Colony: A Study in Sugar* (New York: Vanguard Press, 1928).

3. Challener, *Admirals, Generals, and American Foreign Policy*, pp. 94-98.

4. Enrique Barbarossa, *El proceso de la república* (Havana: Imp. Militar de A. Pérez Sierra, 1911), p. 65.

5. *Diario de la marina*, Oct. 4, 1905, quoted in Thomas, *Cuba*, p. 474.

6. Thomas, *Cuba*, pp. 472-76; Charles Chapman, *A History of the Cuban Republic: A Study in Hispanic American Politics* (New York: Macmillan, 1927), pp. 176-94; Enrique

Collazo, *Cuba intervenida* (Havana: C. Martínez y Cía, 1910), pp. 2-5; Carlos Marquez Sterling, *Historia de Cuba, desde Cristóbal Colón a Fidel Castro* (New York: Las Américas Pub. Co., 1963), pp. 334-35.

7. Jacob Sleeper to Sec. State, Aug. 21, 1906, U.S., Department of State, *Foreign Relations of the United States, 1906,* pt. 1, pp. 454-55.

8. Roosevelt to Sir George Otto Trevelyan, Sept. 9, 1906, Roosevelt Papers, University of Georgia, Athens, Ga. (microfilm), reel 413.

9. Roosevelt to Robert Bacon, Sept. 12, 1906, Roosevelt Papers, reel 413, UG. Roosevelt to Gonzalo de Quesada, Sept. 14, 1906, *Foreign Relations of the United States, 1906,* 1:480-81.

10. Bacon to Roosevelt, Sept. 13, 1906, Navy Area Files, 1900–11, RG 45, NA; Fullam to Sec. Navy, Sept. 14, 1906, ibid.; *La Discusión* (Havana), Sept. 14, 1906; Comdr. J.C. Colwell to Sec. Navy, Oct. 4, 1906, Navy Area Files, 1900–11, RG 45, NA.

Fullam and other naval officers in their "clique," the Marine Corps historian Robert Heinl charged, were determined to abolish the corps. They had a sympathetic supporter in Roosevelt himself, who in 1908 ordered the secretary of the navy to begin reassigning shipboard marines to coastal duty. He told Archie Butt, his private secretary, that the marines should be taken over by the army, "so that no vestige of their organization should be allowed to remain." Heinl, *Soldiers of the Sea,* p. 155. Later research by Graham Cosmas and Jack Shulimson ("Teddy Roosevelt and the Corps' Seagoing Mission," *Heinl Memorial Award Essay, 1982* [Washington: USMC HMD, 1982]), 1-9, indicates that the Marine Corps, ever protective of its interests, misunderstood Fullam's motives. He considered the shipboard marines unnecessary and even a hindrance to ship's discipline. Fullam argued that the marines should be organized into separate assault forces with their own transports. In the end, Congress balked at TR's proposals and sent the shipboard marines back on board navy vessels.

11. Fullam to Sec. Navy, Sept. 15, 1906, William Fullam Papers, LC MS Div.

12. Fullam to Lt. J.V. Klemann, Sept. 16, 1906, Fullam Papers, LC MS Div. On September 18 Fullam did send a contingent to protect the Hormiguero plantation.

13. Taft to Roosevelt, Sept. 21, 1906, William Howard Taft Papers (microfilm), reel 320, University of Georgia, Athens, Ga.

14. Taft to Roosevelt, Sept. 27, 1906, Taft Papers, reel 320, UG.

15. Roosevelt to Taft, Sept. 21, 1906, Roosevelt Papers, reel 413, UG; Allan Reed Millett, *The Politics of Intervention: The Military Occupation of Cuba, 1906–1909* (Columbus, Ohio: Ohio State University Press, 1968), pp. 90-91; Mark Twain, "A Defense of General Funston," *North American Review* 174 (1902):613-24.

16. Roosevelt to Charles E. Eliot, Sept. 13, 1906, quoted in Millett, *Politics of Intervention,* p. 78.

17. Fullam to Lt. J.V. Klemann, Sept. 24, 1906, and Fullam to Comdr. J.F. Newton, U.S.S. *Cleveland,* Sept. 27, 1906, Fullam Papers, LC MS Div.

18. Taft to Estrada, Sept. 24, 1906, Taft Papers, reel 320, UG; Roosevelt to Taft, Sept. 25, 28, 1906, Roosevelt Papers, reel 413, UG.

19. William Inglis, "The Collapse of the Cuban House of Cards," *Harper's Weekly* 50 (Oct. 20, 1906):1505. Reconciliation between the government and the rebels was out of the question. On October 1 a Moderado manifesto announced: "The dignity of the Government does not permit a pact with rebels, considering their principal demand, for to negotiate with them would be tantamount to recognizing their legitimacy." *La Discusión,* Oct. 1, 1906.

4. Cuba Occupied

1. Comdr. Charles Rogers to Asst. Sec. Navy, Aug. 31, 1906, Navy Area Files, 1900–11, RG 45, NA; "La correspondencia," Sept. 6, 1906, ibid.; Chapman, *History of the Cuban*

Republic, pp. 211-23. Enrique José Varona, responding to a Liberal's announcement that "the justice of our cause is fully evident," wrote: "For the modern civilized person, 'right' ceases to be right when it is accompanied by violence." Varona, *Mirando en torno: artículos escritos en 1906* (Havana: Imprenta de Rambla y Bouza, 1910), p. 24. But a Liberal manifesto declared: "We want peace with one condition—that it be a dignified peace for all." *La Discusión,* Sept. 12, 1906.

2. Roosevelt, Sixth Annual Message, Dec. 3, 1906, in Fred Israel, ed., *State of the Union Messages of the Presidents, 1790–1966,* 3 vols. (New York: Chelsea House, 1966), 3:2227.

3. On Magoon, see David Lockmiller, *Magoon in Cuba: A History of the Second Intervention, 1906–1909* (Chapel Hill: University of North Carolina Press, 1938). Hugh Thomas assesses the bitter Cuban characterizations of Magoon in *Cuba,* pp. 482-84.

4. Quoted in Robert Freeman Smith, *The United States and Cuba: Business and Diplomacy, 1917–1960* (New Haven: Bookman Associates, 1960), 25; *El Mundo* (Havana), Oct. 26, 1908.

5. Millett, *Politics of Intervention,* pp. 151-53. On October 11, less than three weeks after Taft's proclamation of a provisional government, the United States had four battleships, four cruisers, and one gunboat in Cuban waters; ashore, it had more than a thousand marines and five thousand army soldiers.

6. Edwin Atkins, *Sixty Years in Cuba* (Cambridge, Mass.: Riverside Press, 1926), pp. 338-39; Taft to Roosevelt, Oct. 6, 1906, Taft Papers, reel 320, UG; *Army and Navy Journal,* Oct. 13, 1906, p. 178, Oct. 27, 1906, pp. 178, 224; *New York Times,* Oct. 4, 1906, 1:3; Upshur to father, Oct. 14, 1906, William Upshur Papers, Southern Historical Collection, University of North Carolina, Chapel Hill, N.C.; George Kase, "Autobiography," USMC History and Museums Division, Navy Yard, Washington, D.C. (hereafter USMC HMD.)

7. Enrique José Varona, in *El Figaro* (Havana), Dec. 2, 1906; Robert Bullard, Diary, Dec. 28, 1906, Bullard Papers, LC MS Div.

8. Provisional Government of Cuba, *Annual Report of Charles Magoon, 1907* (Washington, D.C., 1908), pp. 94-95; Col. O.J. Sweet, 28th Inf., Matanzas, to Military Sec., Army of Cuban Pacification, Dec. 19, 1906, Department of War, Records of the Provisional Government of Cuba, Confidential Correspondence, box 5; RG 199, NA.

9. Bullard, "Education in Cuba," pp. 378-84; idem, "How Cubans Differ from Us," *North American Review* 186 (Nov. 11, 1907):416-21; Allan R. Millett, *The General: Robert C. Bullard and Officership in the United States Army, 1881–1925* (Westport, Conn.:Greenwood Press, 1975), pp. 196-97.

10. Bullard, Notebook, no. 13, Bullard Papers, LC MS Div.

11. On the creation of the Cuban army, see Millett, *Politics of Intervention,* pp. 222-39; and Louis A. Pérez, Jr., *Army Politics in Cuba, 1898–1958* (Pittsburgh: University of Pittsburgh Press, 1976), pp. 21-28.

12. Quoted in Thomas, *Cuba,* p. 504.

13. Bullard, Diary, Feb. 13, 1909, quoted in Millett, *Politics of Intervention,* p. 254.

14. Maj. Frederick Foltz, Memo, Aug. 2, 1907, Records of the Provisional Government of Cuba, Confidential Correspondence, no. 159, RG 199, NA; John W. Furlong, Chief of Military Information Division, Memo, Sept. 17, 1907, ibid.; no. 17, ibid.

15. Thomas, *Cuba,* pp. 514-24; John Gray, "Recollections of the 1912 Cuban Expedition," *Marine Corps Gazette,* May 1932, p. 47; Alexander A. Vandegrift, USMC Oral History Transcript, pp. 95-98, USMC HMD; Theo Brooks to Comdr. G. W. Kline, U.S. Naval Sta. Guantánamo, May 30, 1912, Records of the USMC, no. 161, RG 127, NA. Karmany was ordered to protect American life and property "in accordance with the principle of international law, . . . not for the purpose of intervening in Cuba." Karmany kept a diary of this campaign. Lincoln Karmany Papers, USMC HMD.

16. For a favorable assessment of the Cuban occupation, see Lockmiller, *Magoon in*

Cuba. Cuban historians are uniformly critical: Herminio Portell Vilá, *Historia de Cuba en sus relaciones con los Estados Unidos y España,* 4 vols. (Havana: J. Montero, 1938–41); Rafael Martínez Ortiz, *Cuba: los primeros años de independencia,* 2 vols. (Paris: Le Livre Libre, 1921); and Barbarossa, *El proceso de la república,* condemn the occupation with varying intensity.

5. The Nicaraguan Menace

1. This section is based mostly on Lester D. Langley, *Struggle for the American Mediterranean: United States-European Rivalry in the Gulf-Caribbean, 1776–1904* (Athens: University of Georgia Press, 1976).
2. Charles L. Stansifer, "José Santos Zelaya: A New Look at Nicaragua's Liberal Dictator," *Revista/Review interamericana* 7 (fall 1977):468-85; Raúl Oseguedo, *Operación centroamérica* (Mexico City: Editorial América Nueva, 1957), pp. 38-45; the quotation is from Frederick Palmer, *Central America and Its Problems* (New York: Moffat, Yard, & Co., 1913), p. 178.
3. Munro, *Intervention and Dollar Diplomacy,* pp. 146-51.
4. W.F. Fullam to Gen. Juan J. Estrada, Mar. 29, 1907, Fullam Papers, LC MS Div.; *New York Times,* Apr. 4, 1907.
5. Fullam to Sec. Navy, Feb. 27, Apr. 2, May 8, May 31, 1907; Sec. Navy to Comdr. John Hood, Dec. 1, 1908; Navy Area Files, 1900–11, RG 45, NA.
6. Munro, *Intervention and Dollar Diplomacy,* pp. 151-55; A. Martínez Moreno, *La conferencia de Washington de 1907 y la corte de justicia centroamericana* (San Salvador: Ministro de Relaciones Exteriores, 1957).
7. Hermann B. Deutsch, *The Incredible Yanqui: The Career of Lee Christmas* (London: Longmans, Green and Co., 1931), brilliantly recaptures the adventurer's escapades in Central America.
8. Munro, *Intervention and Dollar Diplomacy,* p. 156.
9. Harold Denny, *Dollars for Bullets: The Story of American Rule in Nicaragua* (New York: The Dial Press, 1929), pp. 71-83.
10. Munro, *Intervention and Dollar Diplomacy,* p. 174; Challener, *Admirals, Generals, and American Foreign Policy,* pp. 72-73.
11. Denny, *Dollars for Bullets,* pp. 74-75.
12. Macario Alvarez Lejarza, *Impressiones y recuerdos de la revolución de 1909 a 1910* (Granada, Nic.: Escuela tip. salesiana, 1941), pp. 302-3, 312-15.
13. For the State Department's outrage over the executions of Cannon and Groce, see U.S. Department of State, *Foreign Relations of the United States, 1909,* pp. 446-51, 455-57.
14. Moffat, Interview with Estrada, July 5, 1909, Navy Area Files, 1900–11, RG 45, NA; Comdr., U.S.S. *Tacoma,* to Sec. Navy, Aug. 29, 1909, ibid.; Comdr., U.S.S. *Des Moines,* to Comdr., shore party, Dec. 21, 1909, ibid.
15. Butler to mother, June 4, 1910, Smedley Butler Papers, Newtown Square, Pa.; Rear Adm. W.W. Kimball, Report, May 25, 1910, "Nicaragua Correspondence," RG 45, NA.
16. Butler to parents, Mar. 1, 1910, Butler Papers; Newtown Square, Pa.; Lowell Thomas, *Old Gimlet Eye: The Adventures of Smedley D. Butler* (New York: Farrar and Rinehart, 1933), pp. 126-29; Butler to father, July 14, 31, 1910, Butler Papers, Newtown Square, Pa.

6. The Nicaraguan War, 1910–1912

1. Pedro Joaquín Chamorro Cardenal, *Orígenes de la intervención americana en Nicaragua* (Managua: Editorial La Prensa, 1951), p. 13.

2. U.S. Congress, Senate, Committee on Foreign Relations, *Nicaraguan Affairs: Hearings,* 62d Cong., 2d sess., 1912.

3. Vicente Sáenz, *Norteamericanización de Centro América* (San José: Talleres de la Opinión, 1925), pp. 45-70; for Zelaya's account of his relations with the United States, see José Santos Zelaya, *La revolución de Nicaragua y los Estados Unidos* (Madrid: Imprenta de B. Rodríguez, 1910).

4. The classic study is Scott Nearing and Joseph Freeman, *Dollar Diplomacy: A Study in American Imperialism* (New York: B.W. Huebsch, 1925), esp. pp. 151-68.

5. Warren Kneer, *Great Britain and the Caribbean, 1901-1913* (East Lansing: Michigan State University Press, 1975), pp. 134-63.

6. A copy of the Dawson agreements may be found in U.S. Department of State, *The United States and Nicaragua: A Survey of Relations from 1909 to 1932* (Washington, D.C., 1932).

7. Munro, *Intervention and Dollar Diplomacy,* pp. 186-204.

8. Langley, *The United States and the Caribbean,* pp. 54-55; Knox, Toledo speech, n.d. [1912], Philander C. Knox Papers, LC MS Div. (italics mine).

9. W.B. Hale, "With the Knox Mission in Central America," *World's Work* 24 (1912): 179-93; Weitzel to Knox, Mar. 5, 1912, Knox Papers, LC MS Div.

10. U.S. Department of State, *Foreign Relations of the United States, 1912,* pp. 1026-33; F.M. Huntington Wilson to Taft, Aug. 30, 1912, Taft Papers, ser. 6, case 456 (reel 395), UG.

11. Munro, *Intervention and Dollar Diplomacy,* pp. 204-6; Huntington Wilson to Taft, Aug. 27, 1912, Taft Papers, case 456 (reel 395), UG.

12. Ellsworth, *One Hundred Eighty Landings,* pp. 126-27; Acting Sec. State to Taft, Aug. 28, 1912; Southerland to Sec. Navy, Aug. 29, 30, 1912; Taft Papers, reel 395, UG.

13. Thomas, *Old Gimlet Eye,* 140-48; Capt. Nelson D. Vulte, Diary, "Expedition to Nicaragua, 1912," USMC Geographical Files, USMC HMD; Alexander A. Vandegrift, *Once a Marine: The Memoirs of General A. A. Vandegrift* (New York: Norton, 1964), pp. 38-41.

14. Thomas, *Old Gimlet Eye,* pp. 151-62.

15. Butler to Mena, Sept. 21, 1912, copy in Mary G. Grist Papers, USMC HMD; Butler to Zeledón, Sept. 15, 1912; Butler Papers, Newtown Square, Pa.; Zeledón to Butler, Sept. 15, 1912; ibid.

American forces in Nicaragua, in fact, had begun enforcing such a strict neutrality that Díaz's commanders were complaining about American officers who prevented them from crushing the rebellion. Southerland had initially forbidden both rebel and government troops from using the railroad, a decision that, in his mind, the situation warranted. But Taft pointed out that the United States had recognized the Díaz government and that the American purpose in Nicaragua was to protect American lives and property so Díaz's troops would be free to deal with the rebellion. Only the rebels should have been denied use of the railroad, Taft believed. Taft to Knox, Sept. 23, 1912, Taft Papers, reel 395, UG.

16. Weitzel to Southerland, copy, Sept. 25, 1912, in Joseph H. Pendleton Papers, USMC HMD.

17. Zeledón to Pendleton, Oct. 3, 1912, copy in Grist Papers, USMC HMD; Thomas, *Old Gimlet Eye,* pp. 166-67; Joseph H. Pendleton, "Battle of Coyotepe Hill," *Army and Navy Register,* May 16, 1941; Undated account of battle, Butler Papers, Newtown Square, Pa. However, the ladies of Granada honored Butler for his services in a public ceremony in the town plaza. Pinned with a medal, Old Gimlet Eye responded: "Woman is at all times a factor in progress because she roused up the courage of the soldiers to go to war." *El Diario nicaragüense* (Managua), Nov. 11, 1912.

18. Ladies of Granada to Southerland, Oct. 11, 1912, *Foreign Relations of the United States, 1912,* p. 1063.

19. Quoted in Denny, *Dollars for Bullets*, p. 122.
With 6,500 rifles and 200,000 rounds of ammunition, Southerland noted later, Mena could have "put up a fight." The admiral believed the arms should have been locked up at Campo Marte or, preferably, thrown in the sea. Southerland to Butler, Nov. 11, 1912, Butler Papers, Newtown Square, Pa.
20. Pendleton to Southerland, Nov. 12, 1912, Office of Naval Records and Library (RG 45), WA-7, Nicaragua, First Prov. Reg., USMC, box 642, NA; *Foreign Relations of the United States, 1912,* pp. 1130-31.
21. Langley, *The United States and the Caribbean,* pp. 57-58.

7. The Mexican Crisis

1. On these themes, see Daniel Cosío Villegas, *The United States versus Porfirio Díaz,* trans. Nettie Lee Benson (Lincoln: University of Nebraska Press, 1963); Albert Tischendorf, *Great Britain and Mexico in the Era of Porfirio Díaz* (Durham, N.C.: Duke University Press, 1961); Daniel Cosío Villegas, ed., *Historia moderna de Mexico,* vol. 7, pt. 2, *El Porfiriato: la vida económica* (Mexico City: Editorial Hermes, 1965); David Pletcher, *Rails, Mines, and Progress: Seven American Promoters in Mexico, 1867–1911* (Ithaca, N.Y.: Cornell University Press, 1958).
2. The literature on Díaz's downfall and Madero's triumph, in English and Spanish, is voluminous; see, especially, the following: Stanley Ross, *Francisco I. Madero: Apostle of Democracy* (New York: Columbia University Press, 1955); Charles C. Cumberland, *Mexican Revolution: Genesis under Madero* (Austin: University of Texas Press, 1952); and Berta Ulloa, "Las relaciones mexicanos-norteamericanos, 1910–1911," *Historia mexicana* 15 (July–Sept. 1965):25-46.
3. Quoted in Kenneth Grieb, *The United States and Huerta* (Lincoln: University of Nebraska Press, 1969), pp. 4-5; see also Henry Lane Wilson, *Diplomatic Episodes in Mexico, Belgium, and Chile* (Garden City, N.Y.: Doubleday, 1927); idem, "Errors with Reference to Mexico," *Annals of the American Academy of Political and Social Science* 14 (July 1914):148-61; and P. Edward Haley, *Revolution and Intervention: The Diplomacy of Taft and Wilson in Mexico, 1910–1917* (Cambridge, Mass.: MIT Press, 1970), pp. 53-73.
4. The literature of Henry Lane Wilson's role in this tragic episode is critical of the ambassador and occasionally bitterly condemnatory. I have followed Grieb, *United States and Huerta,* pp. 13-29, but see also Manuel Marquez Sterling, *Los últimas días del Presidente Madero: mi gestión política en México* (Havana: Impr. El Siglo xx, 1917), by the Cuban minister to Mexico; Jorge Vera Estañol, *La revolución mexicana: origenes y resultados* (Mexico City: Editorial Porrúa, 1957); Ramón Prida, *De la dictadura a la anarquía* (El Paso, Texas: Imprente de 'El Paso del Norte,' 1914); and Michael Meyer, *Huerta: A Political Portrait* (Lincoln: University of Nebraska Press, 1972).
5. George Dewey to Sec. Navy, Oct. 22, 1912, General Board Studies, no. 97-12, NHD; Challener, *Admirals, Generals, and American Foreign Policy,* pp. 351-52.
6. By refusing to protect Madero and Pino Suárez, Hale wrote, Henry Lane Wilson "might be said to have delivered the men to their deaths." Quoted in Larry Hill, *Emissaries to a Revolution: Woodrow Wilson's Executive Agents in Mexico* (Baton Rouge, La.: LSU Press, 1973), p. 37.
7. U.S., Congress, *Senate Documents,* no. 226, 63d Cong., 1st sess., 1913.
8. Berta Ulloa, *La revolución intervenida: relaciones diplomáticas entre México y los Estados Unidos, 1910–1914* (Mexico City: El Colegio de Mexico, 1971), pp. 136-56.
9. Fletcher to Badger, Feb. 24, 1913, Navy Area Files, 1911–27, RG 45, NA; Lt. John Rogers to Senior Off., U.S.S. *Nebraska,* Apr. 1, 1913, ibid.; "The Mexican Situation,"

in Fletcher to Badger, Jun. 23, 1913, ibid.; Fletcher to Comm. Off., Tampico, Nov. 30, 1913, ibid.

10. *Foreign Relations of the United States, 1914,* pp. 443, 444. On Bryan's role in the Mexican crisis, see Paolo Coletta, *William Jennings Bryan* (Lincoln: University of Nebraska Press, 1969), vol. 2, *Progressive Politician and Moral Statesman, 1909–1915,* pp. 147-81.

11. Edith O'Shaughnessy, *A Diplomat's Wife in Mexico* (New York: Harper, 1916), pp. 120-31.

12. Arthur Link et al., eds., *The Papers of Woodrow Wilson,* 35 vols. thus far (Princeton: Princeton University Press, 1966–   ), 29:291-92.

13. Quoted in Arthur Link, *Woodrow Wilson: Revolution, War, and Peace* (Arlington Heights, Ill.: AHM Publishers, 1979), p. 10.

14. Quoted in Harley Notter, *The Origins of the Foreign Policy of Woodrow Wilson* (Baltimore: Johns Hopkins University Press, 1937), p. 274.

15. Lind to Bryan, Mar. 29, 1914, in Link et al., *Papers of Woodrow Wilson,* 29:382-83; Lind to O'Shaughnessy, Apr. 5, 1914, ibid., p. 405.

16. Jack London, "Our Adventurers in Tampico," *Collier's* 53 (June 27, 1914):5-6.

17. Robert Quirk, *An Affair of Honor: Woodrow Wilson and the Occupation of Veracruz* (Lexington: University Press of Kentucky, 1961), pp. 8-9.

18. Ibid., pp. 21-33; Wilson to Bryan, Apr. 10, 1914, in Link et al., *Papers of Woodrow Wilson,* 29:421; Fletcher to Sec. Navy, Apr. 11, 1914, *Foreign Relations of the United States, 1914,* pp. 451-52.

19. Mexico, Ministerio de Relaciones Exteriores, "Cuestiones diplomáticas de la Revolución: desocupación de Veracruz, año de 1914," III/252 (73-72), 1914/1, Archivo de Ministerio de Relaciones Exteriores (hereafter ARE), Mexico City; O'Shaughnessy to Bryan, Apr. 12, 1914, Woodrow Wilson Papers, LC MS Div. (microfilm), reel 56.

20. Quoted in Link et al., *Papers of Woodrow Wilson,* 29:441.

21. Edward House, Diary, Apr. 15, 1914, quoted in ibid., p. 448.

22. Delano to mother, Apr. 18, 1914, Frederick Delano Papers, U.S. Army Research Collection (hereafter ARC) Military History Institute, Carlisle Barracks, Pa.

Kendrick Clements, in a thoughtful assessment of Wilson's Mexican policy, 1913–15, argues that the president was steering a middle course in dealing with Huerta. Wilson, Clements contends, wanted to break the grip of foreign economic power in Mexico and prevent American domination as well, allowing the Mexican people to choose their form of government without outside interference. Clements, "Woodrow Wilson's Mexican Policy, 1913–15," *Diplomatic History* 4 (spring 1980):113-36.

8. Veracruz

1. Comdr. C. L. Hussey, "Estimate of Situation and Campaign Orders for Naval Forces Seizing Vera Cruz, Mexico," Feb. 1913, Department of the Navy, Office of Naval Records and Library, WE-5, box 662, RG 45, NA.

2. Quirk, *Affair of Honor,* pp. 46-47.

3. Ibid., pp. 55-56; O'Shaughnessy, *Diplomat's Wife in Mexico,* p. 269.

4. Michael Meyer, "The Arms of the *Ypiranga,*" *Hispanic American Historical Review* 50 (Aug. 1970):543-56.

5. Quirk, *Affair of Honor,* pp. 64-71; General Board of the Navy, *Proceedings,* 1914, 6:69-70, NHD.

6. Wilson, Address to Congress, Apr. 20, 1914, in Link et al., *Papers of Woodrow Wilson,* 29:471-74; Quirk, *Affair of Honor,* pp. 72-77. The vote was 323 to 29 in the House and 72 to 13 in the Senate.

7. Jack Sweetman, *The Landing at Veracruz, 1914* (Annapolis, Md.: Naval Institute Press, 1968), pp. 52-53.

8. William Canada, "Occupation of the Port of Veracruz, April 21st and 22nd, 1914," Department of the Navy, Office of Naval Records and Library, WE-5, Vera Cruz, box 661, RG 45, NA.

9. *Washington Post*, Jan. 13, 1929. The occasion for the story was the recent death of Admiral Fletcher. Maass's report stated, "My forces and the people showed great enthusiasm in repelling the American insult." Ministerio de Relaciones Exteriores, "Cuestiones diplomáticas," ARE.

10. Sweetman, *Landing at Veracruz*, pp. 69-77; *Mexican Herald* (Veracruz), Apr. 26, 1914; Reports, Office of Naval Records and Library, WE-5, box 662, RG 45, NA; Leonardo Pasquel, *Manuel y José Azueta: padre e hijo—héroes en la gesta de 1914* (Mexico City: Editorial Citlaltep, 1967), p. 55.

11. Paul Foster, Oral History Project, pp. 78-81, NHD; Div. Marine Off. to Fleet Marine Off., U.S.S. *Utah*, May 4, 1914, George C. Reid Papers, USMC HMD.

12. Frank Friday Fletcher, "Report of Capture of Veracruz," May 13, 1914, Department of the Navy, Office of Naval Records and Library, WE-5, box 662, RG 45, NA; Quirk, *Affair of Honor*, p. 97.

13. Quirk, *Affair of Honor*, pp. 98-99, 150-51; Meyer, "Arms of the *Ypiranga*," pp. 543-56; see also Thomas Baecker, "The Arms of the *Ypiranga*: The German Side," *The Americas* 39 (July 1973):1-11.

14. Sweetman, *Landing at Veracruz*, pp. 103-10; Glenn Howell Log, 1:62-63, Howell Diaries, NHD; Louis Botte, "Los americanos en Mexico," in Pasquel, *Manuel y José Azueta*, pp. 143-45; Jack London, "With Funston's Men," *Collier's* 52 (May 23, 1914):9-10.

15. Foster, Oral History, pp. 82-86, NHD; Kase, "Autobiography," USMC HMD; Frederick M. Wise, *A Marine Tells It to You* (New York: J. H. Sears, 1929), pp. 122-25. Foster discovered a cache of Veracruz maps in the palace and had them distributed to unit commanders who, inexplicably, had never been given maps of the city they were occupying.

16. Quoted in Sweetman, *Landing at Veracruz*, p. 81; *Mexican Herald*, Apr. 25, 1914.

17. Arthur Ruhl, "The Unfinished Drama," *Collier's* 53 (May 14, 1914):9-10.

18. Sweetman, *Landing at Veracruz*, p. 123; Howell Log, 1:92, Howell Diaries, NHD.

9. The Rulers of Veracruz

1. *Diario de Centro-América* (Guatemala City), Apr. 24, 1914; *La Epoca* (Mexico City), Apr. 22, 1914; *Japan Times*, Apr. 26, 1914.

2. *Caras y caretas* (Buenos Aires), Apr. 25, 1914; League of Latin American Solidarity, Manifesto, Apr. 26, 1914, in Ministerio de Relaciones Exteriores, "Cuestiones diplomáticas," ARE.

3. Samuel G. Blythe, "Mexico: The Record of a Conversation with President Wilson," *Saturday Evening Post* 186 (May 23, 1914):1-2, 71.

4. *Mexican Herald*, Apr. 27, 1914; Quirk, *Affair of Honor*, pp. 111-13.

5. *Mexican Herald*, Apr. 26, 1914; Fletcher to Sec. Navy, Apr. 24, 1914, Wilson Papers, reel 57; Canada to Sec. State, Apr. 25, 1914, ibid.; Lionel Carden to Mexican Minister of Foreign Relations, Apr. 25, 1914, in Ministerio de Relaciones Exteriores, "Cuestiones diplomáticas," ARE; Herman Brendel to Frederick Bromberg, Apr. 24, May 5, 1914, Bromberg Papers, Southern Historical Collection, University of North Carolina, Chapel Hill, N.C.

6. John Lejeune, *Reminiscences of a Marine* (Philadelphia: Dorrance, 1930), pp. 212-15; *Collier's* 53 (May 30, 1914):9.

234 Notes to Pages 103–109

7. Boaz Long, Latin American Division, Department of State, Memorandum, Apr. 22, 1914, Wilson Papers, reel 274. In 1914, the city was written "Vera Cruz"; in modern times, "Veracruz," which is the spelling I have used.

8. Canada to Sec. State, Apr. 23, 1914, Wilson Papers, reel 56; Fletcher to Sec. Navy, Apr. 23, 1914, ibid., reel 57. Fletcher's staff debated whether or not to raise the flag. In the end, with Lejeune arguing forcefully that the "American flag should fly over American troops no matter where they might be located," the colors were hoisted on April 27 on the spot where Winfield Scott had unfurled his flag in 1847. Lejeune, *Reminiscences of a Marine,* p. 211.

9. Foster, Oral History, pp. 88-93, NHD. When Foster read the story he could not decide whether to "shoot [Davis] or buy him a drink." Another correspondent, Fred Boalt, charged a naval ensign with shooting prisoners under the *ley de fuga* (the law of flight). A naval board of inquiry exonerated the ensign. U.S. Congress, Senate, *Report of Board of Inquiry . . . [of Vera Cruz Occupation],* 63d Cong., 2d sess., 1914, pp. 5-6.

10. *Army and Navy Journal,* Apr. 13, 1901, p. 791; *Dictionary of American Biography* (New York: Scribner's, 1931), 7:74; Thomas Crouch, *A Yankee Guerrillero: Frederick Funston and the Cuban Insurrection, 1896–1897* (Memphis: Memphis State University Press, 1975), pp. 23-55.

11. Daniels to Wilson, Apr. 25, 1914, Wilson Papers, reel 57; Funston to Adj. Gen., May 3, 7, 1914, Records of the Adjutant General of the Army, box 7480, RG 94, NA. Funston's superiors in Washington did send Douglas MacArthur behind Mexican lines to look for locomotives and reconnoiter the territory. MacArthur got into several shooting incidents with Huertistas. See William Manchester, *American Caesar: Douglas MacArthur, 1880–1914* (Boston: Little, Brown, 1978), pp. 73-75.

12. Delano to mother, Apr. 29, 1914, Delano Papers, ARC.

13. H. O. Stickney to Funston, May 4, 1914, Department of War, Records of the Military Government of Vera Cruz, Confidential Correspondence, no. 13, RG 141, Washington National Record Center, Suitland, Md. (hereafter WNRC).

14. Provost Marshal to Military Governor, May 14, 1914, Department of War, Records of the Military Government of Vera Cruz, Confidential Correspondence, no. 13, RG 141, WNRC.

15. Ronald Sharp to brother, Aug. 7, 1914, USMC Geographic Files, "Veracruz," USMC HMD.

16. Jack London, "Lawgivers," *Collier's* 53 (June 20, 1914):15-16. London's colleague, Richard Harding Davis, wearied of Veracruz occupation life and went to Mexico City in a futile effort to get an interview with Huerta. Richard H. Davis, *Adventures and Letters* (New York: Scribner's, 1917), pp. 357, 366-69.

17. Quirk, *Affair of Honor,* pp. 140-42. The Americans set up a claims commission to hear Mexican complaints on property losses. Alexander Vandegrift's marine unit tore down a deserted shack and used the materials to build revetments. An irate Mexican accused him of destroying his home, worth five thousand pesos. Vandegrift, Oral History, pp. 151-52, USMC HMD.

18. Department of War, Records of the Military Government, Confidential Correspondence, nos. 34, 136, RG 141, WNRC.

19. Quirk, *Affair of Honor,* pp. 136-38.

20. Lindsay Garrison to Wilson, May 6, 1914, Wilson Papers, reel 204; *Mexican Herald,* May 8, 1914; Department of War, Records of the Military Government, Confidential Correspondence, nos. 6, 19, 34, RG 141, WNRC; Martín Luís Guzmán, *The Eagle and the Serpent,* trans. Harriet de Onis (Mexico City: Editorial Anahuac, 1941; Gloucester, Mass., 1969), p. 189.

21. Quirk, *Affair of Honor,* pp. 116-17; Francisco Urquidi to Carranza, Apr. 23, 1914, in Ministerio de Relaciones Exteriores, "Cuestiones diplomáticas," ARE.

22.   Min. Rels. Exts. to Mexican Embassy in Washington, Apr. 27, 1914, in Ministerio de Relaciones Exteriores, "Cuestiones diplomáticas," ARE; Grieb, *United States and Huerta,* pp. 159-77; Lind Memo, Apr. 30, 1914, Mexican Mission Papers of John Lind, Minnesota Historical Society (microfilm).

23.   Grieb, *United States and Huerta,* pp. 178-92. Huerta left Mexico for London, then settled on a Long Island estate. Intrigued by the volatile changes of Mexican revolutionary politics, he moved to a small town just north of El Paso, but alert American officials threw him in jail for conspiring to violate U.S. neutrality. Despondent, he resumed his heavy drinking and, in January 1916, died of cirrhosis of the liver.

24.   W. P. Arbuthnot, "With the U.S. Marines in Mexico," *Marine Corps Gazette* 1 (Sept. 1916):246-52; Funston to Adj. Gen., May 25, July 11, 1914, Records of the Adjutant General of the Army, box 7480, RG 94, NA; Delano to mother, July 18, 1914, Delano Papers, ARC.

25.   Quirk, *Affair of Honor,* pp. 158-59.

26.   Funston to Adj. Gen., Aug. 25, Oct. 12, 1914, Records of the Adjutant General of the Army, box 7480, RG 94, NA. On September 9, the General Board of the Navy, alluding to the outbreak of war in Europe, recommended withdrawing all battleships from West Indian and Mexican waters. General Board Studies, 1900–1912, no. 420-1, NHD.

27.   Carranza to Conv. at Aguascaliente, Oct. 19, 1914, in Ministerio de Relaciones Exteriores, "Cuestiones diplomaticás," ARE.

28.   Quirk, *Affair of Honor,* pp. 167-68.

29.   *Foreign Relations of the United States, 1914,* p. 625; G. A. Velásquez to Fabela, Nov. 18, 1914, in Ministerio de Relaciones Exteriores, "Cuestiones diplomáticas," ARE.

30.   *El Pueblo,* Nov. 24, 1914; Quirk, *Affair of Honor,* pp. 170-71.

31.   William B. Caperton, Comdr., Cruiser Squad., to W. S. Benson, June 13, 1915, William Banks Caperton Papers, LC MS Div.

Army-marine rivalry in Veracruz, as might be expected, occasionally disturbed the harmony Funston sought among his military associates. Lejeune's and Waller's records in the occupation offered little out of the ordinary. Butler, however, enhanced his reputation by winning a Medal of Honor and drawing up a war plan for the invasion of the interior. He expertly accomplished the latter by donning civilian clothes and posing as an entomologist on a research trip. Later he wrote an account of his experience in a novel entitled *Walter Garvin in Mexico.*

32.   Mexican accounts, predictably, generally view American occupation of Veracruz as a part of a second Mexican-American war. See, among others, the contemporaneous views of the socialist revolutionary Ricardo Flores Magón, published originally in *Regeneración* and reprinted in *1914: La intervención americana en México* (Mexico City: Ediciones Antorcha, 1981).

10. Civilizing the Tropics

1.   General Board of the Navy, no. 87, Dec. 10, 1900, General Board Files, NHD.

2.   Hill, *Roosevelt and the Caribbean,* p. 167; Roosevelt to Carnegie, Apr. 5, 1907, in Elting E. Morison, ed., *Letters of Theodore Roosevelt,* 8 vols. (Cambridge, Mass.: Harvard University Press, 1951–54), 5:640.

3.   Welles, *Naboth's Vineyard,* 2:640-41.

4.   Ibid., pp. 677-78.

5.   Henry Stimson Diaries, 1:44, Yale University, (microfilm).

6.   Walter and Marie V. Scholes, *The Foreign Policies of the Taft Administration* (Columbia: University of Missouri Press, 1970), pp. 41-44; Special Commission to Knox, Dec. 12,

1912, Department of State, Internal Affairs of the Dominican Republic, 1910–29, RG 59, NA (microfilm).

7. Thomas Morris, Diary, pp. 37-38, U.S. Army Research Collection, Military History Institute, Carlisle Barracks, Pa.

8. Walter Anderson, Oral History, pp. 88-90, NHD.

9. Welles, *Naboth's Vineyard,* 2:693-94.

10. Arthur Link, *Wilson: The New Freedom* (Princeton, N.J.: Princeton University Press, 1956), pp. 106-11.

11. Selig Adler, "Bryan and Wilsonian Caribbean Penetration," *Hispanic American Historical Review* 20 (May 1940):198-226; Coletta, *William Jennings Bryan,* vol. 2, *Progressive Politician,* pp. 182-210.

12. *Foreign Relations of the United States, 1914,* pp. 246-51; Max Henríquez Ureña, *Los yanquis en Santo Domingo* (Madrid: M. Aguilar, 1929), pp. 8-11, 56-57, 114-15.

13. Hans Schmidt, *The United States Occupation of Haiti, 1915-1934* (New Brunswick, N.J.: Rutgers University Press, 1971), pp. 42-58.

14. Sherman to Powell, Jan. 11, 1898, Department of State, Instructions, Haiti; Comdr. Henry McCrae to Sec. Navy, Aug. 25, 1902, Navy Area Files, 1900-11, RG 45, NA; Comdr. John Shipley, U.S.S. *Des Moines,* to Sec. Navy, Dec. 19, 1908, ibid.

15. Munro, *Intervention and Dollar Diplomacy,* pp. 326-51; Dantès Bellegarde, *Histoire du peuple haïtien* (Port-au-Prince: n.p., 1953), pp. 218-45.

16. *Le Matin* (Port-au-Prince), Jan. 15, 1915.

17. Lansing to Rear Adm. James Oliver, Jan. 30, 1918, Robert Lansing Papers, LC MS Div.; Lansing, Diary, July 11, 1915, ibid.

18. William Banks Caperton, "Activities of Rear Admiral W. B. Caperton, U.S.N., While in Command of Cruiser Squadron, U.S. Atlantic Fleet," pp. 4-5, Caperton Papers, LC MS Div.

19. Naval War Plans, portfolio I, 5-D, box 3, NHD; Department of the Navy, Office of Naval Records and Library, WA-7, box 631, RG 45, NA; David Healy, *Gunboat Diplomacy in the Wilson Era: The U.S. Navy in Haiti, 1915-1916* (Madison: University of Wisconsin Press, 1976), pp. 37-42.

20. *Le Matin,* July 27-28, 1915; Healy, *Gunboat Diplomacy,* pp. 53-59; R. B. Davis to Sec. State, Jan. 12, 1916, *Foreign Relations of the United States 1916,* p. 316.

21. Dantès Bellegarde, *La résistance haïtienne* (Montreal: Beauchemin, 1937), pp. 34-35; B. Danache, *Le Président Dartiguenave et les américains* (Port-au-Prince: Imprimeur de l'Etat, 1950), pp. 16-17.

22. *Le Matin,* July 31, 1915; John Russell, "A Marine Looks Back on Haiti," pp. 4-6 (manuscript), USMC HMD.

23. Caperton, "Activities," p. 54, Caperton Papers, LC MS Div.

24. Ibid., pp. 65-66; Healy, *Gunboat Diplomacy,* pp. 96-100. After the election Bobo, fearing for his life, took refuge in the British legation. He was later escorted to the dock by a marine guard and embarked on a vessel for Jamaica. Edward Beach, "Admiral Caperton in Haiti," pp. 169-70, Department of the Navy, Office of Naval Records and Library, ZWA-7, box 850, RG 45, NA.

25. Lansing to American Legation, Aug. 10, 1915, Haiti, Internal Affairs 1910-1929, Department of State, RG 59, NA (Microfilm).

26. Caperton, "Activities," pp. 87-8, Caperton Papers, LC MS Div.

27. Josephus Daniels, "The Problem of Haiti," *Saturday Evening Post,* July 12, 1930, p. 34; Adolf Miller, Diary, 1915-16, p. 12, USMC HMD.

11. The Pacification of Hispaniola: 1

1. Faustin Wirkus and Taney Dudley, *White King of La Gonâve* (Garden City, N.Y.: Doubleday, Doran, 1931), p. 17; Healy, *Gunboat Diplomacy,* pp. 26-27.

2. Wilson to Lansing, Aug. 4, 1915, quoted in Robert and Nancy Heinl, *Written in Blood: The Story of the Haitian People, 1492–1971* (Boston: Houghton Mifflin, 1978), p. 406; Caperton to Sec. Navy, Aug. 19, 1915, in U.S. Congress, Senate, Select Committee on Haiti and Santo Domingo, *Inquiry into the Occupation and Administration of Haiti and Santo Domingo: Hearings,* 67th Cong., 1st and 2d sess. 1922, p. 335.

3. Lansing to Wilson, Aug. 13, 1915, in U.S. Department of State, *The Lansing Papers, 1914–1920,* 2 vols. (Washington, D.C., 1939), 2:526-27.

4. *Foreign Relations of the United States, 1915,* pp. 431-33.

5. Quoted in Bellegarde, *La résistance haïtienne,* p. 41.

6. John Craige, *Cannibal Cousins* (New York: Minton, Balch & Co., 1934), pp. 52-56; Heinl and Heinl, *Written in Blood,* pp. 423-25. The U.S. Senate approved the treaty by unanimous vote on February 28, 1916.

Captain Beach's son, Edward L. Beach, himself a former naval officer and author, states that his father did all the negotiating ashore, reporting to Caperton in the evening, and wrote most of the admiral's reports. Edward L. Beach to author, Feb. 7, 1980.

7. Healy, *Gunboat Diplomacy,* pp. 206-27.

8. Quoted in Schmidt, *United States Occupation of Haiti,* pp. 78-79. See also Robert B. Asprey, "Waller," *Marine Corps Gazette 45* (May 1961):36-41, and (June 1961):44-48.

9. Waller to Lejeune, Sept. 8, 26, 1915, John Lejeune Papers, LC MS Div.; Stephen Fuller and Graham Cosmas, "U.S. Marines in Haiti, 1915–1934," pp. 31-32 (page proofs), USMC HMD.

10. Waller to Lejeune, Sept. 21, 1915, Lejeune Papers, LC MS Div.; Caperton to Adm. W. S. Benson, Sept. 24, 1915, Caperton Papers, LC MS Div.; Rameau to Haitian People, Sept. 5, 1915, in Julian Willcox Papers, USMC HMD.

11. Fuller and Cosmas, "U.S. Marines in Haiti," pp. 38-42; Waller to Lejeune, Oct. 2, 6, 7, 13, 19, 26, Nov. 1, 1915, Lejeune Papers, LC MS Div. The account of the Fort Rivière battle is from the diary of a participant, Capt. Chandler Campbell, USMC HMD. See also Thomas, *Old Gimlet Eye,* pp. 201-7; Senate, Select Committee on Haiti and Santo Domingo, *Inquiry,* p. 1772; and Vandegrift, Oral History, pp. 180-85, USMC HMD.

12. Heinl and Heinl, *Written in Blood,* pp. 431-33. Waller testified at the Senate inquiry of 1921–22 that he knew about the revolt but permitted the conspirators to act in order to discover their supporters. The backers, according to Waller, were German merchants. Senate, Select Committee on Haiti and Santo Domingo, *Inquiry,* pp. 616-17.

13. *Foreign Relations of the United States, 1915,* pp. 336-39; Polk to Wilson, Sept. 21, 1915, Dominican Republic, Internal Affairs, 1910–20, 839.51/1834. In 1915 the investigation of Sullivan's activities in the republic, conducted by Sen. James Phelan, resulted in Sullivan's resignation.

14. Russell to Lansing, Apr. 16, May 15, 1916, Dominican Republic, Internal Affairs, 1910–20, 839.00/1802, 1827; Caperton, "Activities," Caperton Papers, LC MS Div.; F. Wise, *A Marine Tells It to You,* pp. 142-43. Pedro del Valle, who commanded marine forces on Guadalcanal and Okinawa, served under Wise in Santo Domingo and was present at these meetings. Del Valle's command of Spanish was invaluable. About Jiménez's reneging on his "deal," del Valle recalled: "So there we were. They [Jiménez and his cabinet] hauled ass and we had an empty flank." The marines were glad Arias pulled out, remembered Julian Smith, because they were apprehensive about fighting in Santo Domingo. Pedro del Valle, Oral History, p. 27, USMC HMD; Julian C. Smith, Oral History, p. 41, ibid.

15. Caperton, "Activities," Caperton Papers, LC MS Div.

238   Notes to Pages 144–152

16. Dominican Republic, Geographical Files, USMC HMD; Caperton to Daniels, May 15, 26, 1916, Dominican Republic, Internal Affairs, 839.00/1827, 1858.
17. Caperton, "Activities," Caperton Papers, LC MS Div.
18. Dominican Republic, Geographical Files, USMC HMD; Luís F. Mejía, *De Lílis a Trujillo: historia contemporánea de la República Dominicana* (Caracas: Editorial Elite, 1944), pp. 128-29.
19. "Santo Domingo," Geographical Files, USMC HMD; "The Capture of Puerto Plata," *Sea Power,* Aug. 1916, pp. 16-17.
20. Wise, *A Marine Tells It to You,* pp. 146-49.
21. Caperton, "Activities"; Caperton Papers, LC MS Div.; Caperton to Sec. Navy, June 20, 1916, Dominican Republic, Internal Affairs, 839.00/1885.
22. Pendleton to officers, June 24, 1916, Pendleton Papers, USMC HMD.
23. Heinl, *Soldiers of the Sea,* p. 183.
24. Lt. Col. Thomas Saxon, "United States Military Government in the Dominican Republic, 1916–1922" (master's thesis, University of Maryland, 1964), pp. 21-23; Stephen Fuller and Graham Cosmas, *Marines in Dominican Republic, 1916–1924* (Washington, D.C.: USMC History and Museums Division, 1974), pp. 18, 20; Lindsley Allen, "Uncle Joe," *Leatherneck* 32 (Jan. 1949):13-15; Wise, *A Marine Tells It to You,* p. 153; Juan Pérez, "To the People," July 5, 1916, copy in Pendleton Papers, USMC HMD.

12. The Pacification of Hispaniola: 2

1. Munro, *Intervention and Dollar Diplomacy,* pp. 307-14.
2. Carlos V. de León, *Casos y cosas de ayer* (Santo Domingo: Imprenta Nuñez, 1972), pp. 17-20; on the wreck of the *Memphis,* under the command of Capt. Edward Beach, see the work by his son, Edward L. Beach, *The Wreck of the Memphis* (New York: Holt, Rinehart, & Winston, 1966).
3. Fuller and Cosmas, *Marines in the Dominican Republic,* p. 24.
4. *Listín Diario,* Aug. 18, 1916; J. H. Stabler, Memo, Oct. 31, 1916, Dominican Republic, Internal Affairs, 1910–29, 839.00/1951a.
Caperton departed Santo Domingo in the summer of 1916 to assume command of the Pacific Fleet; his successor, Adm. Charles Pond, remained until early November when Capt. Harry Knapp became commander of the Cruiser Squadron.
5. Welles, *Naboth's Vineyard,* 2:797; Daniels to Knapp, n.d. [December 1916], Josephus Daniels Papers, box 86, LC MS Div.; Military Government of the Dominican Republic, *Gaceta oficial,* Dec. 9, 1916, in Archivo General de la Nación, Santo Domingo, D.R.; General Board of the Navy, *Hearings, 1918,* 2:568-71, NHD.
6. Military Government, Provost Court Records, Secretary of the Navy, General Correspondence, 16870-47:33, RG 80, NA; Charles J. Miller, "Diplomatic Spurs: Our Experiences in Santo Domingo," *Marine Corps Gazette* 19 (May 1935):24.
7. Fuller and Cosmas, *Marines in the Dominican Republic,* p. 35; Miller, "Diplomatic Spurs," p. 49; Omar Pfeiffer, Oral History, p. 39, USMC HMD.
8. D. M. Randall to Pendleton, July 16, 1916, Pendleton Papers, USMC HMD; Batt. Comdr. to Reg. Comdr., San Pedro de Macorís, June 1, 1917, USMC Records, RG 127, NA; Fuller and Cosmas, *Marines in the Dominican Republic,* p. 32. For a Dominican interpretation of banditry, see F. S. Ducoudray, "Fueron bandidos los guerrilleros anti-yanquis de 1916?" *Ahora,* July 15, 1974, pp. 36-42; and, for a general account, Bruce J. Calder, "Caudillos and Gavilleros versus the United States Marines: Guerilla Insurgency during the Dominican Intervention, 1916–1924," *Hispanic American Historical Review* 58 (Nov. 1978):649-75.
9. Mejía, *De Lílis a Trujillo,* p. 157; Senate, Select Committee on Haiti and Santo Domingo, *Inquiry,* pp. 116-21, 1140-46; Charles Merkel, Personnel File, USMC HMD.

10. Edward Craig, Oral History, pp. 32-44, USMC HMD.

11. Thorpe to Pendleton, Aug. 18, 21, Pendleton Papers, USMC HMD.

12. Dominican Republic, Geographical Files, USMC HMD; J. Kendrick Noble, n.d. [1918–19], Noble Papers, USMC HMD; Christian F. Schilt, Oral History, pp. 20-21, USMC HMD; Lester A. Dessez, Oral History, p. 26, USMC HMD. On marine aviation in the banana wars, see Edward Johnson, *Marine Corps Aviation in the Early Years, 1912–1960,* ed. Graham Cosmas (Washington, D.C.: USMC History and Museums Division, 1976).

13. Fuller and Cosmas, *Marines in the Dominican Republic,* p. 43.

14. Knapp to Sec. Navy, Jan. 13, 1917, Dominican Republic, Internal Affairs, 1910–29, 839.00/1895.

15. Marvin Goldwert, *The Constabulary in the Dominican Republic and Nicaragua: Progeny and Legacy of United States Intervention* (Gainesville: University of Florida Press, 1961), pp. 2-3, 8-9; Pfeiffer, Oral History, pp. 42-43; USMC HMD; Richard Millett and Marvin Soloman, "The Court Martial of Lieutenant Rafael L. Trujillo," *Revista/Review interamericana* 2 (fall 1972):396-404.

16. Beach, "Caperton in Haiti," p. 15; Eli Cole to Knapp, Apr. 8, 1917, Department of the Navy, Office of Naval Records and Library, WA-7, box 633, RG 45, NA.

17. Danache, *Le Président Dartiguenave et les américains,* p. 54; Waller to Butler, July 13, 1916, Butler Papers, USMC HMD.

18. Heinl and Heinl, *Written in Blood,* pp. 436-42; Thomas, *Old Gimlet Eye,* pp. 211-15; Butler to John McIlhenny, June 23, 1917, Butler Papers, USMC HMD.

19. Senate, Select Committee on Haiti and Santo Domingo, *Inquiry,* pp. 530-31, 540-41, 570-71.

20. Wirkus and Dudley, *White King,* p. 52; the judgment is substantiated by Vandegrift, *Once a Marine,* p. 50. See also "The Haitian Gendarmerie," *Marine Corps Gazette* 11 (June 1926):73-81.

21. William Upshur to family, Oct. 3, Dec. 27, 1915; Jan. 12, 24, 1916; Feb. 8, Mar. 29, May 28, 1916; Jan. 17, 1917; Upshur Papers, UNC.

22. Senate, Select Committee on Haiti and Santo Domingo, *Inquiry,* pp. 684-85; Butler to John McIlhenny, Dec. 31, 1917, Butler Papers, USMC HMD.

23. Senate, Select Committee on Haiti and Santo Domingo, *Inquiry,* p. 530.

24. Heinl and Heinl, *Written in Blood,* p. 450; L. Tom Evans, in Senate, Select Committee on Haiti and Santo Domingo, *Inquiry,* p. 163; Ivan Miller, Oral History, p. 31, USMC HMD.

25. Heinl and Heinl, *Written in Blood,* pp. 449-56; for typical comment on the 1919 uprising, see USMC, Haiti Collection, box 23, WNRC; E. A. Ostermann to Brig. Comdr., Aug. 20, 1919, Louis McCarty Little Papers, USMC HMD; John Russell to George Barnett, Oct. 17, 1919, Clayton Vogel Papers, USMC HMD.

26. USMC, Haiti Collection, box 28, WNRC; R. H. Greathouse, "King of the Banana Wars," *Marine Corps Gazette* 44 (June 1960):29-33; Herman Hanneken, Oral History, pp. 31-34, USMC HMD.

27. Gerald C. Thomas, Oral History, pp. 71-75, USMC HMD; Fuller and Cosmas, "Marines in Haiti," pp. 82-83; Burke Davis, *Marine! The Life of Lt. General Lewis B. "Chesty" Puller, USMC* (Boston: Little, Brown, 1962), pp. 22-23, 26-31; John Gray, "Cul-de-Sac," *Marine Corps Gazette* 16 (Feb. 1932):41-44.

28. Senate, Select Committee on Haiti and Santo Domingo, *Inquiry,* p. 437.

29. Ibid., pp. 434-35, 1642-43.

30. Thomas, Oral History, p. 76, USMC HMD. An early assessment is R. B. Coffey, "A Brief History of the Intervention in Haiti," *United States Naval Institute Proceedings* 48 (August 1922):1325-44.

31. Allan Millett, *Semper Fidelis: The History of the United States Marine Corps* (New

York: Macmillan, 1980), p. 211, concludes: "The Marine Corps became a scapegoat for those who either opposed intervention in principle or were disappointed that the occupation had not civilized Hispaniola."

13. Interregnum, 1921–1925

1. Wallace Irwin, "Uncle Sam—Nursemaid," *Collier's* 33 (July 30, 1904):26.

2. On these points, see John Blassingame, "The Press and American Intervention in Haiti and the Dominican Republic," *Caribbean Studies* 9 (July 1969):27-43.

3. McCormick to Frank Polk, Mar. 14, 1916, Dominican Republic, Internal Affairs, 1910–29, 839.51/2039; Langley, *United States and the Caribbean,* pp. 97-102.

4. Wilson to McAdoo, Nov. 20, 1920, William G. McAdoo Papers, box 526, LC MS Div. On Colby's "good neighbor" policy, see Daniel M. Smith, "Bainbridge Colby and the Good Neighbor Policy," *Mississippi Valley Historical Review* 50 (June 1963):56-78.

5. Welles, *Naboth's Vineyard,* 2:818-19; *Foreign Relations of the United States, 1920,* 2:171-73; Snowden to Daniels, Aug. 5, 1920, Daniels Papers, LC MS Div.; *The Nation* 112 (May 4, 1921):663-64; Military Government, Foreign Relations, *Memorias,* no. 154, Archivo General de la Nación, Santo Domingo.

6. *Foreign Relations of the United States, 1920,* 2:155-60; Josephus Daniels, Diary, Jan. 19, 24, 1921, in E. David Cronon, ed., *The Cabinet Diaries of Josephus Daniels, 1913–1921* (Lincoln: University of Nebraska Press, 1963), pp. 589-91.

7. *Listín Diario,* Apr. 6, 1922; *El Siglo,* May 9, 1922; on the withdrawal, see also Kenneth Grieb, "Warren G. Harding and the Dominican Republic: U.S. Withdrawal, 1921–1923," *Journal of Inter-American Studies* 11 (July 1969):425-40.

8. Welles, *Naboth's Vineyard,* 2:845-46; Harry Lee, Quoted in Robert Kilmartin, "Indoctrination in Santo Domingo," *Marine Corps Gazette* 7 (Dec. 1922):386; Fuller and Cosmas, *Marines in the Dominican Republic,* pp. 64-66.

9. Carson Roberts, Oral History, p. 10, USMC HMD; Merwin Silverthorne, Oral History, pp. 157-59, 167-69, USMC HMD: George Good, Jr., Oral History, p. 33, USMC HMD; Dessez, Oral History, p. 27, USMC HMD; Langley, *United States and the Caribbean,* pp. 102-3.

10. Silverthorne, Oral History, pp. 142-52, 161-62, 165, USMC HMD.

11. Fuller and Cosmas, "U.S. Marines in Haiti," p. 97. See also Yvette Gindine, "Images of the American in Haitian Literature during the Occupation, 1915-1934," *Caribbean Studies* 14 (Oct. 1974):37-52. For a highly critical assessment of the agricultural program see Suzy Castor, *La ocupación norteamericana de Haiti y sus consecuencias* (Mexico City: Siglo Veintiún Editores, 1971), pp. 75-94. On Haitian negritude, see the summary in David Nicholls, *From Dessalines to Duvalier: Race, Colour, and National Independence in Haiti* (Cambridge: Cambridge University Press, 1979), pp. 153-64.

12. Walter La Feber, *The Panama Canal: The Crisis in Historical Perspective* (New York: Oxford University Press, 1978), pp. 74-75.

13. Thomas L. Karnes, *The Failure of Union: Central America, 1824–1960* (Chapel Hill: University of North Carolina Press, 1961), pp. 202-10; Kenneth Grieb, "The United States and the Central American Federation," *The Americas* 24 (Oct. 1967):107-24.

14. Thomas Karnes, *Tropical Enterprise: The Standard Fruit and Steamship Company in Latin America* (Baton Rouge, La.: LSU Press, 1978), pp. 70-88.

15. Aro Sanso, *Policarpo Bonilla: algunos apuntes biográficos* (Mexico City: Imprenta Mundial, 1936), pp. 447-542.

16. Harry Ellsworth, *One Hundred Eighty Landings,* pp. 96-98; J. René, "The Rambling *Rochester,*" *Marine Corps Gazette* 15 (Nov. 1930):13, 169.

17. Karnes, *Tropical Enterprise*, pp. 85-87.
18. Langley, *United States and the Caribbean*, pp. 109-10.

14. The Second Nicaraguan Civil War

1. Langley, *United States and the Caribbean*, pp. 85-90; Thomas A. Bailey, "Interest in a Nicaraguan Canal," *Hispanic American Historical Review* 16 (Feb. 1936):2-28.
2. Denny, *Dollars for Bullets*, pp. 171-202. For a Nicaraguan account, see Chamorro Cardenal, *Orígenes de la intervención americana en Nicaragua*.
3. V. L. Greer, "State Department Policy in Regard to the Nicaraguan Election of 1924," *Hispanic American Historical Review* 34 (Nov. 1954):445-67.
4. Denny, *Dollars for Bullets*, pp. 189-201; William Kamman, *A Search for Stability: United States Diplomacy toward Nicaragua, 1925-1933* (Notre Dame, Ind.: Notre Dame University Press, 1968), pp. 19-36.
5. Denny, *Dollars for Bullets*, p. 203.
6. Ibid., pp. 205-7; Calvin B. Carter, "The Kentucky Feud in Nicaragua," *World's Work* 54 (July 1927):312-31.
7. *Foreign Relations of the United States, 1926*, 2:786. After September 29, not even unarmed soldiers from either side were allowed in Bluefields. Comdr., Special Service Squad., Memorandum, May 14, 1929, in David Sellers Papers, LC MS Div. In 1927 Sellers relieved Adm. Julian Latimer as commander of the squadron.
8. Kamman, *Search for Stability*, pp. 55-68.
9. Howell Diaries, July 30, 1930, vol. 172, NHD.
10. Kamman, *Search for Stability*, pp. 63-65.
11. *Foreign Relations of the United States, 1926*, 2:804.
12. Ibid., p. 813.
13. Ibid., pp. 814-15; Kamman, *Search for Stability*, pp. 69-81.
14. *Foreign Relations of the United States, 1927*, 3:285.
15. Kamman, *Search for Stability*, pp. 78-81; U.S. Congress, House Committee on Foreign Affairs, *Conditions in Nicaragua and Mexico: Hearings*, 69th Cong., 2d sess., 1927, p. 20.
16. *Foreign Relations of the United States, 1927*, 3:310-11; *El Diario nicaragüense*, Feb. 27, 1927 (microfilm).
17. Neill Macaulay, *The Sandino Affair* (Chicago: Quadrangle, 1967), pp. 32-33; for Stimson's account, see Henry L. Stimson, *American Policy in Nicaragua* (New York: Scribner's, 1927).
18. Stimson Diaries, Yale University (microfilm), 17:16, 37-39.
19. Ibid., pp. 40-42, 57, 73-78.
20. Ibid., pp. 100, 107-15; Anastasio Somoza, *El verdadero Sandino; o el calvario de las Segovias* (Managua: Tipografía Robelo, 1936), pp. 20-23. Returning to Washington, Stimson described Nicaraguan behavior during the war as "barbarous." *El Diario nicaragüense*, June 22, 1927.

15. The Sandino Chase

1. Dom Albert Pagano, *Bluejackets* (Boston: Meador, 1932), p. 82; *El Diario nicaragüense*, May 20, 1927.
2. Vernor E. Megee, "Guerrilla Lessons from Nicaragua," *Marine Corps Gazette* 49 (June 1965):35-36; Robert E. Hogaboom, Oral History, pp. 54-55, USMC HMD.
3. Macaulay, *Sandino Affair*, pp. 48-61; Somoza, *El verdadero Sandino*, pp. 42-43;

Gustavo Alemán Bolaños, *Sandino, el libertador, la epopeya, el invasor, la muerte* (Mexico City: Ediciones del Caribe, 1952), pp. 22-23.

4. Wilburt Brown to E. N. McClellan, Nov. 20, 1930, Wilburt Brown Papers, USMC HMD.

5. The Hatfield-Sandino letters are in Somoza, *El verdadero Sandino,* pp. 48-49; Vernon Megee, "The Genesis of Air Support in Guerrilla Operations," *United States Naval Institute Proceedings* 91 (June 1965):49-57; Headquarters, 5th Reg., 2d Brig., USMC, Nicaragua, July 18, 1927, USMC Collection, WNRC.

6. Sandino to authorities, July 17, 1927, in Somoza, *El verdadero Sandino,* p. 56; Floyd to Comm. Off., 5th Reg., USMC, Managua, July 26, 1927, USMC Nicaragua Collection, 27/2, WNRC.

7. Comm. Gen. to Comm. Off., 5th Reg., Aug. 8, 1927, USMC Nicaragua Collection, 27/2, WNRC.

8. Cited in Joseph O. Baylen, "Sandino: Patriot or Bandit?" *Hispanic American Historical Review* 31 (Aug. 1951):394-419.

9. Coolidge, Fifth Annual Message, Dec. 6, 1927; Headquarters, 2d Brig., USMC, Dec. 27, 1927, USMC Nicaragua Collection, 15/1, WNRC.

10. Sellers to CNO, Aug. 20, 1927, in Sellers Papers, LC MS Div.; Macaulay, *Sandino Affair,* p. 87.

11. Xavier Campos Ponce, *Los yanquis y Sandino* (Mexico City: Ediciones X.C.P., 1962), pp. 66, 71; Macaulay, *Sandino Affair,* pp. 97-104; Capt. Francis D. Mulcahy, "Marine Corps Aviation in Second Nicaraguan Campaign," *United States Naval Institute Proceedings* 59 (Aug. 1933):1121-27; Schilt, Oral History, pp. 52-56, USMC HMD.

12. *Literary Digest,* Feb. 4, 1928, p. 42.

13. Carleton Beals, "Sandino: Bandit or Patriot?" *The Nation* 126 (Mar. 28, 1928):340-41; *La Tribuna* (Managua), Sept. 27, 1928.

14. Maj. D. L. Brewster, USMC, to Comdr., Special Service Squad., Feb. 2, 1929, Sellers Papers, LC MS Div.; Morrow to Kellogg, Apr. 11, 1928, copy in USMC, Nicaragua Collection, 10/1, WNRC.

15. Sellers to CNO, Mar. 17, 31, 1928, Sellers Papers, LC MS Div.

16. Matthew Ridgway, *Soldier: The Memoirs of Matthew B. Ridgway* (New York: Harper, 1956), pp. 37-38; Matthew Ridgway, Oral History, vol. 1, ARC.

17. Sandino to Mgr., La Luz Mine, Apr. 29, 1928, quoted in Sellers to CNO, June 2, 1928, Sellers Papers. LC MS Div.

18. Feland to Sellers, May 7, 1928, Sellers Papers, LC MS Div.; *Diario moderno* (Managua), June 3, 1928; Sellers to CNO, Sellers Papers, LC MS Div.

19. Kellogg to McCoy, Mar. 3, 1928, Frank McCoy Papers, LC MS Div.

20. Edwin McClellan, "Supervising Nicaraguan Elections, 1928," *United States Naval Institute Proceedings* 59 (Jan. 1933):37-38.

21. Cornelius Smith (member, McCoy commission) to Maj. Dowell, July 28, Aug. 18, 1928, Smith-Cole Papers, ARC.

22. Craig, Oral History, p. 98, USMC HMD; Samuel B. Frankel, Oral History, pp. 30-32, NHD; Macaulay, *Sandino Affair,* pp. 31-33.

16. The Last Banana War

1. Quoted in Samuel F. Bemis, *The Latin American Policy of the United States: An Historical Interpretation* (New York: Harcourt, Brace & Co., 1943), p. 250.

2. *New York Times,* Feb. 19, 1928.

3. On these points, see Stimson, *American Policy in Nicaragua,* passim; Bryce Wood,

The Making of the Good Neighbor Policy (New York: Columbia University Press, 1967; orig. pub. 1962), pp. 23-24; and J. Reuben Clark, *Memorandum on the Monroe Doctrine* (Washington, D.C.; Government Printing Office, 1930).

4. Sellers to Adm. C. F. Hughes, CNO, Sept. 20, 1928, Sellers Papers, LC MS Div.; Logan Feland to John Lejeune, Jan. 3, 1929, Lejeune Papers, LC MS Div.

5. Willard Beaulac, *Career Ambassador* (New York: Macmillan, 1951), pp. 116, 126-27.

6. Macaulay, *Sandino Affair,* pp. 132-44; Herman Hanneken, "A Discussion of the Voluntario Troops in Nicaragua," *Marine Corps Gazette* 26 (Nov. 1942):120, 247-66; Henry R. Paige, Oral History, pp. 9-16, USMC HMD.

7. Julian Smith, Oral History, pp. 126-131*a,* USMC HMD.

8. H. C. Reisinger, "La palabra del gringo," *United States Naval Institute Proceedings* 61 (Feb. 1935):216-19; Neill Macaulay, "Leading Native Troops: Counterinsurgency Cost Study," *Marine Corps Gazette* 47 (June 1963):32-35; Graves Erskine, Oral History, p. 106, USMC HMD; Hogaboom, Oral History, p. 61, USMC HMD.

9. John Letcher, *One Marine's Story* (Verona, Va.: McClure Press, 1970), p. 43; Robert Denig, "Diary of a Guardia Officer," p. 5, USMC HMD.

10. Hogaboom, Oral History, pp. 73-74, USMC HMD; John Munn, Oral History, pp. 8-12, USMC HMD; Julian Smith, Oral History, pp. 118, 139-41, USMC HMD; William Rogers, Oral History, pp. 29-33, USMC HMD.

11. John A. Daniels, "Don't Plan These Battles," *Marine Corps Gazette* 25 (Sept. 1941):44; Good, Oral History, pp. 57-65, USMC HMD. See also Goldwert, *Constabulary.*

12. E. H. Brainerd, "Marine Corps Aviation," *Marine Corps Gazette* 13 (Mar. 1928):25-36; Charles Sanderson, "The Supply Service in Western Nicaragua," ibid., 17 (May 1932):42-44; John Hart, Oral History, pp. 65-68, USMC HMD; Col. Thomas Turner, "Flying with the Marines in Nicaragua," Lee Conant Papers, USMC HMD; Samuel Jack, Oral History, p. 15, USMC HMD.

13. Davis, *Marine,* pp. 49-50; *El Comercio* (Managua), Mar. 5, 1929.

14. Davis, *Marine,* pp. 51-53; Macaulay, *Sandino Affair,* pp. 161-73.

15. Julian Smith, Oral History, pp. 123-25, USMC HMD.

16. Macaulay, *Sandino Affair,* 184-90; Austin Murphy, "Eyewitness Account of Attack of Sandinista Bandits at Moss Farm, April 11, 1931," Standard Fruit Co. Papers, Tulane University, New Orleans.

17. Jack, Oral History, p. 16, USMC HMD; Beaulac, *Career Ambassador,* pp. 128-30.

18. Karnes, *Tropical Enterprise,* pp. 132-33; Jack, Oral History, pp. 17-20, USMC HMD.

19. Merritt Edson, "The Coco River Patrol," *Marine Corps Gazette* 20 (Aug. 1936):18-23, 38-48, (Nov. 1936):40-41; 60-72, 21 (Feb. 1937):35-43, 57-63; Wood, *Making of the Good Neighbor Policy,* pp. 42-44.

Epilogue

1. Quoted in Jules Archer, *The Plot to Seize the White House* (New York: Hawthorn, 1973), p. 118.

2. *The Nation* 136 (Jan. 19, 1933):49.

3. Richard Millett, *Guardians of the Dynasty: A History of the U.S. Created Guardia Nacional de Nicaragua and the Somoza Family* (Maryknoll, N.Y.: Orbis, 1977), pp. 132-34; Julian Smith, Oral History, pp. 134-37, USMC HMD; Hogaboom, Oral History, p. 63, USMC HMD.

4. Erskine, Oral History, p. 95, USMC HMD.

5.   *Literary Digest,* Feb. 18, 1932, p. 8; Macaulay, *Sandino Affair,* pp. 242-56; Joseph O. Baylen, "Sandino: Death and Aftermath," *Mid-America* 36 (Apr. 1954):116-39.

6.   Samuel Griffith, Oral History, p. 22, USMC HMD.

7.   Oliver P. Smith, Oral History, p. 39, USMC HMD.

8.   Leo Hermle followed Roosevelt and Vincent in the backup car. Leo Hermle, Oral History, pp. 46-49, USMC HMD.

9.   Alfred Noble, Oral History, p. 56, USMC HMD.

10.   Quoted in Heinl and Heinl, *Written in Blood,* p. 514.

11.   The marines' experience in the banana wars produced, among other things, an early theoretical assessment on fighting "small wars." Samuel H. Harrington, "The Strategy and Tactics of Small Wars," *Marine Corps Gazette* 6 (Dec. 1921):474-91; 1 (Mar. 1922):83-92.

12.   Millett, *Semper Fidelis,* p. 263, contends that the Caribbean interventions, especially the second Nicaraguan intervention, "trained a generation of officers in combat leadership . . . [but] demythologized the Marine Corps enlisted man."

Bibliographical Note

This bibliographical comment is intended to identify the major sources, unpublished and published, on which this study is based. For a detailed bibliographical guide to the history of American military interventions in Latin America from 1900 until 1934, the reader should consult the notes.

Among the official records, located in the National Archives (NA) or its branch at Suitland, Maryland (WNRC), the Naval Historical Division (NHD), and USMC History and Museums Division (HMD), the following were most valuable for this study.

For the U.S. Navy, four collections: Record Group (hereafter RG) 80, General Records of the Navy, disappointing because much of the material has been moved to other collections; RG 38, Records of the Chief of Naval Operations (CNO), which contains the records of the Military Government of Santo Domingo, 1916–22; RG 24, Records of the Bureau of Naval Personnel; and RG 45, Office of Naval Records and Library, which has considerable material originally in RG 38 and RG 80, valuable for this study chiefly for its "subject" and "area" files, both of which are voluminous on naval operations in the Caribbean from 1900 to 1927. This collection also contains Capt. Edward Beach's "Admiral Caperton in Haiti," and Marine commandant George Barnett's "Report on Affairs in the Republic of Haiti." Copies of naval war plans and General Board Hearings are located at the Naval Historical Division, Operational Archives.

Since the Marine Corps command in the Caribbean interventions ordinarily came under U.S. Navy jurisdiction, the naval records identified above house Marine Corps material. But the investigator should also peruse three important collections: RG 127, Records of the United States Marine Corps, which contains reports of the Second Brigade in the Dominican Republic; the Marine Corps Nicaragua Collection; and the Haiti Collection, housed in WNRC but available for use in HMD, which contains official memorandums, after-action reports, and special files (e.g., Charlemagne Péralte). Though the National Archives has physical possession of this collection, permission to use it must be obtained from the Director, History and

Museums Division, USMC, Washington Navy Yard, Washington, D.C.

For the U.S. Army, which was twice responsible for the governance of Cuba and for Veracruz from May to November 1914, the following record groups in the National Archives are pertinent: RG 140, Records of the Military Government of Cuba, 1900–1902; RG 199, Records of the Provisional Government of Cuba, 1906–1909; and RG 141, Records of the Military Government of Veracruz (located in WNRC). These contain such predictably mundane materials as outgoing correspondence, military orders relating to civil affairs, newspaper notices, and police affairs—though RG 199 has occasional substantive commentary relating to policy in its "Confidential Correspondence" file. RG 141 should be supplemented with the reports of Frederick Funston in RG 94, Records of the Adjutant General. John R. Brooke, Leonard Wood, and Charles Magoon published detailed reports on the civil operations of their governments in Cuba.

RG 59, General Records of the Department of State, is readily accessible on microfilm for the years embracing this study. Throughout I relied heavily on the published correspondence in the *Foreign Relations* series as general guide to American policy as it was shaped by civilians in Washington. Much of the correspondence of the military government in the Dominican Republic, 1916–22, is reprinted in the State Department series on Internal Affairs of the Dominican Republic, 1910–29.

The most valuable sources for this study were the private papers and oral histories of civilian policy makers and the soldiers, sailors, and marines who fought the banana wars and ruled in America's tropical empire:

Southern Historical Collection, University of North Carolina, Chapel Hill. Frederick George Bromberg; William Upshur, USMC

U.S. Army Military History Collection, Carlisle Barracks, Pa. Albert Clayton Dalton; Frederick H. Delano, USMC; Thomas Morris; Matthew Ridgway (Oral History Collection; hereafter OH); Cornelius Smith

Library of Congress Manuscript Division. Robert A. Bullard, USA; William Banks Caperton, USN (Naval Historical Foundation Collection); Bainbridge Colby; Josephus Daniels; George Dewey, USN; Henry P. Fletcher; William F. Fullam, USN; Charles Evans Hughes; Philander C. Knox; Robert Lansing; John Lejeune, USMC; William Gibbs McAdoo; Hanna-McCormick Family (Medill McCormick); Frank McCoy, USA; Elihu Root; David F. Sellers, USN; Leonard Wood, USA

Naval Historical Division, Navy Yard, Washington, D.C. Walter Anderson (OH); Paul Foster (OH); Samuel Frankel (OH); Kent Hewitt (OH); Glenn Howell

Tulane University, New Orleans. Standard Fruit Company Papers

USMC History and Museums Division, Navy Yard, Washington, D.C. Edward W. Banker; Robert Barker; George Barnett; Charles D. Baylis; David L. S. Brewster; Wilburt S. Brown; Smedley Butler (also at Newtown Square, Pa.); Chandler Campbell; Lee Conant; Edward Craig (OH); Pedro A. del Valle (OH); Robert L. Denig; Lester A. Dessez (OH); Graves Erskine (OH); George Good (OH); Samuel Griffith (OH); Mary G. Grist; Herman Hanneken (OH); John N. Hart (OH); Leo Hermle (OH); Robert Hogaboom (OH); Samuel S. Jack (OH); Lincoln Karmany; George Kase; Louis McC. Little; Adolph Miller; Ivan Miller (OH); Francis P. Mulcahy (OH); John C. Munn (OH); Alfred Noble (OH); James K. Noble; Henry R. Paige (OH); Joseph H. Pendleton; Omar T. Pfeiffer (OH); Louie Putnam; George C. Reid; Carson Roberts (OH); Ford O. Rogers (OH); William W. Rogers (OH); Joseph Rossell (OH); John Russell; Thaddeus Sandifer; Christian Schilt (Papers and OH); Lemuel Sheperd, Jr. (OH); Merwin Silverthorne (OH); Julian Smith (OH); Oliver P. Smith (OH); Gerald C. Thomas (OH); Harold Utley; Alexander A. Vandegrift (OH); Clayton Vogel; William J. Wallace (OH); Littleton Waller Tazewell Waller, Jr. (for L. W. T. Waller, Sr., material); Julian Willcox; Louis E. Woods (OH); Thomas Wornham (OH); William Worton (OH)

Collections on film. Calvin Coolidge Papers, LC MS Div.; John Lind, Mexican Mission Papers, Minnesota Historical Society, Saint Paul; Theodore Roosevelt Papers, LC MS Div.; Henry L. Stimson Diaries, Yale University; William Howard Taft Papers, LC MS Div.; Woodrow Wilson Papers, LC MS Div.

Matthew Ridgway, John Lejeune, Smedley Butler, Pedro A. del Valle, and Alexander A. Vandegrift wrote or dictated published memoirs.

Of the large number of published works I consulted the following deserve special mention: Dana Gardner Munro, *Intervention and Dollar Diplomacy in the Caribbean, 1900–1921* (Princeton, N.J.: Princeton University Press, 1964), and *The United States and the Caribbean Republics, 1921–1933* (Princeton, N.J.: Princeton University Press, 1974), are scrupulously detailed diplomatic histories by a renowned scholar who helped to shape Latin American policy in the 1920s. But Munro relied so heavily on State Department material that his account must be read alongside Richard Challener, *Admirals, Generals, and American Foreign Policy, 1898–1914* (Princeton, N.J.: Princeton University Press, 1973), which superbly integrates military with State Department policy. Both view the Caribbean from the perspective of Washington, D.C. On the Cuban interventions, David Healy, *The United States in Cuba, 1898–1902: Generals, Politicians, and the Search for Policy* (Madison: University of Wisconsin Press, 1962); and Allan R. Millett, *The Politics of Intervention: The Military Occupation of Cuba, 1906–1909* (Columbus: Ohio State University Press, 1968), are essential. For Veracruz, I relied heavily on Robert Quirk, *An Affair of Honor: Woodrow Wilson and the Occupation of Veracruz* (Lexington: University Press of Kentucky, 1961), a sensitive account of the stupidity of Wilsonian policy; and Jack Sweetman, *The Landing at Veracruz, 1914* (Annapolis, Md.: U.S. Naval Institute Press, 1968), which concentrates on the three-day battle for the city. On the Haitian occupation, the most up-to-date accounts are David Healy, *Gunboat Diplomacy in the Wilson Era: The U.S. Navy in Haiti, 1915–1916* (Madison: University of Wisconsin Press, 1976), which evaluates Caperton's role in the occupation; and Hans Schmidt, *The United States Occupation of Haiti, 1915–1934* (New Brunswick, N.J.: Rutgers University Press, 1971), a scholarly account highly critical of American policy. There is lamentably nothing on the same order for the Dominican occupation, though the semiofficial history, Stephen Fuller and Graham Cosmas, *Marines in the Dominican Republic, 1916–1924* (Washington, D.C.: USMC History and Museums Division, 1974), devotes considerable attention to the administration of the military government as well as military activities. Robert and Nancy Debs Heinl devote more than one hundred pages to the Haitian occupation in *Written in Blood: The Story of the Haitian People, 1492–1971* (Boston: Houghton Mifflin, 1978), which is more sympathetic to the marines than the study by Schmidt. U.S. Congress, Senate, Select Committee on Haiti and Santo Domingo, *Inquiry into the Occupation and Administration of Haiti and Santo Domingo: Hearings,* 67th Cong., 1st and 2d sess., 1922, ranks among the most incisive congressional inquiries into American foreign policy in any era. For the 1926–32 Nicaraguan intervention, an essential work, with which I have often disagreed but which I have relied on again and again, is Neill Macaulay, *The Sandino Affair* (Chicago: Quadrangle Books, 1967), which is rightly considered a classic on American intervention in the Caribbean.

Louis A. Perez, Jr., ably provides a historiographical assessment in "Intervention, Hegemony, and Dependency: The United States in the Circum-Caribbean, 1898–1980," *Pacific Historical Review* 51 (May 1982): 165–94. Perez's emphasis is on diplomatic and economic history. For a Marine Corps perspective on the banana wars, see Allan R. Millett, *Semper Fidelis: The History of the United States Marine Corps* (New York: Macmillan, 1980), who devotes three chapters in his monumental history to the Caribbean interventions. The most recent interpretation of Caribbean intervention is Whitney Perkins's *Constraint of Empire: The United States and Caribbean Interventions* (Westport, Conn.: Greenwood, 1981), which covers Cuba, Nicaragua, Haiti, and the Dominican Republic from the 1905 Cuban occupation to the 1965 Dominican intervention, largely from a political perspective.

For this edition, the following deserve special mention: Louis A. Perez, Jr., *Cuba between Empires, 1878-1902* (Pittsburgh: University of Pittsburgh Press, 1983), argues that American intervention in Cuba distorted the "authentic" revolution. Bruce Calder, *The Impact of Intervention: The Dominican Republic during the U.S. Occupation of 1916-1924* (Austin: University of Texas Press, 1984), contends that the American intervention had less impact on Dominican politics than the generation of interveners believed.

Index

254   Index